THE ROUGH GUIDE to

Crime Fiction

by
Barry Forshaw

1st Edition

www.roughguides.com

Credits

The Rough Guide to Crime Fiction

Editing: Andrew Heritage, Ruth Tidball
Layout: Andrew Clare
Proofreading: Anita Sach
Production: Aimee Hampson,
Katherine Owers

Rough Guides Reference

Series editor: Mark Ellingham
Editors: Peter Buckley, Duncan Clark,
Tracy Hopkins, Sean Mahoney,
Matt Milton, Joe Staines, Ruth Tidball
Director: Andrew Lockett

Publishing Information

This first edition published June 2007 by
Rough Guides Ltd, 80 Strand, London WC2R 0RL
345 Hudson St, 4th Floor, New York 10014, USA
Email: mail@roughguides.com

Distributed by the Penguin Group:

Penguin Books Ltd, 80 Strand, London WC2R 0RL
Penguin Putnam, Inc., 375 Hudson Street, NY 10014, USA
Penguin Group (Australia), 250 Camberwell Road, Camberwell, Victoria 3124, Australia
Penguin Books Canada Ltd, 10 Alcorn Avenue, Toronto, Ontario, Canada M4P 2Y3
Penguin Group (New Zealand), 67 Apollo Drive, Mairangi Bay, Auckland 1310, New Zealand

Printed in Italy by LegoPrint S.p.A.

Typeset in Baskerville, Minion and Myriad to an original design by Peter Buckley and Duncan Clark

320 pages; includes index

A catalogue record for this book is available from the British Library

ISBN 13: 978-1-84353-654-3
ISBN 10: 1-84353-654-4

1 3 5 7 9 8 6 4 2

THE ROUGH GUIDE to

Crime Fiction

by
Barry Forshaw

ROUGH
GUIDES

www.roughguides.com

Contents

Foreword

Ian Rankin

Has crime fiction finally achieved the literary respectability that has long been its due? Certainly, crime novels are covered in the books pages of newspapers far more often than they were. But when a famous prize-winning literary novelist recently turned his hand to crime fiction, he felt obliged to put it out under another name. Is there still something disreputable about the genre?

While I have written in a variety of genres, I continue to find the crime novel the perfect vehicle for a discussion of contemporary issues in the most unflinching terms. After all, the detective has an 'all areas pass' to every aspect of the contemporary urban scene, and this is a way for the crime writer to take the reader into forbidden territory; for instance, it was always my mission in the Rebus books to show people an Edinburgh that the tourist doesn't see. And crime fiction has always been good at articulating the fears that society has harboured at all moments of history – such as the stranger who will casually take your life. Equally, the genre is able to deal with high moral purpose in quite as rigorous a fashion as Dostoyevsky did in *Crime and Punishment* and Dickens did in *Bleak House*.

It's difficult these days to write about contemporary life in a crime context and not have violence. Mind you, I don't think that is just an issue for the crime novel – it is a problem for all contemporary fiction. Violence fascinates us because it is deemed unacceptable by society and therefore the people who commit violence are breaking our self-imposed rules, rules that underpin the very notion of civilization. Rule breakers make us curious: why don't they want to be like us? Why do they make the choice not to conform? Do they actually make a choice, or is it made for them (by their genetic coding, their circumstances, etc)? The crime novel should tackle the question of violence whether we reach any answers or not, shouldn't it?

People are interested in crime fiction because they are fascinated by the margins of the world, those places where society's rules break down. They wonder what they would do in similar situations, how they would cope. They learn how to deal with fear and the unknown. And at the end, they have the sense that a certain justice has been seen to be done. Barry Forshaw has tackled these issues (and many others) in a book that covers crime fiction from every part of the world – it's a daunting task.

Ian Rankin
March 2007

Preface

As we settle into a new century, is it possible to predict the direction crime fiction will take? Initially, the auguries are bad: many classic genres (notably the police procedural) have undergone a distinct hardening of the arteries, as inspiration gives way to cliché and innovation to repetition. As all hard-pressed crime writers know, it becomes ever tougher to come up with something new. Editing *Crime Time* magazine, most of the letters I receive lament the difficulties of tracking down that one fresh and inventive novel among much that is – shall we say – warmed over? And yet crime fiction remains (*pace* books about witches, wizards, demons and spurious codes) one of the few evergreen areas of modern publishing. The genre is a broad church, with every level of achievement available, from subtle psychological insight into the minds of murderers to uncomplicated thick-ear action. All sub-genres are covered here, but none are looked down upon. That said, there is no mincing of words when it comes to really bad writing.

The Rough Guide to Crime Fiction comprises a selection of the best in crime writing over the last century or so, organized by subject (or sub-genre). The books that are reviewed represent the best of an author's output, or at least great introductions to often extensive bodies of work. Also included are "top five" lists for the biggest names, brief notes on significant screen adaptations, and profiles of those writers whose contribution to the evolution of crime writing is irrefutable. The book aims to be a truly comprehensive survey, covering every major writer along with many more esoteric choices. It covers everything from the genre's origins and the Golden Age to the current bestselling authors, although a larger emphasis is placed on contemporary writers. The guide is designed to be both an opinionated but unstuffy reference tool and history, and a crime buyer's shopping list that will help the reader to pick their way through some often dire writing to find the real gems in the field.

Barry Forshaw
March 2007

Acknowledgements

Working with three invaluable editors (Joe Staines, Andrew Lockett and the indefatigable Andrew Heritage) has helped me forge this guide – my thanks to them, and also to Caroline Stone, Paul Lunde, Christopher Davis and George and Amelia Heritage for their valuable input.

About the author

Barry Forshaw has written on crime and literary fiction for *The Independent*, *The Express*, *The Times* and *The Times Literary Supplement*. He is the author of *Italian Cinema* and has contributed to *Film Noir* (Penguin). He edits the fiction review *Crime Time*.

Reading the entrails
Origins, motives, sources

With a little ingenuity, it is possible to find literary antecedents to the modern crime novel far back in history. The **Bible** tells how when Cain slew Abel, the third human ever created had managed to murder the fourth. **Sophocles'** *Oedipus Rex* has all the classic ingredients of the psychological mystery, even down to the final painful acquisition of knowledge leading to the destruction of the protagonist, and most of his family. *Noir* territory, indeed. No less dark are **Shakespeare's** pivotal assassination dramas *Julius Caesar* (think conspiracy theories) and the malign 'Scottish play' (for Lady Macbeth read almost every *femme fatale* to glower from the silver screen). But while we can possibly shoehorn the Bible, Sophocles and Shakespeare into the genre as progenitors of crime fiction, the real origins of the genre lie in the 19th century.

Chapter 1

The concept of the cliffhanger mystery novel took off in the 19th century almost simultaneously in Gothic, Romantic and Realist writing. Whereas the **Gothic** writers preferred a darkly supernatural sense of suspense and *dénouement*, horribly real cops, secret agents and villains occur regularly in the work of **Balzac**, while the world's first dogged detective (albeit also a blackguard) trails **Victor Hugo**'s Jean Valjean through almost every page of *Les Misérables* (1862).

An obsession with crime, just retribution and the dark, nefarious underworld was revealed in the popularity of publications such as *The Newgate Calendar*, and by the end of the century lurid 'Penny Dreadfuls' and 'Shilling Shockers' vied for bookstand rack-space with **Bram Stoker**'s comparatively quite respectable parlour-piece *Dracula* (1897). But the most significant innovation of the 19th century was American polymath **Edgar Allan Poe**'s C. Auguste Dupin, who first displayed the requisite cool ratiocination and ability to marshal facts that was to become the *sine qua non* of the investigative detective. Poe even created the less brilliant follower for his detective (in order that the hero's mental pyrotechnics might be displayed more satisfyingly). Poe was greatly admired in France, and translation of his work by Baudelaire (among others) was to spread his influence far beyond the provincial Stateside streets of Baltimore and Richmond.

Leaving aside **Charles Dickens**' Sergeant Clough and Mr Nadgett and his unfinished murder novel *The Mystery of Edwin Drood* (1870), it is tidier to settle on his friend **Wilkie Collins**' *The Woman in White* (1859) and *The Moonstone* (1868) as the first instances of great crime novels. A reacquaintance with these two most readable books demonstrates that many of the key elements we recognize so well (notably the hyper-intelligent, hyper-ingenious villain, the slightly dim hero who we follow as he pieces together the mystery, and a narrative crammed full of delicious obfuscation) are firmly in place. But it is also salutary to note that one element – the elegance and polish of the prose – has become less common since those days.

Edgar Allan Poe (1809–49)

Orphaned, a failed soldier, a bankrupt gambler and an alcoholic incapable of holding down a job, forced to live with his child-wife's mother, and eventually dead in a gutter aged 40. How could this man become an outstanding poet, essayist and progenitor of at least five literary genres: the **short story** (or tale), **horror**, **science fiction**, **psychological fiction** and the **crime novel**? Probably his very background predisposed him to introspection, gloom and despond, but the elegance of his style and intricate intellectual curiosity give even his darkest works a burnished gleam. The obsessive protagonists of many of his tales prefigure both the criminals and sleuths of later writers; *The Tell-Tale Heart* (1843) deals explicitly with a murderer's guilt, as does *The Cask of Amontillado* (1846). But it is the three tales featuring the detective C. Auguste Dupin, who uses observation, logic and lateral thinking to solve crimes, which claim primacy for crime enthusiasts: *The Murders in the Rue Morgue* (1841) is the prototypical 'locked room' mystery; *The Mystery of Marie Roget* (1842) was based on an actual case in New York, and introduces the problem of reconstructing what happened to a murder victim in the last days of her life; *The Purloined Letter* (1845) involves a psychological game to reveal a blackmailer's trophy.

The Mystery Writers of America award, the Edgar, is named in his memory.

Of course, the lean, pared-down prose of many modern crime novels has its own appeal, but whenever the diehard crime reader picks up a modern novel as well written as Collins' were, it's a cause for some celebration.

It was **Arthur Conan Doyle**, a generation later, who was to bring the detective novel to its greatest fruition – a marriage of author and character that few have achieved since. His creation of the master detective Sherlock Holmes owed much to Poe's Dupin (the latter is even discussed in the stories), but his extension of the concept into a considerable canon of work which stretched over 40 years of publication demonstrates a craftsmanship that simply beggars belief. His masterstroke, of course, was to take the relationship between the unconventional, brilliant investigator and his assistant and develop it into something rich and resonant. Again and again, the sheer pleasure of the stories comes from the nuances of the relation between Holmes and Watson as much as from the plot revelations (some of which, as Doyle well knew, were outrageously implausible). The fashion in which details of Holmes' character were freighted in (the violin, the depression caused by inactivity, the '7% solution', etc.) ensured that Doyle's detective became probably the best-known Englishman in fiction, and one of the first true international bestsellers.

At about the same time as Conan Doyle was concocting Holmes, other criminal currents were stirring. In Russia, **Fyodor Dostoyevsky**

Fantomas

The dangerous allure of the fanatical **criminal mastermind** forms a black thread through the history of crime writing, from Holmes' nemesis Moriarty through Bond's many colourful 'welcome to my lair' supervillains to the poisonous attraction of Hannibal Lecter. Fantomas was the original master criminal, created by **Pierre Souvestre** and **Marcel Allain** in 1911. The duo were the French equivalent of later American pulp writers who churned out bloody and sensational fare to order – and Fantomas was designed to inaugurate a series of five novels. But the immense success of the character (a ruthless megalomaniac and master of disguise who always eludes capture) guaranteed him a lengthy literary life, with other authors taking over to chronicle his adventures. That first novel was written in the crudest of styles, but its canny use of crowd-pleasing elements (violence, horror and a bracing amorality) attracted some high-minded disapproval – in turn guaranteeing healthy sales. Intriguingly, the character was taken up by the artistic avant-garde, and the poet Appollinaire was a devoted follower. But it was when Louis Feuillade began his series of Fantomas films that the character's place in the firmament of popular culture was assured (not least because the films were far more accomplished than the novels). By the late 20th century, the novels were only fitfully reprinted; for those who read French, however, Fantomas novels can still be found on the bookstalls along the Seine.

was creating a template for the existential psychokiller (*Crime and Punishment*, 1866) and the familial destruction novel (*The Brothers Karamazov*, 1880). The French Realist **Emile Zola** dealt with a range of shady lowlife scenarios, and godfathered the domestic *ménage à trois* which results in murder in *Thérèse Raquin* (1867). By the turn of the century, the Polish exile **Joseph Conrad** was writing (in English) about terrorism and subterfuge in a pair of mirror novels concerning Anarchists: tragically incompetent ones in England in *The Secret Agent* (1907), and doomed but heroic ones in Tsarist Russia in *Under Western Eyes* (1911). Notions of international conspiracy featured in **Rudyard Kipling**'s Indian Great Game masterpiece *Kim* (1901), but attention soon focused on Germany, as exemplified by two seminal spy novels: *The Riddle of the Sands* (1903) by the Irish Republican gun-runner **Erskine Childers**, and **John Buchan**'s *The Thirty-Nine Steps* (1915).

What follows is a selection of classic crime novels which, between them, definitively established the genre and its various strands.

Trent's Last Case 1913
E.C. Bentley

One of the most celebrated murder mysteries preceding the 'Golden Age', this is also, in fact, one of the most unusual in terms of its unorthodox structure. While the detective protagonist presented to us by Bentley (amateur sleuth Philip Trent) initially appears to conform to the standard requirements for such characters (resourceful, tenacious, cracking a baffling murder case by a steady accumulation of facts), the author has quite a surprise for us in the latter half of the book – a surprise that, at a stroke, makes *Trent's Last Case* a rather modern novel. The eponymous investigator is employed by a London paper to file pieces of investigative journalism, and he is sent to Marlstone to look into the murder of an American money-man named Manderson, who has been shot in his garden shed. Trent (in somewhat unorthodox fashion) begins to dig beneath the surface of the mystery, and finds that the attractive widow of the murdered man, Mabel, was suffering in a loveless marriage to the ruthless financier. Ill-advisedly, Trent finds himself falling in love with the seductive widow, but is still able to solve the murder (in a rather vague fashion that irritated, among others, **Raymond Chandler**). But now comes the surprise that Bentley has up his sleeve: the narrative continues, with Trent relocated to Germany and struggling to shake free from the *amour fou* that has blighted his life. It's this radical shaking up of the standard narrative procedure (almost before the rules of the genre had become set in stone) that now seems postmodern – as if Bentley was uncomfortable with what he perceived to be the demands of the detective story structure. Bentley, essentially a humorist, and inventor of the Clerihew verse form, followed up with *Trent's Own Case* in 1936.

The Thirty-Nine Steps 1915
John Buchan

Without *The Thirty-Nine Steps* the world would be missing such classic novels as **Geoffrey Household**'s *Rogue Male*. Or **Hitchcock**'s matchless British film. Or, for that matter, the spy thriller in the **Ian Fleming** vein (even though the latter adds a libido and classlessness to John Buchan's upper-crust English hero). Buchan's most famous novel, *The Thirty-Nine Steps* remains as much of a delight as when it was written – and is one of the greatest espionage thrillers of all time. Concise and kinetic,

Buchan's story has his mining engineer Richard Hannay returning, at a loose end, from Rhodesia, as the Balkan conflict bubbles away

> **The Thirty-Nine Steps**
> dir. Alfred Hitchcock, 1935
>
> The blueprint for many of Hitchcock's subsequent films (*North by Northwest*, *Saboteur*, *Torn Curtain*), this is one of that rare breed of films (like Curtiz's *Casablanca*) in which absolutely every element (screenplay, direction, cinematography, playing) is balanced to perfection. **Robert Donat** is perfectly cast as the very British hero, and the customary Hitchcock cocktail of suspense and dry humour gets its most adroit workout in the director's English period before he was tempted by Hollywood. Subsequent remakes (with **Kenneth Moore**, 1959, and **Robert Powell**, 1978) were efficient enough, but not remotely in the league of Hitchcock's original.

in the years before the Great War. Hannay is falsely accused of killing an American spy engaged in the Balkan intrigue, and is soon on the run (across a brilliantly realized Scotland – this is the ultimate picaresque thriller) from both police and enemy agents. Those who feel they know Buchan's tale too well from the numerous adaptations should really go back to the irresistible source novel.

The Man Who Was Thursday 1908
G.K. Chesterton

Chesterton was born in London in 1874 and made his mark in speaking out against the Boer War. In many ways, he was the quintessential Edwardian writer, hobnobbing with the likes of Wells and Shaw. From his large range of writing, he is best remembered these days for his **Father Brown** stories, in which the gentle ecclesiastical sleuth solves problems after the fashion of the Ratiocinator of 221b Baker Street. Admirers, however, rate *The Man Who Was Thursday* as his finest work in the crime field. It's a cutting analysis of anarchism (much as **Joseph Conrad** had undertaken in *The Secret Agent* the year before). Chesterton's protagonists are Lucian Gregory and Gabriel Syme, who wear the apparel of poets. One, however, is an anarchist, and the other a policeman. In the dark counter-world they both inhabit, personality and function are defined by a code word, and one of the duo becomes 'Thursday'. This murky universe is not just a place of vaguely surrealistic posing, but one of madness and fear. The London locales are conjured with a disorientating eye (as are the settings for a chase sequence in northern France), and the narrative functions both as a thriller and as a complex symbolist nightmare. The Father Brown books may be Chesterton's most popular work, but this is his best.

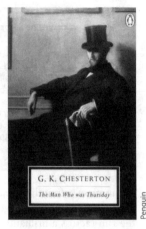

The Riddle of the Sands 1903
Erskine Childers

Highly regarded as an account of small sailing boat cruising, this was also one of the first of many books which raised alarm bells about German preparations for aggressive warfare against her neighbours. Two gentlemen, facing the prospect of an idle London summer, take a sailing holiday off the East Frisian shore. Various encounters lead them to suspect the build-up of German military and naval resources destined to form an invasion force aimed at Britain, and the race is on to alert the British authorities. In no way naïve, the book was not only prescient in historical terms but also laid the foundations for many of the basic formulae of spy novels to follow, notably those of **John Buchan**. Winston Churchill took it seriously enough to instigate the Admiralty's fortification of

---

🎞 **The Riddle of the Sands**
dir. Tony Maylam, 1979

Taking advantage of the maritime setting and slow pace of the novel, the perfectly cast gung-ho British actors **Michael York** and **Simon MacCorkindale** do a fair job of bringing a slightly edited version of the novel to life, as does Howard Blake's fitting score. Both **Hans Meyer** and **Alan Badel** bring suitable menace to their roles as devious Huns Grimm and Dollmann, while **Jenny Agutter** once again dons Edwardian miss threads to bring a feminine element to what is the essential Boy's Own adventure.

England's east coast defences and the creation of naval bases at Scapa Flow, the Firth of Forth and Invergordan. Childers himself, an experienced soldier and sailor, was later executed as a traitor by the newly formed Irish Free State, despite having supported them after the Easter Uprising.

The Casebook of Sherlock Holmes 1927

Arthur Conan Doyle

Conan Doyle's imperishable creation is one of the best-known characters in world fiction. This volume brings together the final 12 stories that Doyle wrote about the detective, which in many ways crystallized the universal appeal of the character. The stories are particularly interesting in their willingness to take on subjects which must have been uncomfortable to a less tolerant readership than that of the present century. In many of them, a dark and destructive secret lies in the heart of rigidly maintained Victorian propriety, and Doyle's dispassionate unearthing of these undercurrents gives the stories a peculiarly subversive charge. Many of the great Doyle classics are to be found here, such as *The Adventure of the Creeping Man* and *The Adventure of the Mazarin Stone*. Doyle had tried to kill off the detective in the Reichenbach Falls struggle with his nemesis, Professor Moriarty, but the writer's affectionate farewell to his greatest creation in the introduction to the stories is genuinely touching.

Sir Arthur Conan Doyle (1859–1930)

While the four novels featuring Holmes and Watson (most notably *The Hound of the Baskervilles*) have their virtues, none is as completely successful as the many perfectly proportioned short stories, originally published in *The Strand Magazine*. Holmes first appeared in *A Study in Scarlet*, published in *Beeton's Christmas Annual* in 1887, and was an immediate hit. By 1891 Doyle was already talking of killing him off. He attempted to do so in 1893, with a plunge down the **Reichenbach Falls**, but public and financial pressure meant that in total some 56 Holmes stories were eventually published.

A famous *Punch* cartoon from 1926 showed Conan Doyle shackled to his celebrated pipe-smoking creation, and the author often voiced his exasperated desire to be remembered for something other than the cocaine-using detective. He was a prolific writer, producing **historical romances** (*The Adventures of Brigadier Gérard*) and even **science fiction** (the *Professor Challenger* stories, including *The Lost World*). But it was Sherlock Holmes, rather than his own preferred historical fiction, that made Conan Doyle (along with H.G. Wells) the most celebrated popular writer of his age.

Conan Doyle famously seemed to lack the rigorous deductive reasoning of his hero. The most infamous incident in the author's non-literary life – recently dramatized in both a film and a TV play – involved Conan Doyle's credulous belief in doctored pictures of **fairies**, produced by two schoolgirls. To modern eyes, Doyle's acceptance of this ludicrous hoax seems astonishing, but the author's personal losses (as so often) seem to have predisposed him towards a belief in the supernatural (a belief which is, surprisingly, not reflected in his fiction), and he famously espoused several very suspect causes – he was, in fact, something of a target for charlatans.

The Casebook of Sherlock Holmes
Granada TV, 1984–94

For many years, the urbane Hollywood expatriate **Basil Rathbone** remained the perfect incarnation of the Great Detective (not least for his Holmesian profile and ability to wear a deerstalker without looking absurd), but his otherwise splendid series of adaptations for Universal Studios in the 1940s were compromised by a fluctuating sense of period, and a doltish Dr Watson. The BBC ran a successful series in the 1960s, with the lugubrious **Douglas Wilmer** in the lead, stolidly supported by Nigel Stock as the Doctor. But two decades later, and at a stroke, the brilliant and neurasthenic performance of **Jeremy Brett** established itself as definitive, aided by his impeccable accent, his fastidious attention to detail and two excellent Watsons (David Burke and later Edward Hardwicke). Granada's cleverly written adaptations consolidated their appeal with vividly evoked period atmosphere and a supporting cast that drew from the cream of the British acting profession. Brett's bipolar depression is thought to have contributed significantly to his interpretation of Holmes' character.

The Sherlock Holmes books

Rivalling both Christie's and Allingham's heroes in longevity, the adventures of Conan Doyle's hero were published for some 40 years, although most were set in a *fin-de-siècle* London.

▶ *Study in Scarlet* (1887)
▶ *The Sign of Four* (1890)
▶ *The Adventures of Sherlock Holmes* (1892)
▶ *The Memoirs of Sherlock Holmes* (1894)
▶ *The Hound of the Baskervilles* (1902)
▶ *The Return of Sherlock Holmes* (1904)
▶ *The Valley of Fear* (1914)
▶ *His Last Bow* (1917)
▶ *The Case Book of Sherlock Holmes* (1927)

Chapter 1

The Amateur Cracksman 1899
Ernest William Hornung

Penguin

While Hornung's debonair criminal protagonist **Raffles** is more remembered than read these days, the author's influence on the genre is still notable. A badge of intellectual respectability was conferred on Raffles in the 1930s, when **George Orwell** wrote a celebrated essay praising the old-fashioned charm of Hornung's well-turned proto-caper novels at the expense of what he (rather old maid-ishly) perceived as the depraved brutality of such then-modern crime novels as James Hadley Chase's *No Orchids for Miss Blandish*. This slightly sentimental view of Hornung's amiable thief is perhaps the best way to approach him. Raffles, however, remains an important prototype of many latter-day crook-heroes (not least Louis Joseph Vance's *The Lone Wolf*, the Falcon movies of the 1930s, and Leslie Charteris's *The Saint*) and, along with his partner Bunny, moves in a charmingly realized English period universe. Raffles (who excelled at cricket) carries his non-professional profes-

---

Raffles
dir. Harry d'Arrast and George Fitzmaurice, 1930

Although previous silent incarnations exist, notably by John Barrymore in 1917, Ronald Coleman's smooth charm is absolutely perfect for the gentleman thief who spins circles around the duffers at Scotland Yard. Today, age gives the film a perfect period feel. Based on *The Amateur Cracksman*, a Sam Wood 1940 scene-for-scene remake featured the only other conceivable actor seemingly born to play the part – David Niven.

sionalism through the picaresque adventures here (with a colourful *dramatis personae* of character types), even though modern readers may look askance at the relationship between Raffles and his adoring ex-fag Bunny. The plotting is loose and discursive, but the gallery of effects remains diverting. Intriguingly this book and later adventures such as *The Black Mask* (1901) and *A Thief in the Night* (1905) could be seen as a refracted critique of British society – after all, Raffles' quintessential English diligence is entirely at the service of crime.

The Golden Age

Classic mysteries

Crime fiction came of age in the years between the world wars, and produced a plenitude of writers who gained enormous popularity. Many continued to publish new work well into the 1950s and 60s, and still sell in substantial numbers today. The most celebrated writer of the period, which many regard as the 'Golden Age' of detective fiction, was **Agatha Christie**. She was canny enough to appropriate several of Conan Doyle's Sherlock Holmes characteristics for her Belgian detective Hercule Poirot. Can we blame Christie for the parodic fashion in which Poirot is customarily played in film adaptations today? God knows, Sherlock Holmes has been parodied often enough, but the strength of that character is such that we remain ready to plunge into the fogbound streets of Victorian London with our sense of irony firmly held in check. Why this distinction between our perception of two eccentric sleuths? Possibly, it lies in the genius of one author as against the craftsmanship of the other. The pleasure of Christie's work doesn't really lie in the creation of Poirot's character (or, for that matter, of her equally distinctive and brilliantly conceived elderly spinster Jane Marple): it's those wonderfully engineered plots of Christie's which still remain as diverting as ever.

There are, of course, two diametrically opposed schools of thought about Christie, mainly concerning social attitudes. If you hate the patronizing attitude to the working classes and the socially stratified never-never-land Britain she nostalgically creates, then nothing will persuade you to open a Christie novel. But as modern crime mistress Minette Walters has pointed out, Christie was later able to take on board social change (albeit peripherally). And, if we can still read John Buchan, happily ignoring those aspects of his work that aren't consonant with current mores, why not Christie? Taking a step on from the 'Locked Room' conundrum, this was the period which gave birth to the 'Whodunnit?', originating in Christie's 'Country House' format in which the murder usually turned out to have been commit-ted by the least likely candidate. Beneath Christie's burgeoning skirts, there are the other giants of the Golden Age: **Allingham**, **Sayers**, **Marsh** et al. And what about **John Dickson Carr**? It's a field richer in mystery and imagination than one thinks at first glance…

Tiger in the Smoke 1952
Margery Allingham

While many writers of the classic British crime novel fought shy (or were unaware) of psychopathic killers in their work, Margery Allingham's signature novel produced one of the most memorable murderers in fiction, and the book's reputation has grown over the years since publication in 1952. In the teeming streets of a fogbound London, a man with a knife is carving a bloody path. Meg is about to be married to Geoffrey Levett, but other things are preying on her mind. She has been under the impression that her unlovable first husband Martin died during the war, until she receives a photograph which appears to prove that he is, in fact, alive. Meg's life is about to change – and very much for the worse. At the same time, the brutal Jack Havoc is summarily dispensing with anyone who gets in his way, including members of his old gang. A wide variety of plots and characters (including Allingham's long-term detective, **Campion**) inter-

Vintage

sect in what is the darkest of the author's many books. While writers such as Agatha Christie largely dealt with death in sedate villages or country houses, Allingham bravely took on the depiction of the urban criminal underworld, and it is here (for the modern reader) that the book comes a little unstuck, with the argot and descriptions now seeming a touch quaint. However, several things in *Tiger in the Smoke* date not a whit, among them the brilliantly evoked post-war setting, and the chilling portrait of pure evil incarnated in the murderous Jack Havoc.

Tiger in the Smoke
dir. Roy Ward Baker, 1956

Roy Ward Baker's creditable stab at Allingham's novel is, to date, the only one of her books to be filmed. It effectively utilizes the Rank organization's 1950s facility for capturing the London milieu; the gritty settings (as crucial here as in the Boulting Brothers' 1947 adaptation of Greene's *Brighton Rock*, see p.193) make up for any inadequacies in the casting. The novel's sense of barely repressed psychosis, however, is only fitfully achieved, which vitiates Allingham's rigorously maintained tension.

The top five Campion novels

Although only a part of Margery Allingham's sophisticated output, the Albert Campion stories spanned an almost unprecedented 40 years of creativity which saw the mysterious and socially ambivalent detective develop from his early career as a loner to family life and maturity, accompanied by his servant and sidekick, the ex-burglar Lugg. They solved cases ranging from 'Country House'-style mysteries to instances of psychological deviance, and one of the first serious serial killer novels.

▸ *Death of a Ghost* (1934)
▸ *Dancers in Mourning* (aka *Who Killed Chloe?*, 1935)
▸ *More Work for the Undertaker* (1948)
▸ *The Tiger in the Smoke* (1952)
▸ *The Beckoning Lady* (aka *The Estate of the Beckoning Lady*, 1955)

The Beast Must Die 1938
Nicholas Blake (pseudonym of Cecil Day Lewis)

Nicholas Blake is not much read these days – a fact that would surprise his enthusiastic following in his mid-20th-century heyday. But are the Blake novels as good as their reputations, or has memory lent enchantment? This most famous of British Poet Laureate **Cecil Day Lewis**'s thrillers still reads in the 21st century as one of the most compelling crime novels ever written. The plot involves a detective fiction writer who plans a perfect murder, one that he himself will eventually commit. When a personal tragedy (the death of a close relative) destroys writer Frank Cairnes' life, his tracking down of the man responsible achieves a pathological intensity, with inevitable death at the conclusion. But the final confrontation is not what the reader expects. With Blake's famous investigator Nigel Strangeways on hand, the sheer pleasure afforded by this book is guaranteed.

> **Que la Bête Meure/Killer!**
> dir. Claude Chabrol, 1969
>
> The brilliant use of Brahms' *Four Serious Songs* (with their death-directed philosophy) in the score establishes Chabrol's remarkable thriller as an arthouse take on Blake's novel; the richness of the subtexts, the flat Gallic tone and the understated performances make for a memorable adaptation, and the translation of the novel's setting into that of a bleached-looking autumnal France is completely successful. As ever, Chabrol freights in his very individual take on Hitchcock's 'Transference of Guilt' concept.

Green for Danger 1944
Christianna Brand

Set in a British military hospital in Kent during World War II, Brand's beautifully turned novel is as celebrated for its perfectly realized milieu (rarely has wartime Britain been so well evoked) as for its unorthodox plotting. If the motivation of the killer does not stand up to rigorous examination, this is hardly ruinous to the spell the book casts. As German air raids pound the country, a group of nurses and doctors carry on as best they can – and all the accoutrements of everyday life (including sex and jealousy) struggle on.

> **Green for Danger**
> dir. Sidney Gilliatt, 1946
>
> Cast the larger-than-life **Alistair Sim** in a movie (as any producer would have known) and you watch him walk away with the film. Fine, if it's a Sim vehicle, and that's what the audience is paying for. But what about a tightly contrived conversation piece like this adaptation of Brand's novel? In fact, the actor shows that he is perfectly capable of reining in his mannerisms and not drawing attention away from the matchless ensemble playing required here (while still affording us the trademark humour). Undervalued for years, this is now seen as a very cherishable miniature in suspense.

When an air raid warden dies a day after an operation, it becomes clear that a killer is at work – and those who discover the murderer's identity die like the victims. As well as the tensely handled plot elements, the characters – all subtly damaged or disappointed in life – are beautifully drawn.

The Hollow Man/
The Three Coffins 1935

John Dickson Carr

The tradition of American writers who opted to set their books in Britain (so strong was their love of the country and its traditions) continues to this day with **Elizabeth George**, but the most distinguished

Crime: a publishing phenomenon

The rise of literacy and popular culture inaugurated by the Great War provided a robust platform for the flowering of crime fiction. Many authors emerged and flourished in the 1920s: **Edgar Wallace**, **H.C. McNeile** ('Sapper') and, in the States, **Sax Rohmer**, **S.S. Van Dyne** and **Edgar Rice Burroughs** became international celebrities. Also many female writers entered the lists, notably **Agatha Christie**, **Margery Allingham** and **Dorothy L. Sayers**. Part of their success was due to a change in the publishing industry, most notably the advent of the paperback, and even more significantly, the paperback 'original'. For the first time, a gripping piece of fiction was available in its entirety (and for only a few pennies). This replaced the old magazine serialization which Dickens, Poe, Collins and Doyle had to deal with. Although Allen Lane's Penguin imprint is frequently credited with inventing the up-market paperback concept in 1935 (and books by Sayers, Christie and Dashiell Hammett were among the first twenty Penguin titles), publishers such as Hodder & Stoughton and Collins had built substantial popular crime lists before Penguin launched its distinctive green crime livery. The Collins Crime Club was launched in 1930. But it was the royalties from popular softback publishing in America, and from the sale of film rights, that created the first millionaire crime writers.

member of this club remains the wonderful John Dickson Carr, a writer who is firmly on the Top Ten list of many a crime fiction connoisseur.

Carr's long-term protagonist, the cultivated sybarite Dr Gideon Fell, is one of the most individual sleuths in the field, and the perfectly judged soupçons of characterization (always economical) that Carr affords Dr Fell are one of the pleasures of the books – along with the impeccable plotting. Those who know Carr's name (but not his books) are usually aware that he excels at the 'Locked

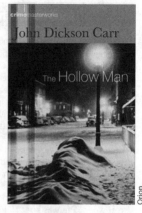

Room' mystery. And the perfect entry point for the author is *The Hollow Man* (retitled *The Three Coffins* in the US), with its nigh-supernatural killer, impenetrable mystery and skilfully conjured atmosphere.

Murder on the Orient Express 1934
Agatha Christie

For those with open minds, *Murder on the Orient Express* is the ideal way to discover what it is that has made the Christie name such a copper-bottomed franchise. Christie's favourite sleuth, **Hercule Poirot**, has solved a case and is taking the Orient Express home when it becomes snowbound. A variation on the 'Country House' scenario sets in with the frost. Poirot's fellow travellers include an unpleasant millionaire, Ratchett, his secretary, MacQueen, and butler, Beddowes. During the night, Ratchett is stabbed to death in what seems like a frenzied attack (there are many stab wounds in the body); it's up

Chapter 2

Agatha Christie (1890–1976)

Despite her unassailable position as Britain's Queen of Crime, there are those who will simply never read an Agatha Christie novel. Endless TV and film adaptations of her many crime stories have created a series of ineluctable images in the public mind: picture-postcard English villages; meddling spinsters whose attempts at sleuthing are welcomed by the police (rather than rebutted as they would be in real life); and Belgian detectives with waxed moustaches and absurd accents. Most damning of all (for many aficionados of the crime novel) is the belief that Christie simply didn't move in the real world. She was after all in reality Lady Mallowan, and also penned romances under the *nom de plume* Mary Westmacott. This litany of complaints is a touch unfair: Christie, after all, is not to blame for the glossy patina which film and TV have added to her work, and the 'real world' of, say, Chandler's novels is scarcely more realistic.

Despite this, she is quoted by *The Guinness Book of Records* as being the best-selling fiction writer ever, with over a billion novels sold in English, and an estimated 1.2 billion in 103 other languages. With over 40 million sales in France, Christie interestingly holds the record as the best-selling author in that country. Her 66 novels and 21 volumes of short stories reflect the not uncommon problem confronting crime writers: how to introduce novelty to a well-worn formula? She solved this by becoming increasingly exotic in her settings after her second marriage to archaeologist Sir Max Mallowan in 1930 (*Murder in Mesopotamia*, 1936, *Death on the Nile*, 1937), although she rarely strayed from the basic principle of the 'country house' or 'country village' mystery. A perfect example of the latter is *Murder is Easy* (1939), in which the killer's imaginative ways of disposing of his victims combines with a nostalgic polished surface and impeccable plotting. Christie also had a particular skill in the distilled short literary form: *The Mysterious Mr Quinn* (1930) was a collection of intricately plotted and atmospheric mysteries, with each story's marvellously beguiling conundrum centred on the shadowy, mysterious presence of Mr Harley Quinn.

As often happens, Christie became the victim of her own success. Her mysterious disappearance for eleven days in 1926 (actually not that mysterious, but a reflection of her celebrity status) dominated the tabloid headlines, an enigma never satisfactorily solved, although Michael Apted's 1976 film *Agatha* (with **Vanessa Redgrave** in the eponymous role) proposed an explanation.

She was created Dame of the British Empire in 1979, but unlike later British crime-writing dames **P.D. James** and **Ruth Rendell**, took little active involvement in parliamentary matters.

The top five Poirot books

Christie's two principal heroes, Belgian detective Hercule Poirot and rural spinster Miss Marple, feature in around half of her novels. Poirot appeared in Christie's first book and pretty much her last, and around 40 in between, plus a similar number of short stories.

▶ *The Murder of Roger Ackroyd* (1926)
▶ *Murder on the Orient Express* (1934)
▶ *Lord Edgware Dies* (1933)
▶ *Evil Under the Sun* (1940)
▶ *The ABC Murders* (1936)

The top five Miss Marple books

Jane Marple is the classic elderly spinster cum amateur detective, whose powers of observation (she is after all a birdwatcher) allow her to unerringly rumble the most innocent-seeming blood-letters. Her ability to attract murders should mean that her mere presence is social poison. But Christie fits her into her social milieu – the English country village – with convincing ease. She has been eccentrically portrayed on screen by English actresses including Margaret Rutherford, Joan Hickson, Geraldine McEwan and Angela Lansbury, who went on to reinvent the role, updated for US TV audiences, in *Murder, She Wrote*. In addition to the thirteen dedicated Marple books, she appears in several collections of short stories.

▶ *The Body in the Library* (1942)
▶ *The 4.50 from Paddington* (aka *What Mrs McGillicuddy Saw*, 1957)
▶ *A Murder is Announced* (1950)
▶ *The Mirror Crack'd from Side to Side* (aka *The Mirror Crack'd*, 1962)
▶ *A Caribbean Mystery* (1964)

Chapter 2

> 🎬 **Murder on the Orient Express**
> dir. Sidney Lumet, 1974
>
> **Albert Finney**'s performance as Poirot may be something of a music hall turn, but (unlike Peter Ustinov in other films) it is at least this side of caricature, and sets the scene for David Suchet's later more sober outings behind the waxed moustache on TV. The star-studded cast incarnate Christie's clearly differentiated characters with aplomb, while director Lumet maximizes one of his key assets: the romance of steam, as embodied in the glittering Orient Express itself (and charmingly enhanced by Richard Rodney Bennett's celebrated orchestral score).

to Poirot and the train's detective Bianchi to track down the murderer from among the variety of suspects (a countess, an imperious American woman and a colonel). The measure of Christie's achievement is that, even though the solution to the mystery is well known to most readers these days (not least because of the many rip-offs of her seminal novel), the impeccable storytelling still grips.

Love Lies Bleeding 1948
Edmund Crispin (pseudonym of Robert Bruce Montgomery)

There are many crime readers (and not just those of a certain age) who would rather turn to one of Crispin's elegant and inventive crime novels than the more gritty offerings of contemporary thriller fiction. His sardonic sleuth, **Dr Gervase Fen**, is one of the great creations of the genre, and *Love Lies Bleeding* is generally felt to be a key outing for the detective. Rehearsals of a play at Castrevenford School are interrupted by high emotion among the cast, and a murder further destabilizes the status quo. Oxford don Gervase Fen investigates, and confronts a mystifying skein of missing Shakespearian manuscripts, violent death and even witchcraft. All of this is handled in prose of quiet and unspectacular skill, with a brilliantly created cloistered world at its centre. Plotting was always a speciality of Crispin's, and the authoritative organization behind this novel is supremely satisfying. In fact, Bruce Montgomery was also a composer, which may explain his close attention to structure.

The Case of the Turning Tide 1941
Erle Stanley Gardner

Renowned for his **Perry Mason** series (at least by those whose memory of the books has not been obscured by the long-running, often by-the-numbers US TV adaptation starring Raymond Burr), in this book Gardner set out to fracture the standardized forms into which he felt the mystery novel (even as early as 1941) had fallen. Instead of allowing his plot to follow a mechanically placed series of clues, he attempted to emulate a natural flow of events. *The Case of the Turning Tide* is one of Gardner's non-series titles. Salesman Ted Shales is walking along a beach, hoping to sell a millionaire paper products aboard his yacht. But he sees a young woman fall from the vessel into the ocean, seemingly unconscious. Going on board, he comes across two bodies – one the man he had hoped to do business with. While still utilizing the intimate knowledge of legal loopholes that was his stock-in-trade in the Perry Mason books, here Gardner spreads the interest among a larger cast of characters, all equally strong, to produce a rich and successful work.

Hangover Square 1941
Patrick Hamilton

Patrick Hamilton came from a family of writers, and this fertile ground produced one of the most striking and individualistic British writers in any field, let alone crime. His 1929 play *Rope* (filmed by

> **Hangover Square**
> dir. John Brahm, 1945
>
> **Laird Cregar** was a heavyweight character actor who always played older than his age – and, regrettably, died young. But among his all-too-brief film legacy is his memorably charismatic turn in this highly professional adaptation of Hamilton's novel. Bernard Herrmann's sinister score complements a dark, Lisztian picture of an off-kilter mind, ratcheting up the tension considerably.

Alfred Hitchcock with **James Stewart** in 1948) demonstrated his interest in malformed psychology, with the real-life Leopold and Loeb case (involving two young apparently motiveless murderers) transformed into an intelligent thriller, while his masterpiece, the trilogy *Twenty Thousand Streets Under The Sky* (1929), has emerged from a period of neglect. But his most celebrated novel, *Hangover Square* (1941), remains his calling-card book in the crime genre. George Harvey Bone is a schizophrenic, obsessed with the calculating Netta. Bone moves from inertia to murder under the influence of a dark mental compulsion. While the take on mental health is hardly a rounded one to modern eyes, it remains a novel of great power.

Rogue Male 1939
Geoffrey Household

'I cannot blame them. After all, one doesn't need a telescope sight to shoot boar and bear; so that when they came on me watching the terrace at a range of five hundred and fifty yards, it was natural enough that they should jump to conclusions…' From the first sentence of Geoffrey Household's lean and powerful novel, the reader is held in the proverbial iron grip. The premise is simple enough: an Englishman (from the hunting set) decides to utilize his shooting skills in a way that will affect (for the better, he hopes) the

Orion

course of world events: he will assassinate a European dictator. The dictator, unnamed in the novel, is clearly **Hitler**, and this 'high concept' premise is an early example of that marketing tool. But Household's wonderfully detailed, high-tension offering is still without equal. The unnamed narrator is viciously tortured, then ruthlessly tracked by secret agents and the police, until he is finally obliged to go to ground, living like a beast beneath the earth in order to survive. And growing ever closer is the sinister nemesis Quive Smith. **John Buchan** was a clear influence on the novel, and the chase across a vividly realized countryside owes something to *The Thirty-Nine Steps*, as does the upper-crust background of the narrator. The book, however, is more than a simple adventure story, thanks to its strongly drawn psychological underpinnings.

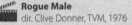 **Rogue Male**
dir. Clive Donner, TVM, 1976

A strong, unmannered performance by **Peter O'Toole** as the English sniper, and an intelligent script by novelist Frederic Raphael, ensures that this pulse-racing TV adaptation of the novel keeps much closer to the original than Fritz Lang's creditable 1941 version (retitled *Man Hunt*, with the American Walter Pidgeon as Household's very British protagonist). Donner's film is a much more faithful take on the novel, retaining the quintessential Englishness of Household's original and evoking far more of the sense of menace beneath the bucolic setting. Lang opted for Expressionist menace, his métier – fine, but some distance from Household.

Malice Aforethought 1931
Francis Iles (one of several pseudonyms of Anthony
Berkeley Cox)

The rediscovery of this well-loved jewel in the crown of crime novels began with a sympathetic TV adaptation some years ago. But Francis Iles, consummate plot-creator that he is, has nevertheless a writer's tone of voice that can only be present in the novel. This was one of those books that reinvented the crime novel form. When Dr Bickleigh decides to murder his wife in the small but exclusive Devonshire hamlet of Wyvern's Cross, the (then) radical concept of revealing the identity of the murderer at the very beginning of the novel created a storm. Amazingly, despite years of imitation, the device functions as compellingly now as when the novel was first written. The beleaguered Bickleigh (consumed by his mounting passion for Gwynfryd Rattery) is rightly recognized as one of the best-remembered protagonists of crime fiction, and there are few who will regret acquainting themselves with this beautifully crafted piece of work.

Malice Aforethought
dir. David Blair, Granada TV, 2005

An earlier TV adaptation (with Hywel Bennett as Bickleigh, 1979) may have had a harder edge, but this version (with **Ben Miller** sympathetically assuming the henpecked mantle of Bickleigh) has its quiet virtues – though the conspicuous production values (always foregrounded, in the manner of most period adaptations on television these days) tend to draw attention away from the central story. Nevertheless, the sense of lower-middle-class orthodoxies destabilized by a single, egotistical act by its central character is nicely captured.

Surfeit of Lampreys 1940
Ngaio Marsh

The **Inspector Alleyn** books of Ngaio Marsh are among the most pleasurable relics of the Golden Age of British crime. Despite Marsh's New Zealand nationality (her forename meaning 'reflections on the water' in Maori), her 32 novels are picture-perfect examples of the genre, and the 1960s Fontana editions of her books remain (like their editions of Eric Ambler) a wonderfully collectable series of beautiful paperbacks. Museum pieces perhaps, but with a vitality that belies their of-the-period accoutrements. Her most celebrated novel – a book that has rarely been out of print since its first publication – begins with the murder of an English aristocrat, pierced through the eye. Alleyn makes heavy weather with a group of English eccentrics, all drawn with Marsh's characteristic humour and affection. The characters may be writ rather large for some tastes, but this is still civilized and ingenious fun. Marsh is less read these days than she should be, but those who pick up *Surfeit of Lampreys* will find it reaching across the years with a vividness that still surprises, still dazzles.

Gaudy Night 1936
Dorothy L. Sayers

The affection with which the work of Dorothy L. Sayers is greeted by crime aficionados remains surprising to the non-initiated. And many would choose this novel as her signature work. Sayers was a far better writer than her contemporary **Agatha Christie**, and her academic background allowed her to freight in serious literary conceits along with the more populist concerns of the crime thriller. Her protagonist, **Lord Peter Wimsey**, with his aristocratic manners and mien, may seem precious in an era of alcoholic, working-class coppers with fractured marriages on their backs, but the books chronicling Wimsey's adventures remain models of their kind. Sayers also showcases her other long-term character, **Harriet Vane**, in *Gaudy Night* (1935), and her tantalizing relationship with Wimsey here approaches resolution. Harriet returns to Oxford after a decade in which she has become a novelist. She becomes involved in the case of a prankster, a seemingly unstable individual who is making life hell for an entire Oxford college. Inevitably, Lord Peter also becomes involved, and (as before) forms a powerful team with Harriet to crack the mystery. The setting of Shrewsbury College is as cannily conjured as anything in the campus novels of **David Lodge** and **Malcolm Bradbury**, and while the central mystery remains the focus, Sayers is able to address such issues as identity and the worth of people's jobs (notably the idea of women's professions in the 1930s is tackled). The relationship between Harriet and Lord Peter is handled with immense assurance, and it's not hard to see why, for many, this remains the great Sayers novel.

The Franchise Affair 1949
Josephine Tey (pseudonym of Elizabeth Mackintosh)

It's comforting to say that a particular book is an author's best – particularly when few well-read people are likely to gainsay you. So, without hesitation, *The Franchise Affair* is Josephine Tey's best book – and that in a career studded with many literary triumphs. Interestingly, this much-loved crime novel doesn't actually contain a murder – though Tey gets away with the omission swimmingly.

The Franchise Affair
dir. Lawrence Huntington, 1950

This adaptation of Tey's novel belongs firmly to the era of buttoned-up, emotionally repressed cinema in the UK – an era that was soon to be violently swept away by the British 'new wave' of such films as *Saturday Night and Sunday Morning*. But that very repressed manner perfectly meshes with the ethos of Tey's original, suggesting dark undercurrents kept ruthlessly in check. The film's structure is as carefully modulated as the novel on which it is based.

Based on a real-life story of abuse and kidnap, the plot (in which a young girl is humiliated and turned into a household slave) seems ever more topical when such events seem to come to light every few months. Robert Blair, a solicitor in a respected firm and a bachelor of mature years, finds his ordered existence disturbed by the appearance of Marion Sharpe who moves, with her mother, into the eponymous Franchise, a local manor house that has seen better times. The couple are accused of kidnapping and abusing a schoolgirl – and all their lives are changed by what ensues. As much a subtle meditation on the nature of appearance and reality as a brilliantly written 'genre' novel, this is a startling product of the Golden Age, and looks forward with unnerving prescience to the darker, psychological obsessions of the next generation of crime writers.

Hardboiled and pulp

Tough guys and tough talk

It is the most beloved – and respected – of crime genres. While the 'Golden Age' of British crime writing is held in high esteem (and America had some similarly classic writers such as John Dickson Carr), the real heavyweight, in terms of literary standing, is the American pulp tradition, forged in the bloodstained pages of the post-war magazines such as *Black Mask*, and boasting the two patron saints of American crime writing, **Dashiell Hammett** and **Raymond Chandler**.

The iconographic elements of the hardboiled world (private eye with a whisky bottle in a filing cabinet, *femme fatale*, rich – and usually corrupt – clients) remain as surefire a combination today as when they were fresh-minted, despite a million parodies. And the image of the lone investigator cutting through the polished surface of society

Chapter 3

Pulp crime: from *Black Mask* to EC comics

Pulp magazines, avidly consumed in America between the world wars (and equally enthusiastically received in Great Britain) were cheap and accessible sources of fiction for non-literary readers, utilizing genres that were then considered to be unsophisticated and meretricious (crime, horror and science fiction). Tempted by the lurid and eye-catching covers of the crime pulps (including the celebrated *Detective Story* and the daddy of them all, *Black Mask*, co-founded by legendary high-end journalist H.L. Mencken, and edited by Joseph T. Shaw), with their half-naked blondes, corpses and blazing guns, readers encountered sensational fiction that ranged from the crudely written to some of the most brilliant and inventive prose produced in the States at the time, from such masters as Chandler, Hammett, Cain and Woolrich. While these writers may now be seen as consummate stylists, they were then admired for the adroit fashion in which they handled all the crucial sensational elements of a genre they were effectively inventing. Others who got their start in the pulps included Erle Stanley Gardner and John D. MacDonald.

Even before the death of the pulps (brought about by a saturated market, the growth of the paperback novel, and the burgeoning medium of televi-

to reveal the decay beneath has an existential force that makes most crime fiction seem trivial. This is a world in which female sexuality is often a snare and a delusion, plunging the hapless protagonist into a hazardous world of carnality and danger; and while the structure of society (manipulative politicians, brutal police) may seem callously efficient, the classic pulp novels present a world in which all is illusion – and fate can randomly destroy the protagonist.

The superficial ease of churning out potboilers attracted many hacks, such as the prolific but now little read Ellery Queen. But more literary sophistication was built into the genre by **Ross Macdonald**, with his private eye Lew Archer often investigating the dark secrets of families with forensic skill, and by **Jim Thompson**, whose chill-

sion), a sophisticated form of crime fiction was quietly flourishing in another despised genre: the comic book. Often produced by the men behind the pulps (such as Martin Goodman), comics – like pulps – contained a considerable level of dross. But at the offices of Entertaining Comics ('EC') in New York, publisher William M. Gaines and editor Al Feldstein inaugurated a cottage industry producing illustrated crime stories quite as ingenious and adult as anything in their prose equivalents (and, in many cases, considerably more accomplished). From 1950 to 1954, in such titles as *Crime SuspenStories* and *Shock SuspenStories* (note missing the 'e'), the duo (aided by the astonishing graphic skills of such illustrators as Johnny Craig, George Evans and Wallace Wood) produced a series of perfectly formed *contes cruelles*, unabashedly adult in their depiction of sex and violence. Massive disapproval from self-styled moral guardians ultimately crushed the company in a wave of media hysteria in the 1950s. However, the EC comics – like the best stories in *Black Mask* – have rarely been out of print, appearing again and again in ever more deluxe editions. Notably, serial killer Ted Bundy, in his eve-of-execution interview with a Christian Right campaigner, directly cited EC comics, with their often lurid sado-masochistic and misogynist covers, as a source of 'inspiration'.

ing, amoral characters earned him the soubriquet 'The Dimestore Dostoyevsky'. And, while the sexual politics of the genre may seem less than enlightened today, the treatment of violence and the erotic is as intoxicating as when these novels were written.

The Asphalt Jungle 1949
W.R. Burnett

Burnett was particularly prolific as a screenwriter in the Hollywood of the 1930s and 40s, and his literary production didn't lag far behind, with over 50 novels to his credit (in crime and other genres). He was one of the progenitors of the gangster genre, and the Edward

Chapter 3

Prion Books Ltd

G. Robinson/Mervyn leRoy film of his novel *Little Caesar* (1930, see p.203) made a considerable impact, inaugurating the famous Warner Brothers cycle of mobster movies. Burnett went on to script both *Scarface* (1932) and *High Sierra* (1941). *The Asphalt Jungle* was one of the first novels to describe a heist (in commanding detail), and remains (with *High Sierra*) one of the author's best-regarded books. His protagonist, Rheimenschneider, is fresh out of prison and keen to get back to the activities that put him there in the first place. Planning a new heist, his financial backer is the corrupt lawyer Emmerich, whose complicated private life has forced him to hire a bent private eye. Other members of the ill-assorted team include the brutal Dix and his girlfriend, the latter yearning for an Arcadian escape from her dispiriting life. The conflicts within the gang are described with a mordant voice that places the reader firmly in the centre of these preparations and the subsequent robbery. When things (inevitably) go wrong, the self-detonation of the group is as fascinating as anything in crime fiction.

The Asphalt Jungle
dir. John Huston, 1950

Huston's first film, a remake of Dashiell Hammett's *The Maltese Falcon* (1941, see p.64), marked him out as a forceful director of crime movies, and his reputation was consolidated by this classic adaptation, shot in a pseudo-documentary style. The script matches the terseness and force of the novel, and the casting (notably **Sterling Hayden** and **Louis Calhern**) do full justice to Huston's vision. Oh, yes – and there's a scene-stealing early performance by **Marilyn Monroe**.

The Postman Always Rings Twice 1934

James M. Cain

This is simply one of the most influential crime novels ever written. The relatively straightforward plot (after a passionate affair, a young woman persuades her lover to kill her older husband, with disastrous consequences) has been ripped off time and again since, and at least three classic movies have been adapted from James M. Cain's slim and trenchant novel (two American and one Italian). A stage production in London drew heavy audiences, and the celebrated EC comics line used the concept so often it became the standard house plot. One would have thought that all the above might lead to over-familiarity, but coming back to *The Postman Always Rings Twice* in its original form is salutary. To call this book seminal is to underestimate its importance: in the relatively few pages of *Postman*, the author burns out a passionate and searing tale of adultery and murder that still manages to make some cogent points about the despair and striving towards hope that are part of the human condition. Frank Chambers is a drifter, deposited after a truck ride at a grimy diner in the country. The café is run by an unsympathetic

---

The Postman Always Rings Twice
dir. Bob Rafelson, 1981

An earlier version with Lana Turner and John Garfield (Tay Garnett, 1946) managed to catch some of the eroticism of Cain's novel but censorship restrictions of the day meant that most of the sensuality had to be conveyed by indirect means. No such restrictions applied when Rafelson made this steamy version, with **Jack Nicholson** and **Jessica Lange** having clothes-tearing sex on the kitchen table. The Italian director Luchino Visconti made a strong neorealist version of the novel in *Ossessione* (1940), again more unbuttoned in its graphic sexuality.

older man, Nick, whose young wife, the seductive Cora, is clearly chafing at the bit in this dead relationship. Frank and Cora begin an all-enveloping carnal affair, and decide to murder her husband. But their actions finally spell catastrophe for them. In its day, Cain's novel was considered to be scandalous stuff; even today its heady eroticism and tensile strength make for a pungent read.

The Big Sleep 1939
Raymond Chandler

Chandler is the master. **Dashiell Hammett** may have been the original progenitor of the hardboiled private eye novel, and many of the elements (tough loner detective, sexually available female clients, uneasy relationship with the police) swam around in the soup of the pulp magazines to which both men contributed gritty work, but Chandler refined the form to its nth degree – and the fact that he was able to write a series of novels featuring his private dick **Philip Marlowe** (as opposed to Hammett's single Sam Spade book, *The Maltese Falcon*) allowed him to introduce refinements that Hammett simply didn't have time to do. *The Big Sleep* is a coruscating diamond of a novel: sardonic, fiercely plotted and boasting a matchless cast of characters. In the confines of a stifling hothouse, the insubordinate Marlowe is hired by the paralysed General Sternwood, who is being blackmailed by a pornographer. The problem lies with his daughters, one of whom is running wild. Marlowe is soon up against murderous gangsters in a plot so tortuous that Howard Hawks barely understood it when he filmed the novel. Reading all the Marlowe novels in succession will make it perfectly clear that the first book is the best.

The genius of the Marlowe books lies both in their evocative picture of a sunbaked Los Angeles (from its down-at-heel Negro bars to the grandest of wealthy estates) and in the impeccable whipcrack dialogue, a yardstick for the genre ever since Chandler refined it.

The following year's *Farewell My Lovely* already displayed signs of the deepening and enriching of character that Chandler was to invest in his books. Marlowe is intimidated by a mountainous ex-con who hires him to track down his mistress. Soon, other cases crowd in involving blackmail, sudden death and precious jewels.

The Big Sleep
dir. Howard Hawks, 1946

Along with Huston's *The Maltese Falcon*, this is the definitive private eye movie. Hawks extracts every ounce from William Faulkner, Jules Furthman and Leigh Brackett's flinty script, and the pairing of **Humphrey Bogart** and **Lauren Bacall** is impeccable (the film was made in 1944, the year Bogart and Bacall first appeared together in another Hawks movie, *To Have And Have Not*). The film famously freighted in some wonderful sexual *entendres* (see the discussion of horse racing – 'depends who's in the saddle', etc), which slipped past an uncomprehending censor. An appalling 1978 remake by Michael Winner, set in England, is best avoided, despite an extraordinary performance by Robert Mitchum and a truly bizarre cast.

Lauren Bacall wonders whether to untie Humphrey Bogart

Raymond Chandler (1888–1959)

Raymond Chandler was born in the 19th century, but remains a modern writer for the 20th century and beyond. While the superficial elements of the sultry 1930s Los Angeles that was his stamping ground are very specifically of their period, the penetrating sensibility of his tough but principled protagonist, Marlowe, remains contemporary even today.

Chandler was born in the States but when his parents divorced he was moved to England, where he attended the prestigious Dulwich School (in light of this, his friendship and literary discussions with the very English **Ian Fleming** do not seem quite so surrealistic). His first literary outings were as a journalist and poet in the UK and created little interest, but after serving in the Canadian army in France in World War I, he went back to his native country. A spell as an oil executive was abortive, mainly due to the author's increasing alcoholism (later to become a professionally crippling addiction), but this was a piece of good fortune for crime readers everywhere, as Chandler began to make a living turning out tough crime stories for such phenomenally popular pulp outlets as *Black Mask* magazine. These early stories now read as fascinating prototypes for later novels such as *The Long Goodbye*, but the richness of characterization that was to make him the best of all the hardboiled writers was some time in future.

In addition to the immense achievement of his Marlowe novels, Chandler did sterling work in Hollywood, producing an original script for George Marshall's *The Blue Dahlia* (1946) and notably working with Billy Wilder on James M. Cain's *Double Indemnity* (1944) and with Alfred Hitchcock on Patricia Highsmith's *Strangers on a Train* (1951). Nevertheless, it is his literary achievement that makes him second to none in the annals of crime writing – and Philip Marlowe remains the key prototype for Chandler's legion of followers, even to this day.

As his correspondence with fellow thriller writer **Ian Fleming** indicated, Raymond Chandler grew tired of his gumshoe, notably so by the time the penultimate Marlowe novel, *The Long Goodbye*, appeared after a gap of a decade, in 1953. Nevertheless, he wanted to invest his writing with more texture and truthful characterization. In many ways, *The Long Goodbye* is his richest book in terms of literary achievement – though its extra *gravitas* saps some of the earlier vitality. In the novel's powerful opening Marlowe encounters the drunken Terry Lennox, and the detective soon finds himself in jail when it's thought that he helped Lennox escape a murder charge. But then Lennox's body is found, and Marlowe is the only person prepared to investigate the death. The narrative process here is far less rigorous than before, with the messiness of real life replacing the tighter structure of the earlier books. And while *The Big Sleep* is the most integrated of the Marlowe novels, there are some who would claim *The Long Goodbye* as his most profound book.

No Orchids for Miss Blandish 1939

James Hadley Chase (pseudonym of Rene Brabazon Raymond)

Many people have picked up this most notorious of pulp crime novels (actually written by an Englishman who at the time had not visited the United States) because of **George Orwell**'s celebrated essay 'Raffles and Miss Blandish'. In this piece, Orwell (in the occasionally old-maid-ish tone he sometimes adopted) had tut-tutted at the immoral sex and violence of Chase's racy tale of kidnapping, rape and murder, extolling in its place the anodyne charms of the classic British crime novel as encapsulated in the gentleman thief Raffles. But those who subsequently picked up *No Orchids for Miss Blandish* in search of the illicit thrills would be dismayed. Orwell would have been deeply disappointed too by later editions of the book, in which Chase, obviously stung by this moral outrage, had toned down the more extreme elements of the novel (no orgasms from the act of murder now). Read today, Blandish is something of a period piece: but it still has a crude energy

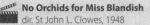

No Orchids for Miss Blandish
dir. St John L. Clowes, 1948

This quaint British film was once excoriated for its immorality (in the same way that Orwell had condemned the original novel). The banning of the film for many years created an underground interest that simply is not repaid by this crude, badly acted farrago (the American accents of the largely British cast are particularly ludicrous, notably **Sidney James** as a Chicago thug!). Robert Aldrich's later stab at the novel (as *The Grissom Gang*, 1971) was much more successful: operatically violent, unsubtle, darkly humorous, and acted with panache.

that sustains the reader's attention. Rural gangs in 1930s Kansas plot to steal the valuable diamonds of the heiress to the Blandish fortune, but her boyfriend is killed in the robbery and they kidnap her. As the ransom demands are delivered, the young woman is subjected to a horrendous sexual ordeal at the hands of the depraved gang (the latter actually modelled on the Ma Barker gang). Chase was no stylist, but the uncomplicated, raw appeal of his books made his name a byword for sexually inflected crime writing for many years. He published well over a hundred novels, in his own name or under the pseudonyms James L. Docherty, Ambrose Grant or Raymond Marshall. Many were set in an America recreated with the help of maps and an American slang dictionary. But time has not been kind to his massive output – only Miss Blandish remains consistently in print.

The Moon in the Gutter 1953
David Goodis

If writers such as David Goodis could look back from beyond the grave at the esteem in which their work is now held, they would be bemused indeed. Goodis and his fellow pulp scribes such as **Cornell Woolrich** regarded themselves as professionals, turning out saleable material by the yard for a tough and demanding market. They didn't write for posterity – but posterity has been kind to Goodis, whose reputation has grown and grown. His big break came in 1946 when his second full-length novel, *Dark Passage*, was filmed by Delmer Daves, with **Humphrey Bogart**. *The Moon in the*

Film noir

Refugee filmmakers from Nazi Europe had a huge impact on Hollywood in the 1940s. Directors such as **Fritz Lang**, **Billy Wilder**, **Robert Siodmak** and **Douglas Sirk** brought with them much of the German Expressionist style, a darkly imaginative *mise-en-scène*, European panache and the often politically driven concerns of their homeland. These sensibilities dovetailed perfectly with the increasing popularity of pulp crime fiction, producing a smoky, shadowy, tersely written style dubbed *'noir'* by the later French critics and *nouvelle vague* filmmakers of *Les Cahiers du Cinéma*, among them **François Truffaut** and **Jean-Luc Godard**. A comparison with the homegrown Hollywood crime movies of the 1930s – the Warner Brothers Mobster cycle, and the jokey William Powell/Myrna Loy *Thin Man* series – makes their impact clear. The *émigrés* also had an immediate influence on many of their American peers, Howard Hawks, Jacques Tourneur, Val Lewton and William Wellman among them.

This new style demanded snappy, dialogue-driven writers. Not only were Chandler and Hammett soon signed up by Hollywood studios, but big guns like William Faulkner, playwright Clifford Odets and the remarkable female writer Leigh Brackett dallied under LA palms, while pulpists such as David Goodis, Kenneth Fearing and Jonathan Latimer were suddenly earning paychecks way beyond their most fevered dreams.

The top five *noirs*

▶ *They Live By Night* (dir. Nicholas Ray, 1949)
▶ *Gun Crazy* (dir. Joseph H. Lewis, 1949)
▶ *Sunset Boulevard* (dir. Billy Wilder, 1950)
▶ *D.O.A.* (dir. Rudolph Mate, 1950)
▶ *Night of the Hunter* (dir. Charles Laughton, 1955)

Gutter was published in 1953, and is proof of the author's stature, with its economical and assertive prose. The anti-hero, William Kerrigan, becomes obsessed by his sister's suicide. Why did she kill herself? Drinking in a rundown bar, Kerrigan meets the seductive Loretta Channing, a woman from a very different social class from his own. And soon Kerrigan finds that she may be a key to the source of his sister's death, along with a tempting opportunity to change his own unsatisfactory life. The descriptive writing of this sordid world is brilliantly sustained, with its tenements and bars and the lost men and women that populate them conjured in transparent prose. Goodis revisited the low-life mien in *Down There* (aka *Shoot the Pianist*, 1956), the tale of a concert pianist whose career nose-dives after his wife's suicide. This is among the most penetrating self-examinations in the writer's body of work, mirroring his own psychological conflicts (which torpedoed his career as a writer in Hollywood) and foreshadowing his own early death. Of all writers of *noir* fiction, Goodis comes closest to the existential angst of Camus and Sartre.

Red Harvest 1929
Dashiell Hammett

If left-wing politics are creeping back into the crime novel today, they'll have some way to go to match the hard-edged commitment of the first great US pulp master, Dashiell Hammett. The hard-drinking writer's streetwise Marxism informed his work in the blistering *Red Harvest*, a ground-breaking work which remains unmatched in cold-eyed cynicism. The novel is crammed with information gleaned from the author's time as a Pinkerton detective, and the edgy authenticity extends to locale: 'The city wasn't pretty... set in an ugly notch between two ugly mountains that had been all dirtied up by mining.'

Sam Spade in Hammett's *The Maltese Falcon* may be the quintessential private dick, but it is *Red Harvest* (1929) which presents his bleakest and most existential vision of a corrupt society. The shadowy protagonist is the middle-aged, overweight Continental Op, hired by the only honest man in the blighted town of Personville (called 'Poisonville' by one of the characters), who is subsequently murdered. The Op decides to hang around and stick it to the killers, which essentially means taking on the entire town. He finds himself playing equally irredeemable rival gangs against each other, and as the gangs bloodily slaughter one other, the Op soon finds that the police force is as corrupt as the gang leaders. Hammett's vision of a society which is only scoured when the Op wipes out every remaining member of the gangs is an uncompromising one; life is shown as a series of brutal encounters that are played out among interchangeable opponents. The lean, pared-down prose is timelessly modern, even in the 21st century.

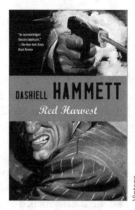

Vintage

Yojimbo
dir. Akira Kurosawa, 1961

This astonishing re-working of Hammett's hardboiled classic sees the cynical anti-hero recast as a masterless samurai in a lawless village in medieval Japan; the only other worthwhile film adaptation is another radical take on Hammett's original: Sergio Leone's *A Fistful of Dollars* (1964) has Personville relocated to an Italianate American West; Leone keeps the body count high, and transforms the overweight protagonist into a grizzled (but prettier) Clint Eastwood.

Chapter 3

Build My Gallows High 1946
Geoffrey Homes (pseudonym of Daniel Geoffrey Homes Mainwaring)

This was the last novel the author wrote under this pen-name (the first being the intriguingly titled *The Man who Murdered Himself*, 1936). It tells the tale of Red Bailey, an ex-New York private eye with shady connections, who has now retired to the countryside, where he hopes to achieve a degree of anonymity. It is not that easy to escape his past, however. Literally out of the past, he is blackmailed back for one last job; but it's a set-up, revenge for a nasty incident involving the fickle dame Mumsie McGonigle – an episode that has funded his retirement. Her current squeeze, mobster Guy Parker, is behind it, and soon Red is caught up in a game of bluff and double-bluff to save his skin. Doom-laden and paranoid, it is no coincidence that Mainwaring went on to write screenplays for Joseph Losey's *The Lawless* (1949) and Don Siegel's *Invasion of the Bodysnatchers* (1956).

Prion Books Ltd

Out of the Past/Build My Gallows High
dir. Jacques Tourneur, 1947

Noir veteran **Robert Mitchum** is forced to abandon his idyllic rural existence, dallying with the girl next door, when his past, in the form of a brilliantly ruthless **Kirk Douglas**, calls in his debt. The debt, in the form of the double-crossing *femme fatale* Jane Greer, is related in classic flashback, and leads the three protagonists to inevitable doom. The contrasts between good life and bad, between now and then, are brilliantly realized in day and night sequences, bridged by Mitchum's extraordinary range of mood and conviction. This is an uncommon instance of the film being better than the book, with Mitchum endowing Red Bailey with a tragic nobility scarcely present in the original text.

The Galton Case 1959
Ross Macdonald

This 1959 novel was Canadian-born Macdonald's favourite among his own work, and is the perfect calling card for the man many feel to be Chandler's true heir apparent. The author's signature theme – the malign influence of childhood events over adult behaviour – is here worked out with true rigour, and while Detective Lew Archer fulfils all the customary behaviour patterns of the tough private eye, the novel itself is in the nature of a psychological investigation. Lawyer Gordon Sable commissions Archer to find Anthony Galton. He is the son of the elderly Maria Galton, who wants to see her long-missing relative before she breathes her last – which will be soon. In the sumptuous Galton residence, Archer also encounters a doctor, August Howell, and his daughter Sheila, along with a companion, Cassie. The search for the prodigal son proves far more complex than Archer expects, but there are other things to distract attention. The lawyer who hired him has a wife with mental problems, and a rude associate named Peter Culligan. Culligan is murdered by a man who then grabs Archer's car, and it soon becomes clear to Lew that all of this is somehow connected to the missing Galton. While the

The top five Lew Archer books

The Lew Archer novels have been described as 'the finest series of detective novels ever written by an American author', by no less than William Goldman. Archer appears in over 20 books.

▶ *The Moving Target* (1949)
▶ *The Ivory Grin* (aka *Marked for Murder*, 1952)
▶ *The Galton Case* (1959)
▶ *The Far Side of the Dollar* (1964)
▶ *Black Money* (1966)

accoutrements of the Chandlerian private dick novel are all firmly in place, Macdonald's prose is heavier and he is far less inclined to embellish the narrative with stinging one-liners. It is this that has prevented Macdonald from ever attaining the reader loyalty that Chandler had, but those who are on to Macdonald know that he is one of the most satisfying practitioners in the field.

Kiss Me, Deadly 1952
Mickey Spillane

Signet

Chandler loathed the brutal Mike Hammer, perceiving him as a coarse caricature of his trenchcoated knight errant Marlowe, and critics delighted in execrating the graphic brutality, blatant sexuality and fervent red-baiting of Spillane's gumshoe. But there are few aficionados of the detective story who won't (privately) admit to having avidly consumed a Mike Hammer novel or two. In Spillane's private eye thrillers, the action exploded in a blood-spurting, cartilage-destroying opera of mayhem. Mike and a bevy of instantly available broads didn't make love – they screwed. The influence on the American public was incalculable (the private eye parody in Vincente Minnelli's classic 1953 musical *The Band Wagon* is a riff on Spillane, not Chandler). With their instantly accessible, fevered prose and helter-skelter pacing, Spillane's Hammer books, beginning with *I, The Jury* (1947), rapidly became one of the great runaway successes of publishing history – a visceral cocktail that went for the reader's killer instinct – and glands. One of the truly iconic titles of the thick-ear school of private eye novels, it's hard (in the 21st century) to disentangle the resonances of this novel from the (far superior) film made of the book. While the brutal Mike Hammer is the

> **Kiss Me Deadly**
> dir. Robert Aldrich, 1955
>
> At a National Film Theatre audience with Mickey Spillane, the author was clearly dismayed that everyone present regarded Aldrich's adaptation as a classic – and (though no one said it) far superior to its source novel. This is one of the key movies of the age of paranoia: Aldrich ditched the drugs MacGuffin and substituted a far more allusive nuclear theme, incorporated in a 'Pandora's Box'. Significantly, Aldrich loathed Spillane's thuggish hero, and encouraged an unsympathetic performance from Ralph Meeker.

least PC of protagonists, that very fact alone makes him perversely attractive. Here, Mike is alternately seduced and beaten to a pulp in a plot involving drug trafficking, with the usual assortment of available females and sinister heavies. The novel, of course, starts with one of the most famous images in the Hammer canon: Mike encounters a girl, naked under a trenchcoat, while driving on a night-time highway. She's been tortured – and Mike is soon driven off the road by the hoods responsible. This time, the luckless woman is killed. Mike finds out that she was working for the FBI, and a bloody reckoning is in the offing. Everything is relatively one-dimensional, but the page-turning quality is undeniable – if you can take Mike Hammer, that is.

The top five Mike Hammer books

Spillane's greatest strength, apart from selling yellow foredge books in truckloads at gas stations and highway diner dimestores, was in his epic, almost Biblical titles.

▶ *I, The Jury* (1947)
▶ *Vengeance is Mine* (1950)
▶ *My Gun is Quick* (1950)
▶ *One Lonely Night* (1951)
▶ *Kiss Me, Deadly* (1952)

Chapter 3

The Grifters 1963
Jim Thompson

One would hardly turn to crime writers of the pulp and post-pulp era (even the best of them) for a balanced and percipient examination of gender issues. After all, everyone behaves badly in *noir* fiction – and if women seem just that much more duplicitous, that's almost a back-handed compliment: the scheming, treacherous *femmes* of crime fiction are usually that bit smarter than the gullible males they put through the wringer. But certain writers were able to present a more nuanced picture of the relationship between the sexes, even within the imperatives of doom-laden novels. Among their number was the gifted Jim Thompson, whose examination of both the male and female psyche was complex and unpredictable. In *The Grifters*, a novel about deception on every possible level, Roy Dillon is a charming and attractive con artist, whose mother, Lily, is involved with the Mob, while his girlfriend Moira has a similarly slippery moral compass. After a con job goes wrong and Roy is left injured, his nurse, Carol, seems to inhabit a different, more innocent universe. However, Roy's largely successful attempts to avoid arraignment for his scams are threatened when Carol – who is not quite what she seems – is stirred into

---

The Grifters
dir. Stephen Frears, 1990

A fearsome array of talent, including **Anjelica Huston**, **John Cusack** and **Annette Bening** playing the versatile but troubled con artists, and a script by Donald E. Westlake helped British director Frears capture a genuinely stark feel for the seamy fringes of American society and, in addition, garner a cluster of Oscar nominations. Huston brings a tragic quality to her role as the stoic failed mother in hock to the Mob, but Westlake dodges the typically Stygian finale of Thompson's novel.

Jim Thompson (1906–77)

Thompson's 30 or so novels were little regarded during his life, despite a highly refined literary sense, and a peculiar mix of raw low-life realism, incisive and often brutal characterization, unusual narrative structures, and a psychological insight second to none in the pulp tradition. Thompson often wrote his novels in the first person, a technique which allowed him to develop the 'unreliable narrator', a theme popular among postmodern novelists today.

Much of Thomson's work was biographical, and most drew on direct experience. He was born in Oklahoma, the son of a county sheriff who was caught up in a corruption scandal. The family later moved to Texas, and most of his novels are set in a drab Southwest. Nearly always on the breadline, and a hardened alcoholic, he worked variously in hotels (as a procurer) and in the oilfields, began writing up true crime stories for pulp magazines, and became head of the Oklahoma Federal Writers Project, a New Deal initiative, in the 1930s. His varied books are united only in their concentration on losers, chancers, nymphomaniacs and psychopaths. The netherworld he portrays is comparable to that of **William Burroughs** in his more lucid moments (*Junky*, 1953) or Nelson Algren on a particularly bad day.

What fame Thompson achieved in his lifetime was established by *The Killer Inside Me* (1952), a masterpiece by any standards. In 1955 he moved to Hollywood, where he adapted the screenplays for **Stanley Kubrick**'s *The Killing* (1956) and *Paths of Glory* (1957) whilst drinking his fees in the bars on Sunset Boulevard. His later books lost some of his inventive and literary verve and, although he was popular in France by the time of his death, none of his books were in print in the US. His reputation revived in the 1980s and, in addition to *The Getaway* (see p.212), several notable films have been made of his novels: *Pop.1280* (as *Coup de Torchon* by Bertrand Tavernier, 1981), *The Kill-Off* (Maggie Greenwald, 1989), *After Dark, My Sweet* (James Foley, 1990) and *The Grifters* (Stephen Frears, 1990). Many of his books, however, remain unfilmable.

The top five Jim Thompson books

▶ *Recoil* (1953)
▶ *Savage Night* (1953)
▶ *A Hell of a Woman* (1954)
▶ *The Kill-Off* (1957)
▶ *Pop.1280* (1964)

the heady brew that is Roy, his mother and mistress. To read *The Grifters* is to be cast into a world where every value is up for grabs, not least sexuality: by the end of the novel, the reader (whatever their gender) will be questioning all assumptions about what might constitute fixed 'male and female' verities.

The Bride Wore Black 1940
Cornell Woolrich

The first of Woolrich's full-length novels, and the first of six written in the 1940s featuring 'black' in the titles (inspiring the French *Série noire*), this is a classic revenge story with, as usual, a twist. The novel opens with a quote from Maupassant: 'For to kill is the great law set by nature at the heart of existence. There is nothing more beautiful and honourable than killing!' Julie Killeen sees her husband mown down outside the church moments after her wedding. She vows to track down the drunk driver and his four passengers, and does so by wooing each of them before settling their hash, and her debt. But through the years she spends stalking and dispatching her prey she is in turn tracked by a homicide cop, Lew Wanger, who finally reveals that her trail of revenge was based on a misreading of the facts. All five men were in fact (if not in spirit) innocent. To reveal the reason would be a spoiler, but this outrageous murder novel is a great six-for-the-price-of-one bargain.

The Bride Wore Black/ La Mariée était en noir
dir. François Truffaut, 1968

Of course, having **Jeanne Moreau** in the lead always helps, as does a Bernard Herrmann score. And for once the self-confessed *noir*/pulp enthusiast Truffaut actually plays along with the qualities of Woolrich's original novel, albeit injecting a strong vein of *sang froid* Gallic humour. Quentin Tarantino was to reference the movie in his *Kill Bill* volumes (2005).

Private eyes

Sleuths and gumshoes

The crime genre has several elements that are absolutely emblematic – but few would deny that the private detective is perhaps the single most important. This is certainly the case where American crime fiction is concerned, and several British writers have successfully translated the necessary accoutrements (guns, seductive clients, sardonic wit) to a British *milieu* – such as, for instance, **Mark Timlin**, with his hyper-violent Nick Sharman series (see p.199).

An early prototype of the investigator-for-hire was **Carroll John Daly**'s Race Williams in the pages of *Black Mask* in the 1920s, while, of course, **Dashiell Hammett**'s Sam Spade and **Raymond Chandler**'s Philip Marlowe (also born in the pulps) remain the benchmark for the figure. Later proponents, such as **Ross Macdonald** (with his well-read Lew Archer), added extra dimensions of psychological acuity – though the irreverent wisecracking was revived in **Robert Parker**'s studiedly brilliant Spenser novels. And the genre continues to offer the possibility for fine writing, quite as accomplished as more overtly 'literary' models – as in the novels of **James Lee Burke** featuring the Cajun detective Dave Robicheaux. One of the most interesting developments of the form – and a relatively recent one at that – is the introduction of female private investigators (notably **Sue Grafton**'s Kinsey Millhone and **Sara Paretsky**'s V.I. Warshawski). Wisely realizing that too thorough a feminization of the private eye parameters would be counterproductive, Grafton and Paretsky invested their heroines with a notable toughness – and the reader is persuaded of the unlikely premise that these distaff gumshoes could survive for as long as they have in a dangerous world. And while current authors are ringing the changes on the professions of their protagonists (from bounty hunters to journos), the private eye will no doubt be pounding those mean streets as long as the crime genre is around.

Case Histories 2004
Kate Atkinson

Is this a crime novel? Or something more 'literary'? Since the award-winning *Behind the Scenes at the Museum* (1996), Kate Atkinson has demonstrated a reluctance to conform to the expectations readers may have of her work – and this hybrid novel (adducing crime novel tropes to more ambitious, non-genre ends) is typical of the surprises that each new book of hers springs on the reader. It delivers the same cool and effortless prose that distinguished both *Behind the*

Doubleday

Scenes and the equally beguiling *Human Croquet* (2006). Part of the pleasure with each new Atkinson book is that anticipation: what has she come up with this time? *Case Histories* is couched in the form of an investigation. The central character is ex-copper Jackson Brodie, who now earns his crust away from the force, tackling small cases privately. His life is in something of a mess (with a dead marriage not the least of his problems), and he is haunted by thoughts of mortality. In the novel he struggles with three cases, involving a disappearance, a murder and a reunion. The plotting here is deliberately amorphous, and Atkinson is more concerned with the emotional chasms between people than the mechanics of the crime genre, though she plays fair by the latter. It's not her best book, but *Case Histories* is still a truly unusual and intriguing crime outing.

Purple Cane Road 2001
James Lee Burke

When it comes to literate, pungently characterized American crime writing, Burke has few peers. His writing has a forceful yet poetic quality that differentiates it from anything else around. His protagonist **Dave Robicheaux**, too, has something new: flawed, yes, and given to some moralizing observations that at times sound like the American Religious Right (surprising from an author who clearly regarded Reaganite USA as a very dark place to be), but Robicheaux is the most fully rounded protagonist in modern American crime fiction. *Purple Cane Road* vaulted Burke beyond genre and into the general bestseller charts, possibly because it is one of his most idiomatic, mature and vivid novels. Dave Robicheaux's mother Mae is dead, murdered by bent policemen. The detective undertakes his most personal journey when he discovers that Mae worked as a prostitute, and that her involvement with the Mob may have led to her death. His subsequent quest is concerned as much with his own

James Lee Burke (b. 1936)

One of the most distinctive crime-cracking protagonists on the scene is James Lee Burke's quick-witted gumshoe Dave Robicheaux. The ex-cop first appeared in *The Neon Rain* (1987), caught up in a morass of violence, and encountering a cast of characters (including drug pushers who target children and CIA agents prepared to provide weapons for foreign death squads) drawn with particular richness and rigour. The novel was the perfect calling card for a striking new author. Burke had enjoyed only small success as a writer of non-crime novels, but his time had come once he fell into the genre, and he quickly made it his own.

His Robicheaux novels are set on the Gulf Coast, where he grew up. Although born in Texas, Burke ensured that the New Orleans and Bayou backgrounds of these books were crammed full of authentic detail about local culture. With *Cimarron Rose* (1997) he introduced a new series set in Texas and featuring wildcat lawyer Billy Bob Holland. Burke's books have also taken on board some cogent socio-political issues: in *Heaven's Prisoners* (1988) a priest involved in a sanctuary movement is killed when a private plane crashes, and the narrative touches on US involvement in Central American terrorism. Although primarily a consummate entertainer, the truly interesting thing about Burke's work is his level of ambition, with such themes as redemption and the horror of the human condition treated with a surprising degree of seriousness in the context of popular novels.

The top five Dave Robicheaux books

▶ *Neon Rain* (1987)
▶ *Heaven's Prisoners* (1988)
▶ *A Morning for Flamingos* (1990)
▶ *A Stained White Radiance* (1992)
▶ *Dixie City Jam* (1994)

identity and antecedents (in flux after his unsettling discovery) as it is with settling old scores. Burke's strategy here is to subtly subvert the standard detective narrative, creating an atmospheric picture of the underbelly of American life.

The Final Detail 1999
Harlan Coben

Harlan Coben's reputation among discerning crime readers is unassailable (even if it's sometimes hard to give a damn about the references to American sports). A key book by this American crime maestro is *The Final Detail*, in which the author delivers a richly detailed essay in human malevolence. Coben's novel features sports agent-cum-detective Myron Bolitar, who is looking into the murder of Clu Haid, a New York Yankees baseball player. Haid (to Myron's dismay) appears to have been shot by Myron's friend and partner in his sports agency, Esperanza Diaz. Has she been the one to pull the trigger – or is the answer closer to home for Myron, with his own murky past at the heart of the killing? Coben, as ever, takes us on a gritty, pungent journey into some of the less savoury byways of human behaviour, but it's a journey shot through with wry humour and trenchant observation.

City of Bones 2002
Michael Connelly

Admirers of Connelly are fiercely loyal, and there was much rejoicing at the return of detective **Harry Bosch** (retired for several books) in this outstanding thriller. *City of Bones* rings some striking changes on previous Bosch outings, and demonstrates a welcome reluctance to repeat a successful formula. Harry opens up a 20-year-old murder case, with devastating consequences (not least for himself). A gruesome discovery is made in Los Angeles: the bones of a 12-year-old boy are found scattered in the Hollywood Hills. The case conjures for Harry dark memories from his past. Seeking to unearth hidden mysteries, he is able to find out who the child was and reconstruct his sad, abused life. Harry determines that the boy will not be forgotten, but a burgeoning affair with a policewoman distracts him. And (as

The top five Harry Bosch books

Kicking off with his award-winning *The Black Echo* (1992), Connelly has to date written 12 Harry (Hieronymus) Bosch books, and one novella. His non-Bosch novels have featured side-characters from the Bosch cycle such as FBI agents Terry McCaleb and Rachel Walling.

▶ *The Black Ice* (1993)
▶ *The Concrete Blonde* (1994)
▶ *The Last Coyote* (1995)
▶ *Lost Light* (2003)
▶ *The Closers* (2005)

so often in crime novels) murders in the distant past have an ineluctable way of bursting to light in the present. Connelly's background as a police reporter gives his books the powerful verisimilitude that few in the field possess. Harry and his new amour are characterized as sharply as ever, and the balance between such detail and the demands of machine-tooled plotting are adroitly choreographed. When so many crime writers are all too happy to repeat themselves, it's refreshing that Connelly clearly rejects such easy options.

The Last Detective 2003
Robert Crais

Former TV cop-show scriptwriter Crais, author of *LA Requiem* (1999), *Demolition Angel* (2000), *Hostage* (2001) and other well-turned thrillers, reversed the trend by leaving Hollywood for his typewriter, and developed an unintentional series by regularly featuring unorthodox private detective Elvis Cole and his intimidating partner Joe Pike. Often accused of being formulaic, his cinematic approach moves the action along. *The Last Detective* is quite his most accomplished novel – even if the first few chapters don't initially exert the customary grip, despite a high-octane opening. The excellent *Hostage* began with a bungled raid on a mini-mart, but the plot engine here is much more personal. Cole is minding his girlfriend's son Ben at his house near LA when the boy is kidnapped from under his nose. The kidnapper taunts the unhappy Cole by phone with the words, 'I've got the boy. This is payback.' But Cole has something to work on: the words 'Five-two', which was Cole's unit's designation in Vietnam. Elvis has put this hellish part of his life at the back of his consciousness for the last 20 years, but he decides that retribution is what the kidnappers are seeking, not money, and the solution to his current predicament lies firmly in the past. Crais has made his mark in an over-crowded field by characterizing his dishevelled private dick with tremendous panache, and by making the kidnapped boy who is the fulcrum of the plot the child of Cole's girlfriend (with the concomitant Crais issues of trust and responsibility) Crais manages to make that old chestnut 'this time it's personal' seem as fresh as new paint.

Calendar Girl 1994
Stella Duffy

The gay crime novel is a tricky tightrope walk for an author. Any special pleading is absolute death to a book's narrative drive, and the best gay crime writers – such as Stella Duffy – are well aware that if points are to be made, it is essential that they simply crop up in the course of the story, rather than drawing attention to themselves. *Calendar Girl* is a good example of just how entertaining Duffy's work can be, for either straight or gay readers (she is also a stand-up comedian). Saz Martin is having a hard time running a private eye business on an Enterprise Allowance

Serpent's Tail

scheme, and is grateful for any clients. When a man named Clark hires her services, he tells her that he's lost £16,000 of redundancy money to a mysterious woman who he knew only as ' September'. They met twice a month for dinner, but she remains an enigma to him. As Saz digs into a dangerous mystery, there are some graphic sex scenes in store for the reader. What makes the book so thoroughly enjoyable, though, is the other main protagonist, stand-up comedian Maggie, who Duffy deals with in alternate chapters. While it is sometimes a bit of a jolt to switch between two very different characters, Duffy handles the change of gear with gusto, and conveys a genuine sense of menace without ladling on the violence. Duffy has proved capable of extending conventional crime scenarios in other ways, as shown by 1999's *Fresh Flesh*, in which Saz Martin is tracking down the natural parents of adopted babies. It goes without saying that if you're someone for whom unblushingly described lesbian sex scenes are a problem, you should steer clear. But Duffy's writing is a delight, and Saz is a strongly drawn heroine.

Steppin' on a Rainbow 2001
Kinky Friedman

There is no one quite like Kinky Friedman. He is the star of his own novels, and his musical private eye persona is a brilliant creation: witty, caustic and highly individual. Not since **Ellery Queen** cast himself (via his various ghost writers) as the hero of his own adventures has this conceit been brought off so imaginatively. Sitting disconsolately in his New York loft, Friedman finds himself musing on friendship and the fact that none of his friends are in town. But then he's contacted by an old acquaintance, Hoover from Honolulu, who tells him that Village irregular Mike McGovern has vanished while researching and writing a cookbook. When last seen, McGovern was heading for the beach. Kinky makes his way to Hawaii to begin a search for his missing friend. What follows is a hilarious (and suspenseful) series of wild goose chases that get Kinky very little closer to the heart of the mystery. But after identifying a corpse whose face is missing and trying to capture hoax kidnappers, he finds (in the local museum) a life-size sculpted wooden head that looks exactly like the missing Mike McGovern. This is thoroughly characteristic stuff from a unique writer. To say that it moves along with the speed of an express train doesn't tell the half of it: the plotting is as bizarre and diverting as ever. There are those who find Kinky a highly irritating figure, but you have to be on the right wavelength. Open yourself up to the quirky delights on offer here (not everyone can), and you'll have a very good time.

S is for Silence 2006
Sue Grafton

The Trojan horse for women crime writers in the States, Grafton possesses a laser-sharp ability to read (and reproduce) human behaviour while not giving too much away about herself, a skill parleyed into her long-running female private eye series, which began in 1982 with *A is for Alibi*. While the adjective 'feisty' is routinely applied to **Patricia Cornwell**'s pathologist heroine Kay Scarpetta, Grafton's gumshoe Kinsey Millhone does not lend herself so readily to easy categorization. While undoubtedly a survivor, and preternaturally gifted in getting under the skins of those she encounters, Kinsey has a chameleon-like quality that helps put her witnesses and suspects at ease (very often so they will betray themselves); in this, she is something like a American distaff George Smiley (with an added taste for junk food and rather more changes of brassiere). *S is for Silence* demonstrates why Grafton has such a dedicated following, with Kinsey Millhone as dogged (and perceptive) as ever, trying to crack a particularly intractable mystery. In July 1953, the promiscuous Violet (married to the abusive Foley) disappeared, driving off in her new Chevy, blowing a kiss to her daughter. Thirty-five years later, that daughter, the unhappy Daisy, has decided that finding out what happened to her mother is the only way she can put her own unresolved life in order. She hires Kinsey, who questions all those who knew Violet before her disappearance. Was she murdered by the brutal Foley? Or is the reason behind her vanishing a more complex affair? As Kinsey gets closer to the truth she finds the easy cooperation of the townspeople hardening into something more hostile, and the slashing of her car tyres is the first sign that things will turn very nasty. Grafton eschews the synthetic climaxes that lesser writers inject into their narrative to add spurious excitement, and provides a more steady and realistic unravelling of the central mystery. If there's a problem with that approach here, it's possibly the fact that Kinsey is told over and over again how sluttish the missing Violet was, and any description of the latter's husband is incomplete without the information that he used to beat her. But just as we're getting impatient, Grafton cannily moves things onto another level, and the revelations begin to come satisfyingly thick and fast. Like her great predecessor **Ross Macdonald**, Grafton foregrounds idiosyncratic characterization at all times, and some of the observation of small-town American life here has the acuity of **Richard Ford**.

The Maltese Falcon 1929
Dashiell Hammett

The definitive Sam Spade adventure is also the definitive private eye novel, forging the template from which all future practitioners would draw. Initially serialized in *Black Mask* magazine (and filmed on several occasions), the novel features the ultimate literary MacGuffin (the object which all the characters kill or die for) in the eponymous *objet d'art*. As so often in the genre, the plot and its machinations very much play second fiddle to the wonderfully

Alfred A. Knopf

Dashiell Hammett (1894–1961)

Raymond Chandler may have burnished the crime novel to its brightest gloss, but he was undoubtedly building upon the foundations of the godfather of the genre, Dashiell Hammett. Hammett's first work was published pseudony-mously in the late 1920s, and he spent his last 30 alcohol-fuelled years without producing any novels or stories. But for the brief time that his flame burned, none burned brighter.

Hammett served in World War I, and his first contact with crime was with the real thing – he was employed for eight years as a detective for the famous Pinkerton agency in Baltimore. His varied experiences with the agency were later transmuted into the stories and novels featuring his overweight, middle-aged sleuth, the Continental Op, always unnamed. On leaving the agency, and dogged by lung complaints, he paid the bills by writing advertising copy, but he found his *métier* writing crime stories for such pulp magazines as *Black Mask*, gradually expanding his pieces into longer, serialized novels. His first, *Red Harvest* (1929, see p.44), was a bleak and compelling portrait of a corrupt city, and defined his pared-down, economical style. In the same year came *The Dain Curse*, and then *The Maltese Falcon*, which encapsulated all the great themes of the private eye novel. *The Glass Key* (1932), about corruption and friendship, was his favourite, and he created an equally enduring staple of the private eye genre in *The Thin Man* (1934), in which the wisecracking husband-and-wife detective team Nick and Nora Charles embodied a lighter, more comic style without the bleakness of his earlier books.

All of Hammett's work retains its freshness and vigour, constantly reminding the reader what a loss the writer's final decades of non-productive alcoholism were. He did see service in World War II, however, and consistently spoke out for left-wing causes alongside his second wife, Lillian Hellmann; both were blacklisted during the McCarthy witch hunt.

sharp characterizations: of the dogged Sam himself, of course, of the urbane villain Casper Gutman and of his homosexual henchman Joel Cairo. There is, too, the archetypal literary *femme fatale* in the beguiling and treacherous Brigid O'Shaughnessy. The novel begins with Sam tracking down the killers of his partner Miles Archer, and the blunted but resilient code of honour that is the private eye's stock in trade is given a definitive airing. While Sam may lack the more

> **The Maltese Falcon**
> dir. John Huston, 1941
>
> From John Huston's impeccable screenplay (wisely utilizing whole swathes of Hammett's dialogue) and direction (his debut), through **Humphrey Bogart**'s matchless Sam Spade, to the most memorable duo of villains in crime movies (**Sydney Greenstreet**'s saturnine, overweight Gutman and **Peter Lorre**'s effeminate but dangerous henchman), all the elements in this definitive cinematic incarnation of the novel simply could not be improved upon.

subtle characterization that Chandler was to bring to his heir apparent Marlowe, the economical, diamond-hard and witty dialogue is there, and the stripped-down prose echoes the contemporaneous writing of **Ernest Hemingway**. There are those who would claim that Hammett's work (in this less respectable genre) is the equal of his more fêted colleague.

Gravedigger 1982
Joseph Hansen

Probably the most celebrated name in gay crime fiction, Joseph Hansen combines the flinty narrative skills of his many predecessors with a totally modern (and radical) gay sensibility. His protagonist, Dave Brandstetter, is probably the only gay character to make a mark comparable to the many straight heroes of the genre. Dave's humanity and professionalism are always to the fore, and make all his appearances very welcome indeed. *Gravedigger* is one of the more enjoyable Hansen novels: Charles Westover is a lawyer who has been disbarred from his profession and files an insurance claim when his errant teenage daughter is murdered. Dave is assigned to the case, and discovers that several young women had been killed by the guru of a sinister cult. But is the dead girl, Serenity, one of these victims? As Dave moves into more and more disturbing territory, he finds that even his own unshockable character is to be tested – not for the first time, as 1979's *Skinflick* dragged him from the evangelical church through a sordid underworld of prostitution and drugs. *Gravedigger* is played out against brightly realized settings: the sultry Californian locales and the snowbound mountain camps are evoked with all the customary Hansen aplomb.

A Season for the Dead 2004
David Hewson

In a hushed Vatican reading room, a professor is shot dead after brandishing evidence of a grisly crime. Moments later, two bodies are found in a nearby church, each with a gruesome calling card from the killer. Thus begins David Hewson's electrifying novel, a bewitching blend of history and drama, set amidst a bizarre killing spree in modern Rome. As the August heat has it in its grip, the news of the two murders holds the Holy City in thrall. And as the media gathers and Vatican officials close ranks, a young detective is sent to the forefront of the case. Nic Costa is the son of an infamous Italian Communist, a connoisseur of Caravaggio, and a cop who barely looks his 27 years of age. Thrust into the midst of a slaughterfest that will rattle his city down to its ancient bones, Nic meets a woman who will soon dominate both his consciousness and his investigation. A professor of early Christianity, the elegant Sara Farnese was in the Vatican library on that fateful day, a witness to her colleague's strange outburst and death. But her role will become even more puzzling as more bodies are found: each victim is killed in a gory tableau of a Christian martyrdom. And each victim had intimately known Sara, whose silence Costa cannot quite crack and whose carnal history becomes more lurid and unfathomable with every revelation. Soon, a nightmarish chase is implicating politicians and priests. A beguiling mystery, and a more fascinating tour of the streets and alleyways of Rome, Nic Costa's suspenseful debut is a treat.

Sunset and Sawdust 2004
Joe R. Lansdale

Among writers in what is loosely called the crime and thriller genre, Joe Lansdale is a unique talent. In fact, his sardonically funny, atmospherically realized novels barely fit in any recognized genre (although violent death can be counted on as a recurring factor). This is unsurprising as he has also written Westerns, sci-fi, horror, and even (pseudonymously) porn titles. But the 'Mojo' series featuring Texan sleuths Hap Collins and Leonard Pine, which launched in 1990 with *Savage Season* and which includes such books as *Bad Chilli* (1997) and *Captains Outrageous* (2001), has carved out a Lansdalian universe, unlike any other writer (apart, of course, from his growing host of imitators). *Sunset and Sawdust* is something of a new departure: Sunset is the widow of a constable who has been shot dead at a Texan sawmill camp, and she undertakes to look into a double murder. But her assumption of her husband's position is looked at askance by the uncooperative townsfolk – and some bizarre encounters are in store for the gun-toting Sunset. Over-the-top characters, delirious plotting, a vividly drawn *milieu*, and coruscating dialogue: all the customary Joe Lansdale fingerprints are in place.

Prayers for Rain 1999
Dennis Lehane

With a background as a counsellor specializing in disturbed and abused children, Lehane writes with authority. His *Mystic River* (2001, see p.98), filmed by Clint Eastwood, vaulted him to fame, but

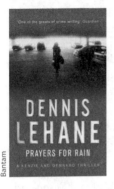

Bantam

his Kenzie-Gennaro novels, beginning with *A Drink Before the War* (1994), established a firm basis for his growing reputation. In *Prayers for Rain*, the fifth in the cycle, Boston private investigator Patrick Kenzie meets an intriguing young woman, Karen Nichols, who six months later jumps from one of Boston's most cherished monuments. As Patrick finds himself becoming obsessed with the truth behind the tragic events that befell Karen, he soon becomes engaged in psychological warfare with a lethally intelligent sociopath who specializes in making his victims' lives hell. The byplay between Patrick, his ex-partner Angela and his eccentric friend Bubba Gennaro are a particular pleasure, and even the shopworn theme of the hyper-intelligent villain is handled with a freshness that keeps cliché at bay.

One Fearful Yellow Eye 1966
John D. MacDonald

American master John D. MacDonald's Travis McGee novels (all with a colour in the title) made him a very rich man – and though he is far less consistent than his namesake in the private eye genre, **Ross Macdonald**, at his best he brings an energy and forcefulness to his material, married to a keen social concern (as voiced by his gumshoe hero, who lives on a Florida houseboat called the 'Busted Flush'). *One Fearful Yellow Eye* is the perfect entry point for MacDonald. McGee is commissioned

Fawcett Books

by the wife of an old friend to retrieve the missing money that a celebrated surgeon (mortally ill) was to leave to his long-suffering family. MacDonald's plotting here is tortuous, but in the best possible fashion, and the sense of the fragility of life and of the social order is as acute as it was in that other McGee novel which many consider to be among MacDonald's best, *The Green Ripper*.

The Moving Target 1948
Ross Macdonald

One of Ross Macdonald's most popular novels, *The Moving Target* is in some ways the quintessential outing for his Marlowesque private eye **Lew Archer**, with an ambitiously large *dramatis personae*, all impeccably characterized. A great many people are going to a great deal of trouble to get their hands on a hundred grand in small notes. Archer finds himself running up against Elaine Samson, the disenchanted wife of a millionaire, ex-D.A. Albert Graves (not a man noted for philanthropy), and the violent chorus boy Dwight Troy. All of this is vintage Macdonald and one of the best post-Chandler private eye novels, with a palpable sense of evil.

Harper
dir. Jack Smight, 1966

Paul Newman plays an oddly renamed Lew Archer in this updated adaptation of *The Moving Target*. He works on some levels: at the height of his career, an obvious choice, serious, handsome and enquiring, and bringing something of his Tennessee Williams stage experience to the role. And he is surrounded by a clincher cast (**Lauren Bacall**, **Shelley Winters**, **Arthur Hill**). But is he Lew? Not really. Nevertheless, the success of the film was enough to ensure a follow-up adaptation of *The Drowning Pool* (1976).

Murder at the Nightwood Bar 1987
Katherine V. Forrest

The Kate Delafield mysteries of Katherine V. Forrest are always stylish, with crisply written dialogue that marks the author out as one of the most proficient in the mystery, let alone the lesbian mystery, genre. Here, Kate investigates the murder of a prostitute named Quillin, whose body has been found outside a lesbian bar. An addict who had been living on the streets, she was only 19 years old when she died, and her death leads Kate into a tortuous mystery. There is zero cooperation from the girl's strict and repressive parents, nor even, surprisingly, from the women who might be thought to be her friends – the lesbian patrons of the Nightwood Bar. Things are further complicated by Kate's attraction towards one of these women, the alluring Andrea Ross. All this is handled with the quiet skill and authority that are Forrest's trademarks, and the sexual politics are never allowed to get in the way of some solid storytelling.

Sex Dolls 2002
Reggie Nadelson

Since 1995, Nadelson's crime series featuring Moscow-born New Yorker Artie Cohen has built up a considerable following, with such books as *Hot Poppies* (1997) and *Bloody London* (1999) full of the quirky, irreverent writing that is Nadelson's stock-in-trade. *Sex Dolls* struck out into new territory in its unflinching depiction of a snowbound Paris in thrall to a grim trade in sex slaves. Artie Cohen, disturbed by changes in his long-term girlfriend Lily, is summoned from London to Paris, where he finds that Lily has been savagely raped and beaten in an unused apartment. Her amnesia offers Artie few clues, and he finds that he must investigate a very seamy side of Paris, one little known to the tourists. Artie's interest in jazz and the darker side of life is not, he finds, sufficient preparation for the world of abused hookers and human enslavement he finds. And as his search for Lily's attackers leads him into considerable danger, he is pitched into a truly international trade that takes no prisoners. New York-born Nadelson (she also lives in London) has created a strongly drawn, engaging protagonist in the womanizing Artie, and his encounters with the various low-lifes of *Sex Dolls* makes for scabrous and involving reading. Nadelson is good, too, on the various locales of the novel: drawing on her journalistic background, from London to Paris, from Vienna to New York, all Nadelson's destinations are etched with colour and atmosphere.

Blacklist 2003
Sara Paretsky

Despite this book marking a reappearance of Sara Paretsky's dogged heroine V.I. Warshawski after a lengthy layoff, *Blacklist* is quite as vibrant and astringent as the author's earlier work. V.I. remains the best single female private investigator in American crime fiction, and her survival (after numerous pummellings, both physical and emotional) is both plausible and (for readers) very welcome. Here, we're concerned with cover-ups and conspiracy: familiar Paretsky terri-

The top five V.I. Warshawski books

▶ *Indemnity Only* (1982)
▶ *Killing Orders* (1985)
▶ *Blood Shot/Toxic Shock* (1988)
▶ *Burn Marks* (1990)
▶ *Total Recall* (2001)

tory. A dead woman journalist turns up on the grounds of an upscale mansion (it's V.I. who discovers her body), and when the police take very little interest, she is convinced that the race of the victim is a determining factor. V.I. begins to dig into the background of the victim, and family secrets begin to crop up – much as in the great Lew Archer novels of **Ross Macdonald**, families can be threatening things in V.I.'s world. The police, of course, are no help – and are even physically obstructive. Who is manipulating the police agenda? As often in Paretsky's books, the emotional involvement of V.I. in the case is both ill-advised and inevitable. In interviews, Paretsky has made it clear that this is one of her most personal books – that involvement is framed in every word here.

Stone Cold 2003
Robert B. Parker

Parker's tough private eye Spenser has long been recognized as one of the most accomplished facsimiles of **Raymond Chandler**'s definitive gumshoe Marlowe, and it might have been seen as a foolhardy move to introduce another series character. But Parker clearly needed to recharge his batteries, and the introduction of Jesse Stone had a galvanizing effect. Stone's chequered career in the LAPD has pushed him into the backwoods of Paradise, Massachusetts, where he holds down the job of Chief of Police and tries to keep his alcoholism in check. In *Stone Cold*, Jesse is on the trail of two random killers, but the number of victims – from all walks of life – begins to stack up at an alarming rate, and Jesse realizes that he may be dealing with a serial killer. Jesse has another problem too: the pressure-cooker atmosphere of Paradise is putting a merciless spotlight on him, and his personal problems (his wife, his drinking) have to be sorted out before he tackles the greatest professional challenge of his life. The dialogue and the sense of locale here are as acute as in vintage Parker.

The top five Spenser books

When Robert Parker's Spenser first appeared in *The Godwulf Manuscript* (1973) he was immediately hailed as a successor to Chandler's Marlowe: snapshot dialogue, LA settings, improbably complex plots inhabited by richly drawn and eccentric characters. No wonder then that, in 1989, he was authorized to complete Chandler's unfinished *Poodle Springs*, and in 1991 published an authorized sequel to *The Big Sleep* in *Perchance to Dream*. That said, Spenser is his own man with, to date, some 34 novels charting his career.

▶ *God Save the Child* (1974)
▶ *Mortal Stakes* (1975)
▶ *Promised Land* (1976)
▶ *The Judas Goat* (1978)
▶ *Valediction* (1984)

Hell to Pay 2002
George Pelecanos

Pelecanos' second book to feature black private dick Derek Strange and his white colleague Terry Quinn (the first was *Right as Rain*, 2001) signals that he may be digging into the messy emotional lives of its tough heroes. But Pelecanos also has bigger fish to fry: the hard-edged scenario on offer here is really a frame for a piece of scabrous sociological writing, in which urban deprivation darkens the future of generations of young black males. Pelecanos has written cogently before about the cycle of violence that cripples the potential of so many young men, and his anger has a keen personal edge (the author has a black wife and son). Here, his two tarnished heroes become involved in the death of a youth, gunned down as an innocent bystander in a drug shooting, and Strange feels he must take out the killers in bloody ghetto fashion. But he's forced to confront some unpalatable truths about himself. The writing at times has a genuinely epic quality, with an excoriating analysis of the dark underbelly of society echoing both **Dostoyevsky** and **Nelson Algren**. The bizarre juxtaposition of privilege and decay that is the city of Washington DC has rarely been anatomized as acutely as here, with drug lord Granville Oliver given the gravitas and influence of one of Washington's uptown senators.

Angel on the Inside 2003
Mike Ripley

Angel enthusiasts know what to expect from the ever-reliable Ripley: crime writing shot through with humour of a Stygian hue. *Angel on the Inside* delivers the usual sharp-edged antics. So why is Ripley's wry protagonist Angel trying to break *into* a prison? The trouble starts when the ex-husband of Angel's wife Amy is re-arrested, having been released from prison only a month before. Some very seedy characters start taking a close interest in what the ex-husband was doing in the period between his release from prison and his subsequent re-arrest for stalking Amy – but Amy's not talking. It's up to Angel to find out why his wife is being so reticent and why another mystery person is so fascinated by the ex's movements – and the only way to do that is to discover what was going on in prison prior to his release. So Angel has to figure out how to break in; he doesn't yet know how he'll do it, only that it's going to be just like breaking out – only in reverse... Grab some hard liquor and curl up with this.

The No.1 Ladies' Detective Agency 2002
Alexander McCall Smith

Talk to readers about the phenomenally successful Alexander McCall Smith, and you'll find there are no half measures. People

The No.1 Ladies'
Detective Agency

'One of the International Books of the Year'
Times Literary Supplement

Alexander McCall Smith

Abacus

either see this Scottish writer's Botswana-set crime series as a breath of fresh air in an increasingly clichéd genre, or find their gentleness and whimsy totally resistible. Mostly, however, the naysayers are outnumbered; Sandy McCall Smith's books featuring the lovable Precious Ramotswe have gleaned a massive following, mainly through something that most publishers would dearly like to buy (but can't): word of mouth.

Born in Zimbabwe but living in Edinburgh, McCall Smith was a professor of medical law and a member of UNESCO before turning his hand to fiction. The series may initially have had something of a cult following, but this quickly burgeoned into massive sales. The secret of this success is not hard to fathom: firstly, the universe of the books is not a million miles from **Agatha Christie** (they're ingenious, non-violent mystery narratives; the author has made clear his objections to the sex and violence of most contemporary crime writing). But, added to this, the beautifully realized Botswana settings were quite unlike anything crime readers had encountered before, while the beguiling Precious and her assorted associates were a unique cast, singularly unlike the burnt-out alcoholic coppers that seemed to be populating every other crime novel. There is no plot, as such: more a succession of small puzzles that the amiable Precious and her eccentric group takes on – if everything is a touch decorous, the wit and invention continually sparkle. And it might be argued that Precious is a very original riff on **Miss Marple** – but owing less to her matrix than, say, Poirot does to Holmes.

Black Maps 2004
Peter Spiegelman

A palpable sense of danger haunts the pages of *Black Maps*, and that pleasurable unsettling of the reader is a constant factor. Spiegelman's shop-worn hero, private eye John March, is struggling to pull himself together after the misfortunes that have blighted both his life and his career. Manhattan is his beat, but when a Park Avenue client employs him, he finds himself in a case that has a million ramifications – most of them dangerous. Rick Pierro, March's client, is a self-made man who has transcended his low-rent origins to become a star performer on Wall Street. But everything that Rick has acquired – including his desirable wife – is on the line, when an unwelcome communication threatens to pull him into a massive financial scandal. John March tracks down a ferociously intelligent opponent who has left banks and people bleeding in his wake, and he discovers that the layers of corruption run very deep indeed. It's no longer a novelty for a thriller writer to have a financial background, but Spiegelman spent some 20 years in the banking, brokerage and software sectors, and there's no denying that he uses his knowledge more impressively than most.

Mr Clarinet 2006
Nick Stone

Let's face it, it's much easier to pick up a thriller by an author whose work we know well than to take a chance on a debut novel by some-one we've never heard of. But sometimes playing safe is the wrong option – and readers would be doing themselves a disservice by ignoring Nick Stone. *Mr Clarinet* comes weighted down with some heavy pre-publicity hype from its publishers, clearly hoping that Stone will be the Next Big Thing. Certainly, his biography is unusual: born in Cambridge to a Scottish father (in fact, the noted historian

Chapter 4

Norman Stone) and a Haitian mother, with a great-grandfather who used voodoo remedies, Stone was sent to live in Haiti with his hard-drinking, gun-brandishing grandfather. After studying at

Sleuths on screen

'You could imagine Powell playing chess', said Raymond Chandler of **Dick Powell**, who played Philip Marlowe in Edward Dmytryk's *Murder, My Sweet* (an adaptation of *Farewell, My Lovely*, 1944). Chandler's preference for the somewhat smart-assed Powell's interpretation of the character may seem perverse. This is because for most it is the inimitable **Humphrey Bogart**'s performances as both Marlowe and Sam Spade that appear definitive, casting a shadow it was difficult to best. The diminutive **Alan Ladd** proved irritating in Hammett's *The Glass Key* (1942), and **Robert Montgomery** rather too chirpy and earnest directing himself as Marlowe in *The Lady in the Lake* (1946). The only other viable 1940s candidate, **Robert Mitchum**, had such an air of moral ambiguity about him (both on screen and off) that he only got the chance to portray Marlowe as an old man (tremendous in Dick Richards' *Farewell, My Lovely*, 1975, and barely retaining his dignity in Michael Winner's ludicrous *The Big Sleep*, 1978).

In fact, on screen, the knight errant P.I. became something of a figure of derision by the 1950s, when hard-bitten cops were in the ascendant. Affectionate nods were made by **Albert Finney** in the British-based *Gumshoe* (Stephen Frears, 1972); by **Jack Nicholson** in Roman Polanski's *Chinatown* (1974), in which the hapless Nicholson sports an absurd plaster across his nose for most of the movie; and by **Steve Martin** in Carl Reiner's hilarious tribute *Dead Men Don't Wear Plaid* (1982), which interposed real footage from a range of Hollywood *noir* classics. Meanwhile an off-screen Bogart prompted **Woody Allen** on romantic gambits in *Play it Again, Sam* (1972). Less affectionate was **Elliot Gould**'s absurd postmodern anti-Marlowe in Robert Altman's *The Long Goodbye* (1973). Altman presented Marlowe as a loser and an anachronism in modern-day LA: Gould's shambling, ineffectual detective – whose most significant relationship is with his cat – will not be to the taste of most Chandler admirers.

Interestingly, few of the modern private eyes have made it to the screen (although Kathleen Turner's feisty V.I. Warshawsky made a great BBC radio series), and Robert Crais for one refuses to license his characters, preferring his readers' images of them to remain unadulterated.

Cambridge, he was back in Haiti when the country went down another bloody path.

Of course, none of this guaranteed that he'd be able to turn out a novel as interesting as his life has been. But a few pages of *Mr Clarinet* are enough to prove that Nick Stone is indeed the find that his publishers were clearly hoping for. For a start, his scene-setting is a revelation: the terrifying narrative plays out against a pungent, massive Haitian canvas. Stone is able to make impressive capital from his years in this violent and exotic country. Miami private investigator Max Mingus will pocket $10 million if he can track down Charlie Carver, scion of an extremely rich family. Charlie has gone missing in Haiti, as have many young people. As Max digs ever deeper into the mystery surrounding Charlie, he finds that voodoo is not just a come-on for the tourists, but an extremely sinister and forceful presence, behind which hovers the mysterious figure of Mr Clarinet, who the natives believe has been luring children away from their families. All of this is dispatched with tremendous brio by Stone, who never gives the slightest impression of being an apprentice novelist. Many elements are stirred into the heady brew: black magic, Baby Doc Duvalier, the cocaine trade and the incipient civil war in the country. Stone even persuasively draws parallels between the 1994 US invasion of Haiti and the current situation in Iraq. If he doesn't pull together every strand in this ambitious enterprise, few readers will have cause to complain when the experience of reading the novel is so exhilarating.

Penguin

Cops

Police procedurals and mavericks

The private eye in crime fiction is always a maverick – it goes with the territory. But protagonists who earn their crust as policemen may fall into one of two categories. There are plenty of maverick cops: just as much of a loose cannon as the private eyes, even though they are paid by the state, they are always a whisker away from sacking – or violent death, if they're corrupt (the Old Testament morality of even the most anti-establishment crime writers usually surfaces in a savage reckoning before the last page). But there are also the organization men (and women), who may be at daggers drawn with their superiors but who (largely speaking) buckle down and get the job done. There are the usual broken marriages, alienated children and battles with the bottle, but an innate professionalism always – finally – sustains them.

On the other hand, there are also the police procedurals, godfathered by **Ed McBain**, which set themselves the task of ensuring that the quotidian details of a cop's life are handled in an absorbing fashion (an ever-more daunting task, as readers and viewers go glassy-eyed under an avalanche of cop novels and TV shows, endlessly rehashing the familiar tropes). But the very best writers of novels featuring coppers are always aware that it's the character of their hero that keeps us reading quite as much as the impenetrable mysteries that they're solving. The dichotomy between the deeply flawed man and his professional responsibilities is a sand and oyster scenario that has produced some shining pearls of crime writing. As with the private eye novel, the job of the literary copper – to strip bare the human soul – has often proved a fertile area for writing of penetrating psychological acuity, quite the equal of non-genre fiction.

Echo Burning 2001
Lee Child

Since the British writer Lee Child inaugurated his series of kinetic and compelling thrillers (notably *Die Trying*, 1998, and *Tripwire*, 1999), he has maintained the standard of excellence that finds its apogee in *Echo Burning*. As ever, locales and characters are shot through with a pithy sense of the American landscape (Child now lives in New York, so it's easier for him to get things right). Ex-military policeman Jack Reacher, at a loose end (as so often), finds himself in Texas and hitches a ride with a striking young woman – a ride that will have serious consequences for him (Child often has Jack bump into his adventures in this fashion). Her name is Carmen, and she tells Jack that she has a daughter who is in danger – not least from her thuggish husband, who is in jail, ready to murder her when he gets out. Clearly, what Jack shouldn't do is journey to Carmen's secluded Echo County ranch and get mixed up in the mess that is Carmen's life. So, of course, that's exactly what he does. Bent cops and lawyers add to the lethal mix. It's an exhilarating ride – for both Jack and the reader. Nothing gives Child more pleasure than to be told by American readers that they were convinced that his novels were written by someone from their own country. It's a measure of how much things have moved on from the days when novels which appeared to be American but were actually the work of British writers (such as **James Hadley Chase**'s *No Orchids for Miss Blandish*) could be a little haphazard when it came to details of setting and society. These days readers on both sides of the Atlantic require total verisimilitude – and that Lee Child delivers in every sentence. For an early glimpse at Jack in his MP outfit, try *The Enemy* (2004).

The High Commissioner 1966
Jon Cleary

Jon Cleary has long enjoyed a reputation as one of the most accomplished of Australian crime novelists (though he has worked in several genres), with a productivity of over half a century (he has over 50 novels under his belt) and a particular skill at the use of international backdrops, always realized with great vividness. Although the award-winning *Peter's Pence* (1972), concerning an IRA plot to murder the Pope, is one of his most impressive novels, *The High*

Nobody Runs Forever
dir. Ralph Thomas, 1968

While this adaptation of Cleary's novel is undoubtedly a misfire, indifferently scripted and directed, it maintains a watchability through two canny pieces of casting: **Rod Taylor** as the bolshie Oz cop Malone and the urbane **Christopher Plummer** as the High Commissioner he has been instructed to bring back. The treatment of the action sequences is perfunctory, and the political dimensions are similarly underplayed, but the performances of these two veterans ensure interest throughout. Taylor, in particular (using his own accent for once), is great value for money.

Commissioner (1966) is perhaps the best entry point for those new to Cleary. The Australian High Commissioner has been accused of murder, and rough-edged Sydney cop Sydney Malone is handed the assignment of travelling to London to bring him back for trial. But on arrival in the UK, Malone discovers that the High Commissioner is marked for murder, and saving his life becomes as much of a priority as bringing him back to Australia to face justice. The political dimension is intelligently handled, but the real skill of the novel lies in the creation of the tough, out-of-his-element cop, Malone.

Broken 2000
Martina Cole

The amazing success of all Martina Cole's dozen or so crime novels must be a source of despair to those writers who have struggled for years. Right from the start, she has enjoyed unqualified approval for her distinctive and grittily written fiction. Even the workaday TV adaptations of *Dangerous Lady* and *The Jump* merely brought more kudos her way. A child is abandoned in a deserted stretch of woodland and another on the top of a derelict building. D.I. Kate Burrows makes the inevitable connections, and when one child dies, she finds

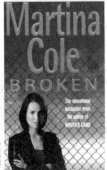

herself up against a killer utterly without scruples. Her lover Patrick offers support in this troubling case, but he is under pressure himself. A body is found in his Soho club, and Patrick himself is on the line as a suspect. And Kate begins to doubt him... In prose that is always on the nail, Cole weaves her spell throughout this lengthy and ambitious narrative. Kate is an exuberantly characterized heroine, and the sardonic Patrick enjoys equally felicitous handling from the author.

Headline

The Blue Nowhere 2001
Jeffery Deaver

Some authors are content to plough the same furrow for most of their working lives, while others need the re-charging of batteries that a totally fresh approach brings. Jeffery Deaver is clearly in the latter camp, for despite the success of the seven **Lincoln Rhyme** books, such as *The Bone Collector* (1997) and *The Devil's Teardrop* (1999), *The Blue Nowhere* moved off in a very surprising direction, with little of the Doyle-in-the-20th-century approach of its predecessors. He pulled off the coup of introducing two distinctive new heroes: Frank Bishop, a flawed but ruthlessly effective cop, and his reluctant associate, Wyatt Gillette, a talented young computer hacker released from prison to help Frank track down that most topical of modern criminals, the überhacker. The villain in this novel is a kind of online Hannibal Lecter, a criminal genius (without the taste for fava beans) whose trawling off and on the net allows him to follow every move and detail of a victim's life, before moving in for the kill. Working against the considerable disadvantage of an online villain (Deaver has to work hard to make him truly sinister), he has created a hi-tech thriller that suggests he need never go back to his Lincoln Rhyme books.

The Way Through
the Woods 1992
Colin Dexter

Dexter is, of course, the poet laureate of Oxford crime, and his long-running series of **Inspector Morse** novels (shored up by a remarkably successful series of TV adaptations with John Thaw as the morose, crossword-solving, opera-loving copper) has been something of a publishing phenomenon. These are gracefully written, atmospheric

The top five Morse books

If you, or your children, are wondering which university to apply for, then Oxford should be avoided at all costs, if Colin Dexter's Morse novels are to be believed. But, unlike Leonard's Miami or Detroit, or Burke's New Orleans, or indeed Pelecanos' Washington DC, where the levels of criminality are all too credible, Dexter's Oxford body-count should be taken novel by novel, and certainly not be aggregated against the affectionate portrayal of the university city which emerges from Dexter's Morse series. This is England, after all, where suspension of disbelief arcs from the comforting 'naturalism' of domestic soaps like *The Archers*, *Coronation Street* and *EastEnders* (all of which have had their fair share of nasty and mysterious moments) to the chocolate-box village bloodfests of Christie's Miss Marple and the blood-stained shores of Bergerac's Channel Islands.

▶ *Last Seen Wearing* (1976)
▶ *Service of all the Dead* (1980)
▶ *The Dead of Jericho* (1981)
▶ *The Wench is Dead* (1989)
▶ *The Jewel That Was Ours* (1991)

essays in classic crime, with the cultivated, beer-loving Morse one of the great literary curmudgeons (his sniping relationship with his sidekick Lewis is wonderfully entertaining). Dexter himself is notably wry about the sheer amount of Oxford mayhem that Morse encounters, reasoning that there would hardly be an Oxford don left alive if his novels were true to life. But that hardly matters, given the achievement of the individual books. Of these, *The Way Through the Woods* is one of the best. Morse is on holiday in Lyme Regis where he finds himself caught up in the case of the disappearance of a Swedish girl who may have been murdered. But he's soon back in Oxford, where he encounters a multi-layered mystery involving both pornography and bird fancying. As so often, of course, a variety of plot strands are drawn together – and another characteristic of the Morse books is given an airing here, his sentimental attachment to a

> ![icon] **The Way Through the Woods**
> dir. John Madden, TVM, Zenith Productions, 1995
>
> This is one of the better TV adaptations in the much-loved **John Thaw** Inspector Morse series – and further proof that the late actor supplanted any mental image readers may have possessed of the character. Running to 33 episodes aired from 1987 to 2000, many with an unprecedented two-hour primetime slot, what makes the series particularly pleasurable is its willingness to allow the mystery to unspool at its own natural pace. Thaw's often glacial but always considered performances were perfectly judged. The use of the Oxford locations – always a plus in this series – is as skilful as ever.

variety of intelligent women. The final icing on the cake is provided by literary allusions, another favourite device of Dexter, who knows his A.E. Housman quite as well as his Conan Doyle.

Medusa 2003
Michael Dibdin

Dibdin began his writing career with *The Last Sherlock Holmes Story* (1978), in which he had the Master Detective take on the case of Jack the Ripper. Outrageous but brilliantly ingenious, the book truly put Doyle purists' noses out of joint. He followed it up with a quirky outing for the poet Robert Browning as a sleuth in *A Rich Full Death* (1986). Each new Dibdin book is quite unlike its predecessors – except in terms of adroit plotting. His series detective, Italian Police Commissioner Aurelio Zen, is an individual creation. But it's the informed, non-tourist renderings of Italian settings – Venice, Rome, Florence – that really give the books their insidiously gamey flavour. Government corruption (as we all know) seems to be endemic under Italian skies – and Zen's bruising encounters with more and more levels of bureaucratic chicanery make for riveting reading. In *Medusa*, Zen's Roman superior Brugnoli unofficially assigns him to look into the grisly discovery of a corpse in a disused military tunnel in the Dolomites. But then the body is mysteriously removed from the morgue by the military police, the Carabinieri, and Zen (as so often before) finds government interference tying his hands. While he's trying to figure out the significance of the tattoo of the Medusa's head on the corpse, the Defence Ministry has dropped a curtain over the case, describing the death as accidental (Dibdin always has his finger on the political pulse – Italian politicians moulding the law to their own ends seems more plausible than ever these days), and Zen stumbles across the mysterious 'Operazione Medusa'. We're into extreme right-wing conspiracies here, with a back-story of Red Brigade-style left-wing terrorism.

LA Confidential 1990

James Ellroy

Is this the most impressive crime novel produced in the US in the last couple of decades? Many would argue so, and considering it in its context as the third volume of Ellroy's ambitious *LA Quartet* (preceded by *The Black Dahlia*, 1987, and *The Big Nowhere*, 1988, and completed by *White Jazz*, 1992) would seem to make the claim irrefutable. Starting with a relatively simple premise (a killing at an all-night diner is under investigation by three LA cops, each of whom has a very different agenda), Ellroy utilizes the discursive narrative to produce a massive panoply of Los Angeles in the 1950s, more assiduously detailed than that other great chronicler of the area, **Raymond Chandler**. Blending his fictional scenario with real events and characters, the picture-postcard vision of the city (with its non-stop sunshine, glistening beaches and universal prosperity) is swiftly undercut by Ellroy's penetrating vision of the darker side; but his real subject is the psyches of his three very different policemen. It is in this area that the true greatness of the novel lies, for while the psychology of his protagonists is laid open with a scalpel-sharp precision, the task is always accomplished in prose which is clean, unfussy and pared-down. It's Christmas, 1953. Bud White is young, brash and eager to make his mark in the LAPD, by whatever methods it takes. Sgt Jack Vincennes has the glamorous sideline of being consultant on a popular TV cop show, and revels in his celebrity, while Ed Exley tries to do his job without bending the rules (unlike

LA Confidential
dir. Curtis Hanson, 1997

Curtis Hanson's triumphant version of Ellroy's brilliantly written labyrinthine novel does it full justice, not least with its three star-making turns by **Kevin Spacey**, **Russell Crowe** and **Guy Pearce**, who between them perfectly encapsulate the ruthlessness, glossy likeability and boy-scout incorruptibility (in a deeply corrupt world) of their respective characters. The film, which seemed to herald a revival of the period-set crime movie, and which brought Ellroy to a much wider audience, has proved to have no offspring: Brian de Palma's subsequent film of Ellroy's *The Black Dahlia* (2006), while stylish, proved stillborn.

LAPD's finest: James Cromwell, Guy Pearce, Russell Crowe, Kevin Spacey

his fellow officers). Associates of an LA kingpin are dying messily, and one of the suspects is a rich pornographer with a sideline in plastic surgery that transforms prostitutes into simulacra of movie stars. As the three cops dig deeper into a very complex mystery, they encounter departmental corruption and find their lives changed forever. Ellroy's novel is a *tour de force*, one of the most complex and fully achieved works in the field. It has proved to be a difficult act to follow, not just for his imitators, but also for Ellroy himself.

The Scholar of Extortion 2003
Reg Gadney

Readers still demand one key element in crime novels that may be quite as important as the protagonist: an atmospherically realized and vividly detailed locale. Yes, we still want to be taken places, however dangerous. And the art of scene-setting is not a lost one: *The Scholar of Extortion* has a Hong Kong setting so pungent and distinctive that the reader will be checking their pockets for passports. Gadney has long been the least parochial of English writers, sporting a gift for vivid foreign settings. His hero here is Winston Lim, a stalwart of the Hong Kong Police Force whose palm has resisted greasing; he spends his time struggling against the bureaucracy and teeming chaos of his city. When Lim gets wind of a bloody act of terrorism that is to take place on the Hong Kong seas, he plunges into the city's fetid back streets to nail the instigator. This turns out to be Klaas-Pieter Terajima, the so-called 'Scholar of Extortion', a sadistic assassin hired by the ruthless Zhentung clan to facilitate their murky activities in southern China. While the trappings here are ostensibly modern and hi-tech, this is basically an old-fashioned, rip-roaring tale of piracy in the Far East, with Winston Lim as doughty and winning a protagonist as one could wish for. The governmental corruption angle that surfaces seems a tad warmed-over, but there's little authors can do these days when this particular cliché beckons. Does it matter? If your nightmares are filled with terrorist bombs ticking in the luggage compartment of your plane, a smaller expenditure on this novel will give you a distinctive holiday you won't forget, and all from the safety of your armchair.

The Third Victim 2001
Lisa Gardner

The quality of crime writing on offer today ranges from the indifferent through the workmanlike to the genuinely inventive. Lisa Gardner has demonstrated in such books as *The Other Daughter* (1999) and *The Perfect Husband* (1997) that she's more than capable of delivering the genuine article: thrillers always couched in smart, well-turned prose. If *The Third Victim* isn't quite as involving as her earlier books, it's still a very impressive piece of work. A grim crime has torn apart the pleasant town of Bakersville and the residents are insistent that justice is done. But although a boy has confessed, some of the evidence suggests that he may not actually be guilty. Officer Rainie Conner, assigned to her first homicide investigation, is caught up in the controversy. And it's hitting too close to home, bringing back memories of her past, and her worst nightmares. With the help of FBI profiler Pierce Quincy, Rainie comes closer to a deadly truth than she can imagine. Because out there in the shadows, a man watches her and plots his next move. He knows her secrets. He's already brought death to Bakersville. But what he really wants is Rainie – and he won't give up until he has destroyed her. Gardner is a skilled writer, and this is com-

IT'S HER FIRST CASE. BUT SHE'S *HIS* NEXT VICTIM.

the **third** victim

LISA GARDNER

Orion

pelling stuff. We've encountered the policewoman struggling with her first case before, but the device is handled with freshness and imagination here.

A Traitor to Memory 2001
Elizabeth George

Don't underestimate the professional who knows exactly what he or she is doing – even if (superficially) the use of the crime genre (as here) is comfortingly familiar rather than innovative. Concert violinist Gideon Davies is playing a piece by Beethoven when he realises that his ability has totally deserted him – nothing connected with music remains in his mind. But a woman's name is embedded in his consciousness: Sonia. And the sound of a woman crying. He finds himself part of the investigation into the death of a young woman, Eugenie, killed after being hit by a car. Seeking her murderer, aristocratic detective Thomas Lynley investigates connections he has discovered between the violinist and a shadowy group of individuals who share a secret involving a 20-year-old crime. As ever, Elizabeth George (an American who chooses to set her mysteries in the UK rather than on her native shores) plays fair by all the rules of the classic English detective story, and it's a pleasure to see the machinery of the genre functioning with such smoothness.

A Ghost in the Machine 2004
Caroline Graham

For anyone familiar with the crime novels of Caroline Graham (perhaps inspired by the workaday TV adaptations, the *Midsomer Murders* series), one word will spring to mind again and again: plotting. This is what Graham does; impeccably. In such books as *Death in Disguise* (1992) and *A Place of Safety* (1999), Graham has conjoined persuasive characterization with narrative assurance of an impressive order. In *A Ghost in the Machine*, we're given a comfortable, in-each-other's-pockets community which is party to a dark secret. Kate and Mallory Lawson take possession of a relative's well-appointed house in the village of Forbes Abbot, and pleasurably anticipate the de-stressing that the move from metropolitan life will hopefully bring. But they're in for a disappointment: the village's internecine feuds seem to have a lethal edge. When violent death ensues, the doughty D.C.I. Barnaby finds himself with a very tangled web – quite as baffling as the many Midsomer murders which have kept him occupied. Lively, vigorous stuff.

The Big Thaw 2000
Donald Harstad

Having served as a sheriff in northeastern Iowa for 26 years, Harstad used his accumulated experience of the darker side of human experience to create the acclaimed *Eleven Days* (1998). And, pleasingly, he broke the 'Second Novel Curse' to produce another thriller shot through with the intensity of its predecessor. This time, Nation County is suffering as the dead of winter exerts a paralysing grip. Deputy Sheriff Carl Houseman is dealing with the usual criminal fraternity of Iowa, while his partner and friend Hester Gorse has undertaken security duty on the floating casino *Colonel Beauregard*. Both will find themselves fighting for their lives when a ruthless group of men attempt a million-dollar siege of the economic assets of the state. Harstad's unerring tactics here involve a carefully orchestrated double jeopardy for his beleaguered protagonists: while Carl fights for control of the investigation, and finds himself at the extremes of his survival skills, Hester is trapped on the *Beauregard*, firmly in the eye of the storm. We've read the 'conflict between lawmen' scenario before, but rarely as adroitly handled as here – this is down to a combination of economical but rounded characterization, and a sense of verisimilitude that no doubt results from Harstad's long experience as a law officer. Hester, too, is a highly plausible creation – and her more direct experience of dangerous situations in the narrative means that she must carry the weight. That Harstad pulls this off as convincingly as Houseman's clashes with his fellow law enforcers is an index of his considerable skill.

The Murder Room 2003

P.D. James

For 30 years, P.D. James has been firmly at the top of the tree in British crime writing stakes. The secret of her success is a combination of elements: elegant writing, striking characterization (notably her long-time protagonist Commander **Adam Dalgliesh**) and a refusal to write the same book over and over, even though certain tropes often reappear. More than any other British writer, James has elevated the detective story into the realms of literature, with the psychology of the characters treated in the most complex and authoritative fashion. Her plots, too, are full of intriguing detail and studded with brilliantly observed character studies. Who cares if Dalgliesh

---

The Murder Room
dir. Diarmuid Lawrence, TVM, 2004

If Ian Rankin was initially unlucky in the TV casting of Rebus (John Hannah was far too young and lightweight – the weightier, more mature Ken Stott is much better casting), James has been luckier with (the unlikely) **Roy Marsden** as Dalgliesh for most of her TV outings. In this otherwise capable adaptation, however, **Martin Shaw** (replacing Marsden) is clearly miscast as the poetry-reading copper. Other casting decisions in the piece seem odd also, and the sections involving Dalgliesh's love life don't really work. Leaving that aside, James' beguiling plotting remains substantially intact, and the director makes strong use of his locations.

P.D. James (b. 1920)

P.D. James has a busy lifestyle which keeps her diary full: her commitments in the House of Lords, her foreign travel (including transatlantic voyages to meet her legions of American fans), her role as a wry TV pundit on *Late Night Review* for the BBC (she was a BBC governor). Oh yes – and that little matter of writing the most elegant and ingenious crime novels around, featuring her saturnine and cultivated copper **Adam Dalgliesh**.

What distinguishes James from her illustrious predecessors is her refusal to sanitize the murders in her books and her care to ensure that they are committed by individuals for real reasons, rather than simply to provide a body for the sake of plot mechanisms. It seems James has taken to heart **Raymond Chandler**'s famous dismissal of the classic English murder mystery along these lines. She is also an author not afraid to take her time over exposition, and eschews any artificial ratcheting up of tension: if suspenseful situations arise, they are invariably generated by the plot rather than a feeling that several chapters have passed without something sanguinary happening.

Many crime aficionados have a pronounced affection for the book in which James's female private eye Cordelia Gray first appeared, *A Suitable Job for a Woman* (1972), but the best entry point for new readers remains *A Taste for Death* (1986), which is also a good introduction to her beloved Adam Dalgliesh. The novel begins when a woman stumbles across the bodies of a tramp and an important Tory politician in her local church. Dalgliesh is charged with finding out whether or not the MP (subject of a smear campaign) killed himself after murdering the tramp.

The top five Dalgliesh books

▸ *A Mind to Murder* (1963)
▸ *Shroud for a Nightingale* (1971)
▸ *The Black Tower* (1975)
▸ *Innocent Blood* (1980)
▸ *Death in Holy Orders* (2001)

belongs more in the pages of a book than poking around a graffiti-scrawled council estate? A particular speciality is the isolated setting (a nod back to her predecessors, and none more isolated than 2001's *Death in Holy Orders*). So where does *The Murder Room* stand in her particular pantheon? The doughty Dalgliesh finds himself obliged to take a trip to the Dupayne, a private museum on Hampstead Heath. One of the family trustees has been killed, and the future of the museum is in the balance, as a new lease was on the point of being signed, while the trustees were at daggers drawn over whether or not the museum should remain open. In one of the galleries, the eponymous Murder Room, there is a recreation of Scotland Yard's famous Black Museum. But as Dalgliesh peels back the layers of deceit, his attraction to the beguiling Emma Lavenham begins to interfere with his job, and he finds himself having to make some stark choices. For years, James promised to give the lonely Dalgliesh a new relationship, and the fact that she delivered on her promise is particularly pleasurable, as the handling of the relationship is sympathetic and intelligent. But the real pleasure here lies in the black deeds in a classic cloistered setting, and there is no denying that James is unbeatable in this area.

Head Shot 2002
Quintin Jardine

Jardine's novels split into two series: the nine novels featuring reluctant actor/private detective Oz Blackstone, and the fifteen or so following 'Britain's toughest cop', the resourceful Edinburgh-based

D.C.C. Bob Skinner, which has been one of
the most consistent sequences in the crime
field since he appeared in 1993's *Skinner's
Rules*. For some time, the best entry was
probably *Gallery Whispers* (2001), in which
Bob Skinner tackled a terrorist attempting
to murder various heads of government.
But *Head Shot* is one of the most interesting Skinner books – not least because the
author cannily relocated his protagonist to
a different country (the US), with all the
extra problems such a move creates. And

there's a personal element this time: Bob Skinner is obliged to identify the murdered bodies of his wife's parents, and exerts pressure on
his colleagues to become part of the investigation. But this is New
York State, and American policing methods are very different from
those on his home beat of Edinburgh. Skinner is not persuaded that
the killings are part of a series of bungled burglaries (the prevailing
theory), and finds himself tackling the usual recalcitrant witnesses
and false leads. The switch this time, though, is the fact that Skinner
is something of a fish out of water. Although not all his Stateside
colleagues are unhelpful, his approach has to be less intuitive than
usual – and considerably more direct. Meanwhile, things are not
going well for Skinner's team back in Edinburgh, where a whole
slew of problems cry out for the boss's attention. A quirky and
individual work.

Breaking and Entering 2000
H.R.F. Keating

It is amazing to think that Keating wrote his first Inspector Ghote
novel, *The Perfect Murder*, in 1964, and was thereafter a stalwart

of the *Collins Crime Club* stable. Here we are in the 21st century, and Keating is still delighting us with such expertly turned tales of Bombay-set mayhem as *Breaking and Entering*. The city is alive with the news of local bigwig Ajmani's savage murder, and the police force is unable to solve the mystery of how he could be stabbed in his heavily guarded mansion. Ghote has been given the less prestigious task of tracking down a cat burglar, who bears the nickname Yeshwant. With the dubious help of his old friend Axel Svensson, Ghote is on the point of revealing the cat burglar's true identity, and (needless to say) his investigation looks likely to throw light on the murder of Ajmani... What has made the Ghote series so beguiling is Keating's effortless conjuring up of the sultry Indian locales, along with the perfectly anatomized jealousies and infighting of the local police force. Ghote remains one of the most individual sleuths in crime fiction, although he has managed to ring changes with his character including a fish-out-of-water novel, *Go West Inspector Ghote* (1981), in which the detective finds it difficult to function professionally outside of India. Nevertheless, Keating owes little to other classic models (except, perhaps, Holmes – but which literary sleuth doesn't?). *Breaking and Entering* has some of the smoothest and most ingenious plotting of the series, and there are no signs that Keating has lost the freshness and inspiration that characterized his very first Ghote book.

The Business of Dying 2002
Simon Kernick

This is the inaugural novel in a series of London-set thrillers by a British writer who has all the hallmarks of a forceful and original stylist. After a rather discursive opening, the plotting is as cogent as you'll find this side of the Atlantic. D.S. Dennis Milne is a rogue copper with a speciality sideline in killing drug-dealing villains. But everything goes pear-shaped when (on the basis of some bad advice) Milne kills two straight customs officers and an accountant. At the same time, he is looking into the savage killing of an 18-year-old working girl, found with her throat ripped open by Regent's Canal, and his investigation draws him towards other police officers. Soon, it's a throw of the dice as to whether Milne will go down for his own dodgy dealings before he cracks a case that is steeped in blood and corruption. This is vigorous stuff that delivers all the grimly authentic storytelling

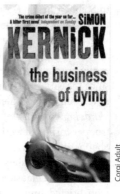

Corgi Adult

that is the *sine qua non* of the best crime thrillers. But it's something more than that – there's a touch of **Graham Greene** in the redemption that's within the grasp of the hopelessly compromised D.S. Milne, a character with as many edges as you'll find in any first-rate novel, crime or otherwise. Another theme is the transitoriness of so much that we hold dear in life: ironically, even before the novel was published, two of the three Kings Cross gas rings that adorned the jacket of the original hardback were swept away by the Eurostar extension... nothing is permanent, as Kernick's rugged novel coolly argues.

Soft Target 2005
Stephen Leather

Let's face it: most thrillers are little more than a series of tenuously connected action set-pieces with grudging, cursory moments of characterization – the latter clearly of little interest to many big-name writers. It's a formula that works; **Robert Ludlum** salted away a tidy fortune working in this fashion. But it clearly doesn't appeal to Stephen Leather. An ex-journalist who divides his time between the UK and Hong Kong, Leather can dispense high-adrenaline plotting, but never at the expense of remembering that his characters are human beings rather than Action Man dolls. He is also phenomenally productive, turning out an original thriller at least once a year since the early 1990s. In such books as *The Long Shot* (1994), the plot never pulls along wafer-thin characters in its trail, Dan Brown-style. *Hard Landing* (2004) introduced Dan 'Spider' Shepherd, an SAS trooper turned detective in an elite undercover squad. In *Soft Target*, Shepherd takes on a maverick police unit that has a sideline in ripping off drug dealers. As always with Leather, the technical detail here is totally plausible (the author has a police contact within SO19 who briefed him on the elite unit). And there's another plotline: Shepherd is also investigating a woman who wants her gangster husband killed. Shepherd pretends to be a hitman-for-hire as he gets the woman to incriminate herself, but the closer he gets to her the more he realizes that she is the victim rather than her husband. If all of this suggests an over-egged pudding, nothing could be further from the truth – this isn't just thick-ear action: moral questions are incorporated into the set-pieces. Leather is fascinated by the psychology of hired killers, both the professionals themselves (often terrorists) and their customers. How can an individual disarm all moral constraints and commission murder for hard cash?

Mystic River 2001
Dennis Lehane

For quite some time now, Dennis Lehane has been firmly in the lists of must-read novelists on the strength of such gritty and forceful novels as *Darkness, Take my Hand* (1996) and *Gone, Baby, Gone* (1998) featuring private investigators Kenzie and Gennaro (see p.66). Praised for his taut, carefully orchestrated storylines and expressively

> **Mystic River**
> dir. Clint Eastwood, 2003
>
> Clint Eastwood's experience as an actor has always allowed him to get the best out of his casts when he directs; here, **Sean Penn**, **Tim Robbins** and **Kevin Bacon** give career-best performances as Lehane's childhood friends dealing with their blighted adult lives. One of the many admirable qualities of the film (as with so many of Eastwood's later films as director) is its readiness to allow things to fall into place at a judicious pace, rather than pitching things at an audience with the attention spell of a gnat.

drawn, vulnerable characters, Lehane is the kind of writer who has achieved his position by stealth rather than massive advertising campaigns. *Mystic River* confirmed his status as one of the most vigorous and skilful American talents in years. Childhood friends Sean, Jimmy and Dave have their lives changed when a strange car turns up in their street. After one boy gets into the car and two don't, a terrible event happens which terminates their friendship and changes their lives. Twenty-five years later, Sean is a homicide detective, while Jimmy has taken a criminal route. When Jimmy's daughter is found savagely killed, Sean is assigned to the case. And with his own personal relationships in deep trouble, he finds he is obliged to go back to the life he thought he had left behind, coming to terms with his ex-friends and a confrontation with a human monster. As a character study and psychological thriller, *Mystic River* is without equal, and has to be read.

Uniform Justice 2003
Donna Leon

How does she do it? Other crime writers falter – even the best – but not Donna Leon: each outing for the urbane Commissario Brunetti is every bit as impressive as the last – and reading a Leon novel is almost as good as a trip to Venice, so evocative is the expat Leon of her adoptive city. Not that Signor Berlusconi and his successors would necessarily approve of the multiple levels of Italian corruption and double-dealing that Leon has stripmined for her novels – and her view of the dark sides of Italy strays quite some way from the tourist's point of view.

Leon's cunningly wrought plots often take their own sweet time to establish an inexorable grip. This is particularly the case in this outing for Commissario Brunetti, but, boy, does it pay dividends. A mysterious death has Brunetti stumped. A cadet at a highly respected military academy has died – is it suicide? Or is a murderer stalking the academy? Brunetti discovers that the boy's parents are separated, and that his father – who has had a chequered career in both medicine and politics – is a man with a lot to lose. What's more, the boy's sister has vanished. An implacable silence greets Brunetti – par for the course in his investigations – but he's soon uncovering institutional skulduggery and forbidden sexual behaviour. Leon winds things up in a surprising fashion – as always, she's too canny a writer to allow the reader to second-guess her when it comes to her dénouements.

The Empty Hours 1962
Ed McBain (pseudonym of Salvatore Lombino)

Ed McBain is one of the true immortals of the crime writing field, with his **87th Precinct** series freighting in a whole host of highly influential innovations – not least the large ensemble cast, all developed to precisely the right degree (while never getting in the way of the exigencies of the plot). His second career (under the name of Evan Hunter) produced some notable successes (such as the juvenile delinquency drama *The Blackboard Jungle*, 1954), but it's for this long-running 87th Precinct series that he will be remembered. In

Ed McBain (1926–2005)

One of the most influential of American crime writers, Ed McBain wrote children's books, science fiction and Westerns before making an indelible mark on the crime genre. Under his other *nom de plume*, Evan Hunter (his 'real' name was Salvatore Lombino), he utilized his background as a teacher to create *The Blackboard Jungle* in 1954, which was a massive hit (as was Richard Brooks' film version in 1955, which spawned cinema riots with its Bill Haley soundtrack).

McBain's greatest legacy lies with his 87th Precinct books, beginning with *Cop Hater* in 1956. The series initiated the theme of the tightly functioning team of cops, all strikingly (if economically) drawn, and McBain showed a readiness to tackle the grimmer aspects of police work (*Calypso* in 1980 had elements as grim as anything to be found in the work of later writers such as **Thomas Harris**). The 87th books appeared in quick succession (there were thirteen from 1956 to 1960), but the standard was remarkably consistent. And McBain still found time to produce a slew of other books, principally as Evan Hunter. In the 1960s he moved into film writing with a brilliant screenplay for **Alfred Hitchcock**'s *The Birds* in 1963. He also produced the Matthew Hope books (with over a dozen from 1977 to 1998) but they were less successful. Tough cop Steve Carella remains probably his strongest creation. McBain also created the forensic crime genre – and was notably nettled when other writers (such as **Patricia Cornwell**) picked up the ball and ran with his innovations.

The top five 87th Precinct books

▶ *Cop Hater* (1956)
▶ *The Heckler* (1960)
▶ *He Who Hesitates* (1964)
▶ *Hail, Hail the Gang's All Here!* (1971)
▶ *Calypso* (1979)

The Empty Hours, one of his most distinctive books, we're given three razor-sharp episodes in the life of the 87th Precinct. The title tale has a young and well-to-do woman found strangled in a down-at-heel block of flats. Doughty cop Steve Carella has little to work with: just a handful of cancelled cheques. The second tale, *J*, centres on the bloody murder of a rabbi, with the letter 'J' painted on the wall of the synagogue. And *Storm* features (surprise!) another murder: Cotton Hawes, officially on holiday, mixes it with the local police when a girl is found dead in the snow. McBain confidently delivered the goods, as ever.

The Marx Sisters 1994

Barry Maitland

Australian-resident but Scottish-born Maitland's novel *The Marx Sisters* inaugurated the much-admired Brock and Kolla series, featuring D.C.I. David Brock and D.S. Kathy Kolla. As a tyro detective, Kolla is assigned to a murder in Jerusalem Lane, a decaying part of London about to fall into the hands of developers, in which a group of aging refugees from Central Europe are still living. The murder victim and her sisters are the eccentric descendants of Karl Marx, who has perhaps provided for them an unexpected legacy. Kolla's investigation is made more difficult by a senior officer, D.C.I. Brock, supervising her every move. The Brock and Kolla series has subsequently developed into nine novels, in the course of which the relationship between the two protagonists is fascinatingly developed. The locales for the novels, each in a distinct area of London, are a key element, as are the disparate concepts embedded in the murder investigations, from naturopathic medicine to modern art, from philately to the growth of the shopping mall. Maitland trained as an architect, but his claim to fame rest with these quirky crime novels.

Arabesk 2000
Barbara Nadel

Barbara Nadel continues to go from strength to strength with her atmospheric and idiosyncratic Istanbul-set thrillers featuring the unorthodox Inspector Ikmen as their protagonist. The first, *Belshazzar's Daughter* (1999), was immediately successful. The third book, *Arabesk*, provoked some to describe her as the Donna Leon of Istanbul, but Nadel needs no comparisons with other authors: she is very much an individual talent in her own right. The scion of one of Turkey's most aristocratic families, Inspector Suleyman,

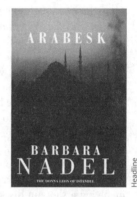

is unfamiliar with the downmarket, noisy world of Arabesk singers. And when the peasant wife of one of its star performers is killed in a sumptuous Istanbul apartment, he finds himself unable to cope with the case. Needless to say, Suleyman's mentor, Inspector Ikmen, is persuaded to become involved (despite being on sick leave), and both are plunged into a world that hides depths of menace beneath its beguiling exterior. As before, Nadel presents a gallery of richly created characters, along with the assured scene-setting we expect from her. If at first it seems that a certain freshness is lacking from this third outing for Ikmen, this is probably due to the fact that Barbara Nadel has now made us thoroughly familiar with his world. Nadel's day-job as PR officer for the National Schizophrenic Fellowship in London (she's an East Ender) gives her an edgy insight into mental disorder. Nevertheless, this remains one of the most original crime series currently in progress – though the author has begun a second series set in World War II Britain.

Chapter 5

Jacquot and the Angel 2005
Martin O'Brien

Those lucky enough to have picked up O'Brien's debut crime novel, *Jacquot and the Waterman* (2005), will have discovered an inventive detective story, with vivid French locales creating the perfect backdrop, satisfying the English middle-class obsession with all things French. O'Brien, who lives in Gloucestershire, was, in fact, travel editor of *Vogue*, and it's hardly surprising that he utilized his globetrotting to produce his first crime novel. But, as many a disappointed crime aficionado will tell you, the second novel is often the fence at which new writers fall. Not so with O'Brien's *Jacquot and the Angel*. Daniel Jacquot of the Regional Crime Squad is not happy with the work of his colleagues after a well-to-do German family living in Provence is savagely killed. It's a particularly grisly killing, involving a shotgun discharged over and over again at point-blank range. A gardener from the region is the chief suspect, but Jacquot isn't convinced. The answer to the mystery lies some 50 years in the past, when (during World War II) the Gestapo murdered a group of resistance fighters. As Jacquot struggles with intractable facts, an enigmatic young woman appears, and claims to have crucial knowledge that might crack the case. And Jacquot finds that even his own family plays a significant and tragic role. It takes a matter of only two or three pages before it's perfectly clear that O'Brien is no one-trick pony, and that this second outing for Jacquot is quite as involving and forceful as the first. French country life has never been so fraught with sinister atmosphere, and the beauty of the settings is shot through with the heavy legacy of the past. It is only a matter of time before readers will be eagerly anticipating each new trip to Daniel Jacquot's France.

The Falls 2001

Ian Rankin

The impatience with which Ian Rankin's admirers await each new publication by the author grows ever keener: each fresh novel is more authoritative and incisive than the last. Rankin is now incontrovertibly the bestselling male crime writer in the UK, and his tough Scottish copper **Inspector Rebus** a part of the zeitgeist. Of course, the acclaim garnered by Rankin's Edinburgh-set crime novels has set high standards for the author to maintain. How does he keep his laconic copper John Rebus from merely repeating the tics and tricks of earlier books?

In *The Falls*, the twelfth Inspector Rebus novel, Rankin wisely sidelines the detective's strip-mined private life in order to focus on a highly involving (and topical) plot. A student disappears in Edinburgh, and Rebus is assigned to track her down, with added pressure coming from the fact that she is the daughter of a family of moneyed bankers. At first it looks like an instance of a rich girl striking out on her own, away from family responsibilities. But a wooden figure in a coffin circuitously leads Rebus to an online role-playing game in which she was involved. And when one of Rebus' most valued team members, D.C. Siobhan Clarke, takes on the Virtual Quizmaster, is she to share the same fate as the vanished girl? All the fingerprints of Rankin's best work are evident in this tight and beguiling thriller. A considerable plus is the welcome development of Siobhan Clarke as a powerfully realized character in Rankin's arsenal – we are quite as concerned with her dangerous situation as we are with Rebus's bushel of problems, and the tension is maintained whichever character is centre-stage. The following year's *Resurrection Men* (2002) drove deeper into the groove, sidelining the aspects of Rebus with which we had become all too familiar, bringing forward Siobhan Clarke and, in an entertaining inside joke, having Rebus sent off to be 'retrained'. Rankin is clearly capable of running and running, and sharing the problem of how to maintain the pace with his readers.

Ian Rankin (b.1960)

It must be something of a burden to be the most successful male crime writer in the UK, but Ian Rankin (who was born in Scotland in 1960) carries his responsibilities lightly, and continues to produce a body of work that will ensure his pre-eminence in the field for some time to come. If **Charles Dickens** is the ultimate chronicler of London, then there are those who would argue that Ian Rankin has performed a similar function for his beloved Edinburgh: his novels featuring the wry, damaged Detective Inspector John Rebus have produced a cumulative picture of the city – in all its splendour and squalor – that is quite as rich as anything in more explicitly literary novels. While Rebus may be cut from a familiar cloth (messy private life, conflicts with his superiors, alcoholism), Rankin's skill as a novelist makes Rebus quite as rich a character as (for instance) the protagonists of **John Updike**. The first book to feature Rebus, *Knots and Crosses* in 1987, demonstrated that Rankin's skills were already burnished to perfection, while such subsequent books as *Dead Souls* in 1999 treated issues such as paedophilia in a harrowing (yet responsible) fashion. His most complex novel is possibly *The Hanging Gardens* (1998), with its issues of war criminals and sexual slavery as persuasively handled as one could wish.

The top five Rebus books

Another in-joke Ian Rankin shares with his readers is using Rolling Stones songs as titles for his books. Spot any below?

▶ *Knots and Crosses* (1987)
▶ *Strip Jack* (1992)
▶ *Black and Blue* (1997)
▶ *The Hanging Gardens* (1998)
▶ *The Name of the Dead* (2006)

The Babes in the Wood 2002
Ruth Rendell

Rendell's books continue to grow in clarity and craftsmanship. *The Babes in the Wood* is one of her most trenchant and stylish offerings featuring her long-term protagonist **Inspector Wexford**. Rendell usually saves her most disturbing writing for her non-Wexford books, and her more psychologically driven plotlines for her alter ego **Barbara Vine**, but this novel imports all those elements into a narrative that begins in a typically macabre fashion and inexorably moves into the darker reaches of the human soul. The River Brede near Wexford's territory of Kingsmarkham has burst its banks after a torrential downpour. When a colleague tells him about a woman who believes that her two teenage children and their babysitter have drowned (even though all three could swim), Wexford finds himself launched into an investigation that has him questioning some basic assumptions of human behaviour – even those of himself and his family. Wexford himself is delineated as economically as ever, but remains the most persuasive of literary coppers, and Rendell's matchless plotting skills ensure the usual seamless marriage between carefully structured storytelling and a restless probing of the psyche. As so often, Rendell writes unsparingly about the façades we all carefully maintain – and which can so easily slip.

Playing With Fire 2004
Peter Robinson

Peter Robinson has never quite achieved the upper echelons in terms of sales for his highly efficient crime novels, but those familiar with his work quickly realise that he's one of the most reliable practitioners around. *Gallows View* in 1987 established Robinson as a fresh and astringent voice in the field, and his hero, the tenacious Inspector

Alan Banks, has proved to be the perfect conduit for Robinson's canny narratives. However, the key to the appeal of a Peter Robinson book is not just the plotting, but a vividly conveyed sense of place: the tales of murder and deception are set in the Yorkshire Dales, and after a book like *Playing with Fire* the reader feels very familiar with this atmospheric terrain. On a cold winter's day, fire destroys two narrowboats on the Eastvale Canal. Inspector Banks and his colleague D.I. Annie Cabbot are examining the charred corpse found in what's left of the boats. Who are the victims? There are several possibilities – and several possible killers, including the father of a girl who perished in the flames, and an art dealer with some dark secrets. And then the arsonist killer makes things hot again. Perhaps not the equal of the assured *In a Dry Season* (1999), this is a more rounded piece of work by Robinson that weaves a binding spell.

The Madman of Bergerac 1932
Georges Simenon

Over the years, the standard of Belgian-born Georges Simenon's books featuring his dour and doughty French copper **Maigret** was remarkably consistent. And Simenon was notably prolific (despite the time he says he spent seducing thousands of women), retaining through nearly all his novels the literary strain that elevated his work above all other police procedurals; more than most, Simenon is responsible for the high critical standing of crime novels today. In *The Madman of Bergerac* Maigret leaves a train to pursue a man, and ends up being shot by him. As he recovers in the small village of Bergerac, he is occupied with the eponymous madman, who has driven a needle through the hearts of two women. This is a wonderfully structured novel – with an almost Proustian sense of the past forcing its way through into the present. The unlikely plot is given total verisimilitude by Simenon's art-that-conceals-art.

Gorky Park 1981
Martin Cruz Smith (born Martin William Smith)

After the phenomenal success of Martin Cruz Smith's *Gorky Park* (with his brilliantly realized pre-*perestroika* Russian settings and wonderful Russian copper Arkady Renko), it was obvious that a major new talent had arrived on the crime scene, along with a detective who (at a stroke) had joined the ranks of the most memorable in the field. But some disappointment was in store for new Smith readers: many of his 17 earlier books began to appear on the back of the success of *Gorky Park*, and readers were reminded that this former reporter had had a lengthy career as a novelist before this breakthrough book. And although the re-issued books were perfectly capable pieces of work, they didn't begin to match the achievement of the most recent novel. The novel won the C.W.A. Gold Dagger, and few previous novels had ever utilized a foreign locale with such attention to detail. Renko, Chief Homicide Investigator for the Moscow Prosecutor's Office, is handed a triple murder to investigate. Why have three corpses been mutilated and buried in the Moscow park of the title? As Renko tries to deal with intractable government departments and the whole vodka-swilling apparatus of the Soviet

---

Gorky Park
dir. Michael Apted, 1983

The excellent **William Hurt** as Renko; **Lee Marvin** as a duplicitous American businessman; a screenplay by no less than **Dennis Potter**. The auguries were all in place for a movie that would have done full justice to the novel. So what went wrong? Many things: Hurt's performance is so low-key as to be almost invisible, director Michael Apted is not able to marshal the elements of the complex plot with sufficient rigour, and Dennis Potter gives every impression of being out of sympathy with the material. The film was shot in Helsinki, which makes a passable substitute for Moscow. And Marvin was, of course, characteristically great.

state, he finds that the solution may lie with some dangerous (and influential) foreigners. Renko is a classic creation, and has been utilized almost equally well in later books such as *Polar Star* (1989) and *Red Square* (1992) – though the novelty was, of course, diminished. But it is the Russian setting, with its unremitting snow, May Day celebrations and indomitable – if repressed – citizenry, that both made this novel one of the most popular crime thrillers ever written and, of course, led to a whole army of imitators.

Hollywood Station 2006
Joseph Wambaugh

It's truly a cause for celebration that one of the most influential and important of police crime novelists is back in the spotlight again in the 21st century (after some neglect) with a 'comeback' book, *Hollywood Station*. The contemporary police novel owes a great deal to such Wambaugh classics as *The Choirboys* (1975) and *The Onion Field* (1973); in these novels, Wambaugh's experience on the force evokes the immense pressures that officers on duty are forced to experience, and the breakdowns of several of his characters have a power that is charged by

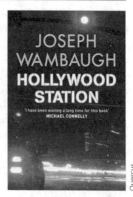

this verisimilitude. *Hollywood Station* is proof that he hasn't lost his touch. His strikingly drawn protagonists here are Hollywood cops Fausto Gamboa and Ron leCroix, who deal with the kind of outrageous situations that one might expect of Tinseltown. Unsurprisingly, things turn very dark indeed – although Wambaugh's knowing authorial tone always informs his kinetic narrative.

Sideswipe 1987
Charles Willeford

Although well known to the cognoscenti, ex-boxer, painter, actor and journalist Charles Willeford remains unknown to the great mass of crime readers – and that's undoubtedly their loss. Namechecked by **Elmore Leonard**, **Carl Hiaasen** and **James Hall** as a key influence, it was only with George Armitage's 1990 film of *Miami Blues* that he really came to public attention. Hardened cineastes might also remember him as the author behind Monte Hellmann's controversial 1974 movie *Cockfighter.* Always one of the most individual of stylists (and one of the first crime writers, like James Hall, to run a university creative writing course), Willeford combines a cockeyed view of the world with an inimitable prose style and wonderfully drawn characters – such as *Sideswipe*'s beleaguered Hoke Moseley (who also features in *Miami Blues*). Hoke is a cop who has struggled through a none-too-shining career when he decides to retire and attempt to run a down-at-heel hotel. This proves to be a mistake: he has got his girlfriend pregnant, and his two daughters are rapidly going off the rails. If this wasn't bad enough, a gang of wackos turns up at the hotel. All of this is handled with the kind of delirious energy that is Willeford's trademark, and his influence on later writers (and even filmmakers) will be evident to anyone who makes an acquaintance with his work. In some ways, it would be nice for Charles Willeford to remain a hidden pleasure for the chosen few – but that would be selfish, wouldn't it?

The Silent and the Damned 2004
Robert Wilson

They are a proud band, the knot of readers who extol the virtues of Robert Wilson, with such books as *A Darkening Stain* (2004)

Chapter 5

categorical proof that their man is something unique in the ranks of current crime writers. His sagas of twisted loyalties and middle-level corruption in pungently evoked foreign settings are reminiscent of an earlier generation of writers (grimy urban *noir* is not for Wilson). He gleaned much praise for *A Small Death in Lisbon* (2000, see p.276), and although *The Company of Strangers* (2002, see p.255) was less well received Wilson followers were pleased to receive *The Silent and the Damned*, an outing for his conflicted detective Javier Falcon that pressed all the right buttons. It is summer in Seville. Falcon is investigating what appears to be a suicide pact in an upscale area. Needless to say, nothing is as it seems; Falcon dispenses with the obvious and begins to see the hand of a criminal strategist at work. Another double suicide follows – and one of the dead is a police colleague of Falcon's. Ukrainian prostitutes and people-smuggling Russian Mafia are soon stirred into the brew – but then Falcon makes a significant discovery... While the trademark Wilson gift for vividly drawn locales is in evidence, he never forgets that the key to the best crime writing is sharp characterization, and his large *dramatis personae* is drawn with skill. If some plot elements seem a tad warmed-over, Wilson still delivers a carefully structured but exuberant piece of work.

Professionals

Lawyers, doctors, forensics and others

Barely a week passes without a well-paid lawyer deciding that they can become an even better-paid writer of legal thrillers – for that dubious pleasure we can blame the unprecedented success of **John Grisham**. But the law has featured in fiction as a source of destruction in the lives of the protagonists as far back as Dickens' *Bleak House* – the modern riff on the theme involves placing the lawyers centre-stage, often functioning as detectives-by-default. It was a source of some annoyance for the late **Ed McBain** that the two major innovations he brought to the crime novel were developed (and thoroughly colonized) by others: the police unit functioning as a tight-knit team, and the importance of forensics in detection. But McBain could hardly complain that his achievement in the field was undervalued – and there is no denying that two phenomenally successful American female crime novelists in particular, **Patricia Cornwell** and **Kathy Reichs**, have parleyed forensic anthropologist heroines into total bestsellerdom. It was clearly time for something other than the policemen or private detective in the crime field – and it's interesting that the other highly influential 'alternative profession' for a crime novel protagonist is the criminal profiler. There, **Val McDermid**'s unassumingly brilliant Dr Tony Hill is almost as imitated as Cornwell's heroine Kay Scarpetta. The public's taste for the often gruesome technicalities of crime-solving has been reflected in the popularity of TV series such as *Cracker* (criminal profiling), *Silent Witness* (forensic pathology) and *CSI* (crime scene investigation). And there are other verdant areas of crime-related professionals ripe for development: insurance investigators and bounty hunters for instance.

Double Indemnity 1943

James M. Cain

James M. Cain's second most famous book is as febrile and hard-edged as *The Postman Always Rings Twice* (see p.37). Insurance investigator Walter Huff falls for the middle-class *femme fatale* Phyllis Nirdlinger and (as in *Postman*) is persuaded to kill her husband for his insurance. This most cold-eyed of crime novels is one of the most impressive in the genre (hardboiled or otherwise), with

---

Double Indemnity
dir. Billy Wilder, 1944

While many a *noir* masterpiece has undergone an ill-advised re-make, no one has yet had the temerity to try to match Billy Wilder's ice-cold classic, burnished with work on the screenplay by no less than **Raymond Chandler** (although Lawrence Kasdan's *Body Heat*, 1981, came close). **Barbara Stanwyck**, **Fred MacMurray** (the definitive fall guy) and **Edward G. Robinson** as the insurance fraud investigator who rumbles the plot are a matchless cast for this reptilian tale of lust, greed and betrayal.

---

nary a wasted word – the concision of Cain's prose is even more bracing today, when elephantiasis has taken hold of the crime novel. The basic scenario – the anti-hero led by his genitals into a murder for gain by a ruthless, predatory woman – was to become the most crucial of blueprints for the genre, never more coolly articulated than here. The famous **Billy Wilder** film consolidated the success of the book, but it would still be remembered today even without this helping hand, not least for Cain's very modern cynicism.

Seizure 2003
Robin Cook

The name of the doctor/novelist Robin Cook has long been a byword for impeccably detailed, plausible thrillers, and even if his later work is not always as powerful as his early books such as *Coma* (1977) and *Outbreak* (1987), he is always totally professional, guaranteeing the reader a well-turned piece of work. That's very much the case with *Seizure*, where Cook's skills in the plotting arena are quietly brought into play. Biotechnology is the theme here, and an implacable opponent of all research in

the field, ultra-conservative Southern senator Ashley Butler, enjoys chairing a committee to put the brakes on cloning technology. Stem cell researcher Dan Lowell is, of course, a key opponent, but both men have strange and conflicted personalities. When Butler contracts Parkinson's disease, he is forced to enlist the aid of his former enemy. But too-precipitate use of the new advances in the technology has disastrous consequences for both men. All of Cook's best thrillers utilize medical and scientific concepts like this (highly topical as America moves further to the right in such areas), and *Seizure* satisfyingly incorporates such ideas into a sprawling but taut narrative.

Blowfly 2003
Patricia Cornwell

After *Postmortem* (1990) launched her series of **Kay Scarpetta** novels – and created an army of imitation female pathologists – Patricia Cornwell seemed to lose her way. But this outing for the resourceful Scarpetta has all the energy and invention of the earlier work – although the levels of blood-boltered horror here make even the sanguinary excesses of the earlier books look restrained. Scarpetta's independence has made her *persona non grata* with her long-suffering bosses, and she's pursuing a freelance career in Florida. But the monstrous Chandonne, a serial murderer with lycanthropic tendencies who she tackled in the past, is not quite out of her life. And if this doesn't make Kay's life complicated enough, her niece Lucy, no longer in the employ of the FBI, has Chandonne's bent lawyer in her sights, with intentions quite as murderous as the serial killer had towards Kay. As so often before, Kay is forced to juggle her personal and professional responsibilities, with her emotional life a hostage to fortune – a settled love life is not on the cards for her. What follows is a richly unsettling mélange of tortuous plotting (the above synopsis only hints at the complexity of *Blowfly*'s multi-layered narrative) and the usual full-throated bloodletting, all hurtling along at a pace that rarely gives pause for breath. What a dark world the beleaguered Scarpetta plies her trade in! Being aware of the skull beneath the skin leaves her with few illusions about the imperfections of the human race.

Patricia Cornwell (b.1956)

Patricia Cornwell is so unassailably at the top of the crime-writing profession that her name is routinely used to sell the books of the legions of imitators who have followed in her path. Approbation arrived immediately for her first book, *Postmortem* (1990), and the astonishing success of this debut (and the multiple prizes it gleaned) acted as a spur for her successive books, in which the forensic anthropologist Kay Scarpetta (with her messy private life) encounters a series of increasingly grisly puzzles (Cornwell is at the forefront of women writers who match their male counterparts in horrific detail). It was no surprise when she received the Crime Writers' Association Dagger, about which she remarked that to receive it in the home country of **Agatha Christie** was a tremendous honour ('after all, in terms of plotting, we're all her heirs'). When Cornwell changed direction, temporarily abandoning Kay Scarpetta for the Judy Hammer books (Hammer being a more straightforward female cop), she took a measure of flak. Why wasn't she continuing to produce something that was a proven quality? But clearly Cornwell had to keep the experience of writing fresh for herself, and the Hammer books have their charms. However, most loyal Cornwell fans were glad to see Kay Scarpetta back, in re-invigorated novels. On the faintly risible subject of the painter **Walter Sickert** (who Cornwell identified as the most famous of all serial killers in her controversial book *Jack the Ripper: Case Closed*) the author brooks no argument, and she spent a great deal of money adducing scientific opinions for her case.

The top five Kay Scarpetta books

▶ *Postmortem* (1990)
▶ *Cruel and Unusual* (1993)
▶ *The Body Farm* (1994)
▶ *From Potter's Field* (1995)
▶ *Point of Origin* (1998)

Hard Eight 2002
Janet Evanovich

Bounty hunting is a relatively new profession in the crime genre, but one that was sparked off by several high-profile real cases. And with the ever-reliable Janet Evanovich, you know you're in safe hands. In the comedy thriller stakes, she has few equals – even if, at times, her splenetic imagination falters, and the farcical takes over. Not here, though: *Hard Eight* is vintage Evanovich, firing on all cylinders and throwing out the one-liners in a positively spendthrift fashion. Bombshell bounty hunter Stephanie Plum is back on her Harley – so we're in for another wild ride. Sardonic, fresh and full of surprises (if a touch self-conscious), Evanovich's adroit thriller is crammed full of more diverting misadventures for Stephanie. As she spirals and tumbles through her customarily frenetic and incendiary world, she can hardly catch her breath, let alone her man – even if she could decide which one to chase. The author now lives in New Hampshire but (like Stephanie) grew up in New Jersey and cannily draws on her background for some evocative scene-setting (the comedy and thrills are always anchored in a plausible world). She has won major crime fiction awards for her Stephanie Plum novels; *One for the Money* (1994) bagged a Crime Writers' Association Award, as did *Two for the Dough* (1996). It's always good to spend time in the company of the feisty Ms Plum and her ingeniously numbered series.

Avenger 2003
Frederick Forsyth

Enthusiasts of the early diamond-hard thrillers of Frederick Forsyth have had something of a dry time lately. What was The Master up to, aficionados wondered? Had he grown disenchanted with the thriller genre? Forsyth, as we all know, is a man who easily grows disenchanted with things. Would our encounters with the man now have to consist of his splenetic outbursts in his new role as in-your-face political pundit? But perhaps the bafflement that greeted his *Phantom of the Opera* sequel *The Phantom of Manhattan* (1999) forced a recharging of his batteries, helping him to deliver *Avenger*, a lean and mesmerizing thriller with all the hallmarks of his vintage work. His protagonist here is Cal Dexter, a survivor of the Vietnam War who is making an unexceptional living as a

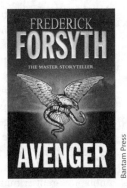

Bantam Press

small-town lawyer. But his real *métier* is his role as 'Avenger', a clandestine righter of wrongs who tackles jobs unsuited to standard law enforcement agencies (any echoes of comic book superheroes are quickly banished by the dark tone here). Dexter is commissioned to revenge the brutal murder of a multi-millionaire's son by callous Serbian militants, with plentiful (and bloody) action in store for the reader. Motivations are presented in primary colours, and a pulse-racing narrative is the overriding imperative (nothing wrong with that, of course) – although the millionaire Steven Edmond is made more complex than the simple plot device he might easily have been. Perhaps we'd like to dig a little deeper into the psychology of Dexter but it hardly matters, given the sheer momentum of the author's machine-tooled plotting.

A Dark Devotion 1997

Clare Francis

The reach of Clare Francis as an author is wide indeed: at least six of her bestselling thrillers (including *Red Crystal*, 1985, *Wolf Winter*, 1987, and *Deceit*, 1993) are among the most trenchant in the field, and her three non-fiction books describing her epic ocean voyages have become classics in the field. Like many a crime writer, however, she is interested in blurring the boundaries between crime fiction and literature and, latterly, some may feel that she has been lost to the crime fraternity. But for the enthusiast there are still books as impressive as *A Dark Devotion*, in which Norfolk's salt marshes are put to masterful use as a backdrop for an atmospheric tale of murder, legal skulduggery and sexual passion. Criminal lawyer Alex O'Neill is enjoying the rewards that her successful career is bringing her, but there is a fly in the ointment: her husband, a partner in a London legal firm, is becoming an alcoholic. The couple move among low-rent criminals, with petty crime on the everyday menu. Then Alex is contacted by the man she was in love with as a child in Norfolk, Will Dearden. His wife has gone missing, and Alex finds herself drawn into a complex web of intrigue, which will irrevocably change her personal life. What makes this such a forceful read is the elegantly textured prose, in which characterization is allowed to emerge skilfully alongside the adroit plotting. It's to be hoped that Francis's move into more literary realms won't deny readers books as enjoyable as this.

Body Double 2005
Tess Gerritsen

Tess Gerritsen's *Body Double* is a reminder that – Mo Hayder apart – the toughest female writers hail from America. This is as visceral a thriller as one could wish for, with Gerritsen maintaining her characteristic unrelenting grasp of the reader's attention. She has upset some of her fellow crime writers (curiously, only the female ones) with her readiness to hit her readers in the face, with absolutely no concessions to the squeamish. But – honestly – who would pick up a Tess Gerritsen novel expecting something suitable for readers of *The*

Lady? Her heroines, detective Jane Rizzoli and medico Maura Isles, are memorable figures, with a whole slew of memorable character traits (and, what's more, they are two very different women – something Gerritsen emphasizes). Building on the success of her already impressive body of work, *Vanish* (2004) was a book that consistently (and pleasurably) accelerated the reader's pulse rate. And that's something Gerritsen pulls off once again with *Body Double*, even though this novel has a deceptively slow-burning start. Detective Jane Rizzoli is shown a woman stretched out on a slab – a woman who seems to share her appearance, age and blood group. While a killer is wreaking havoc across the country, Jane has to journey to Maine to find out the truth about a mother she never knew. In Gerritsen novels, things are seldom what they seem – and that's very much the case here, as layers of reality are ruthlessly stripped aside. Once again, the author pulls no punches when it comes to confronting the most extreme and disturbing outer reaches of human behaviour, and (as they used to say on the BBC) 'those of a nervous disposition' should take care. But Gerritsen fans are a hardy breed, and this scarifying novel delivers everything they go to her for.

The Broker 2005
John Grisham

One writer who has never let carefully textured writing get in the way of page-turning is John Grisham. The massive popularity of his novels (and the workaday movies that are usually squeezed from them) is down to a killer combination of sheer storytelling and stripped-down, no-nonsense prose. Not to mention an authoritative way with the details of the milieux in which he sets his fast-moving tales (usually the American legal profession). But *The Broker* is proof that Grisham has found other fish to fry. All the customary narrative muscles are exercised (ostensibly, the plot concerns slippery

Washington power broker Joel Backman being sprung from a high-security cell by a departing president, principally so that the CIA can see who murders him first: the Russians, the Israelis, the Saudis or the Chinese). But something more ambitious peeks out: this is Grisham's State of the Nation novel, masquerading as a chase thriller;

John Grisham (b.1955)

Not many authors can bask in the knowledge that their very name defines a genre – but John Grisham is in that select company. There's barely a legal thriller that doesn't invoke the author's moniker as a selling tool – but few of the army of Grisham wannabes have the sheer storytelling *nous* that the prototype possesses. The standard Grisham fare: penny-plain prose, but sporting a plausible, engrossing plot that makes up in sheer page-turning stickiness for what it might lack in sophistication.

As a trial lawyer, Grisham had the notion of using details of an existing case for a novel (a career trajectory emulated by all too many lawyers since), and the result was the excellent *A Time to Kill* (1989) – which remains a justified favourite of the author. And *The Firm* (1991), with its young lawyer protagonist who finds his hands are dirty with mob business, demonstrated that Grisham was no one-hit wonder. While subsequent titles have not all maintained the impetus of the early books, *The Summons* (2002) is interesting: the central conceit echoes **Jonathan Franzen**'s 2001 novel *The Corrections*, with two dysfunctional brothers living unsatisfactory lives in the shadow of their withholding, bone-headed father. The brothers (alienated law professor Ray and wastrel Forrest) travel to their reclusive father's home in Clanton, Mississippi, for a final settling of the dying ex-judge's estate. There's no sex, of course, and virtually no violence (Grisham has railed against the excesses of Hollywood in these areas), but (in what seems like a reaction to the author's much-trumpeted born-again Christianity) religion is given very short shrift – sanctimonious preachers are characterized as having little sympathy for the Civil Rights movement. Grisham is always professional, and has recently added a strain of sharp social comment to his books.

some excoriating points are made about high-level corruption in the US (and, *inter alia*, the UK), in between heads falling under car wheels, and one doubts that *The Broker* will be on any White House bedside tables. It's a cold eye Grisham casts on his country, and its (fictitious?) president. Given that Michael Moore's unnuanced attacks barely dented George W.'s triumph in the last election, will a thinly veiled attack by America's most popular thriller writer influence any hearts and minds?

The Rat on Fire 1981
George V. Higgins

What to choose from the man whom **Ed McBain** described as 'The le Carré of classy sleaze'? All the books are great, and Higgins' background in the Boston legal scene gave him access to an enormous range of criminal briefs. But strangely, few of his books focus on legal practitioners – it was the clients (or defendants) which fascinated him. With *The Rat on Fire* he picked up on a bog-standard insurance scam, when torching a tenement full of blacks who default on their rent seems like a perfect way to make some easy money.

Constable and Robinson

But when the scheming landlords choose a couple of incompetent low-lifes, Leo and Jimmy, to do the dirty deed, the plot unravels horrifically and, oddly, comically. Anyone with an ear for dialogue will enjoy Higgins' work, and the uneasy feeling that he actually likes the scummy crooks who populate his pages gives him a serrated edge as a chronicler of quite where, and how, the American Dream went off the rails.

George V. Higgins (1939–99)

When aficionados of crime fiction have a need to silence someone extolling the verities of some overrated, bestselling writer, there's one name that will do it: one of the most underappreciated writers in the genre – the late, great George V. Higgins. His specialities were threefold: his enormous reservoir of specialized information, gleaned from his work as an attorney and assistant D.A. in Boston (which provided a rich brew of Jewish, Irish and home-grown hoods to reinvent in his fiction); characters and *mise-en-scène* as quirky and brilliant as anything in **Elmore Leonard**; and then (like Leonard) there was the dialogue: what dialogue! Higgins' ear was unique, giving him the ability to reproduce the quotidian patterns of everyday speech, so that the exchanges between his low-life protagonists were utterly cherishable. In fact, most of his novels read like plays, almost entirely dependent on dialogue, with stage directions kept to a minimum; strangely, reading Higgins evokes strong echoes of **Harold Pinter**. His first novel, *The Friends of Eddie Coyle* (1972) is his masterpiece, but equally splendid work is to be found in *A Choice of Enemies* (1984), with its mordant take on political corruption, and *The Judgment of Deke Hunter* (1976), sporting a memorable cast of minor criminals. The verisimilitude that Higgins' personal experience gave him is splendidly transmuted into his first-rate novels.

The top five George V. Higgins books

▸ *The Friends of Eddie Coyle* (1972)
▸ *The Judgment of Deke Hunter* (1976)
▸ *The Rat on Fire* (1981)
▸ *Outlaws* (1987)
▸ *Wonderful Years, Wonderful Years* (1988)

The Last Temptation 2002
Val McDermid

There was a time when McDermid was just a solid, reliable crime novelist producing series featuring lesbian journos Lindsay Gordon and Kate Brannigan. But then something happened: imperceptibly, McDermid joined the elite ranks of those 'Serious Novelists Who Write Crime Fiction'. Had her work really changed? Did it justify the new gravitas she seemed to have acquired? Her early books were diverting, but better was to come. McDermid's series featuring profiler and clinical psychologist Tony Hill was quite her strongest work yet, creating one of the richest pieces of characterization of her career. And she now has the best of both worlds – a dedicated crime readership eager for every new offering, and the kind of serious attention her more literary peers might envy. *The Last Temptation* addresses all these various audiences – and takes her best-loved characters into truly disturbing new territory. Tony Hill is up against a truly terrifying killer, who has very specific targets in his sights: psychologists, no less. He has brutally murdered top names in the profession across Europe, and Hill has urgent reasons for cracking the *modus operandi* of his nemesis. But complications are added by the dangerous job that Hill's erstwhile partner, D.C.I. Carol Jordan, has undertaken: she is doing undercover work in Berlin, with a well-heeled criminal in her sights. Long-time thriller aficionados will not be surprised to discover that Hill and Jordan are soon pooling their resources to confront a force of evil that stretches back as far as the Nazi era. Both protagonists are wrenched from their controlled environments and fighting for their lives. *The Torment of Others* (2004) was a resounding follow-up, and despite the question marks currently hanging over the value of criminal profiling, McDermid remains utterly convincing.

HarperCollins

Ties that Bind 2003
Phillip Margolin

One of the reasons that readers go back to the legal thriller genre again and again is the delicious pleasure of plotting: nothing exhilarates more than some ingenious and surprising narrative, and that's something Phillip Margolin delivers with *Ties that Bind* – and in spades. Defence attorney Amanda Jaffe is saddled with what seems like an impossible case: not only is her client facing execution for a double murder, he has added to his crimes by killing his previous lawyer. John Dupre is, self-evidently, a nasty piece of work – a wheeler-dealer in the dirty world of selling both drugs and women – and his fate is clearly sealed. But as Amanda digs beneath the surface of the case, she finds herself with the proverbial can of worms: Dupre can claim friends in the most unlikely of places; and not just at the criminal end of society. He is the custodian of some very dark secrets, and there are people who will go to considerable lengths to prevent him spilling the beans. Apart from the satisfyingly convoluted narrative, Margolin's skill here (evident in such earlier books as *The Burning Man*, 1996, and *The Associate*, 2002) lies in the creation of a strongly drawn, conflicted protagonist – and Amanda is certainly that. We've met her type before, but Margolin rings the changes with aplomb.

Blind Eye 2004
John McLaren

The author John McLaren has more strings to his bow than most. As well as producing such well-turned novels as *Black Cabs* (1999) and *Running Rings* (2001), McLaren has made his mark as a diplomat, a venture capitalist and director of two major investment banks. For *Blind Eye*, the author mingled with the top brass of the naval establishment, who granted him unprecedented access in his research for the novel, and the direct experience of officers and sailors incorporated here has unquestionably ensured that the detail in the book is strikingly plausible, making the unorthodox behaviour of his hero, Captain Chris Cameron, seem acceptable (if unlikely). Cameron commands H.M.S. *Indomitable*, an aircraft carrier dispatched by the Foreign Office to handle a delicate assignment off the west coast of Africa. Cameron and his crew are to monitor Numala, once a British colony, but now about to fall into the clutches of a dictator with ambitions towards some ruthless ethnic cleansing once his power base is secure. Vote-rigging is on the agenda, and Cameron is furious when the British government, bowing to pressure, recalls the *Indomitable*. Cameron takes a decision that he knows may destroy his career: he will not abandon Numala to a despot's rule, and opts to stay. The screeching jets that kick off the novel are a harbinger of the technology-savvy derring-do that follows (it's a fairly safe bet that McLaren's target readers are men), and it's a clever touch to introduce us to Chris Cameron going through a relationship crisis in this country before he's plunged into risky international waters – we're drawn into his thinking on a personal level before Cameron is foolhardily taking on the assembled might of two governments.

Déjà Dead 1997
Kathy Reichs

As debut thrillers go, Kathy Reichs' *Déjà Dead* made more of a mark than most. Employing her background as a forensic anthropologist in North Carolina, Reichs ensures that the tradecraft of Reich's heroine, Temperance Brennan, has complete verisimilitude. A woman's bones are found within the grounds of a monastery and Tempe, assigned to the case, suspects the work of a serial killer. The victim, she believes, is not the first woman to die at the hands of the killer before being

Chapter 6

Kathy Reichs (b.1950)

In an overcrowded field such as crime writing, it's difficult to establish a solid reputation. To achieve the acclaim that Kathy Reichs has – and in a relatively short time – is quite an achievement. Reichs, like **Patricia Cornwell**, has utilized her medical background to create a series of tough and uncompromising thrillers. She was forensic anthropologist for the office of the Chief Medical Examiner of the State of North Carolina, and worked in a similar capacity in the province of Quebec. Her massive experience in the area of forensic science has been heavily drawn on, and at present she is one of only 50 people certified by the American Board of Forensic Anthropology, and very few of those individuals are women.

Like her leading character, Dr Temperance Brennan, Reichs found herself obliged to distinguish herself in the male world of law enforcement. *Déjà Dead* established her reputation in 1997, and Tempe Brennan made an immediate mark as a solid and reliable heroine. Brennan was, of course, similar to Patricia Cornwell's Dr Kay Scarpetta, but Reichs nevertheless rendered her a fully rounded character in her own right, and managed to build new elements through three successive books. The first novel had a relatively cool tone, but in *Death du Jour* (1999), Reichs refined elements such as character interaction, and the emotional temperature was higher. This new level of energy and invention clearly established Reichs as a more impressive writer than had been originally thought, and decisively moved her out of the shade of Patricia Cornwell. In *Deadly Decisions* (2000), bikers are engaged in a war, and two of them appear to have blown themselves up. Brennan is largely unconcerned with what the bikers do to each other, until a 9-year-old girl is killed in the crossfire. Not all Reichs' novels maintain the same level of achievement, but *Bare Bones* (2003) and *Monday Morning* (2004) have much to offer, while *Grave Secrets* (2002) saw Tempe investigating mass graves, serial murders and corruption in a brilliantly realized Guatemala, an interesting finger-on-the-pulse new direction. *Break No Bones* (2006) is categorical proof that the author still knows how to intelligently ring the changes on concepts from her earlier work. There are undoubtedly too many feisty female forensic experts in the field now, but Tempe Brennan remains one of the best. The Reichs trajectory has been decisively upwards.

brutally eviscerated. Her point of view is not shared by the detective on the case, but Reichs' heroine is a woman who is always driven to prove herself, and soon changes her colleague's mind. As the protagonists draw ever nearer to their quarry, the author is able to create a vivid and pungent picture of the province of Quebec as a backdrop to the tension. Other details shore up the power of the narrative: the internal politics of a police division (with Tempe riding roughshod over some of the more fondly maintained protocols); the carefully maintained duality in the nature of the heroine, her professionalism sometimes at odds with her enthusiasm; and the steady accretion of flesh-creeping detail – this is not reading for the squeamish.

Presumed Innocent 1987
Scott Turow

Turow's most famous novel is a virtual blueprint for the legal thriller which has subsequently become such an oversubscribed genre. Turow was himself Assistant US Attorney in Chicago (1977–86) and the blizzard of legal detail with which the book is crammed ensures a strong sense of verisimilitude underneath the dirty dealings. *Presumed Innocent* is narrated by Rusty Fabich, a prosecuting attorney who is happily married. After an ex-work colleague of his is savagely raped, Rusty finds himself on a fatal collision course in both his professional and his private life. When his ex-lover Carolyn is murdered, Rusty finds – to his horror – that he himself is accused of the murder. It isn't just the photographically detailed picture of the legal universe (with its internecine squabbles and courtroom dramas) that distinguishes *Presumed Innocent*: Turow is well aware that characterization remains paramount, along with the kind of plotting that can constantly take the reader by surprise. Of the many legal thrillers that followed this, few were able to capture the gusto of Turow's remarkable book, and the only source of regret concerning it is that other lawyers felt obliged to give up their legal careers and write indifferent photocopies of this book. The background to his work is intelligence: Turow has talked about his faith in science, and is dismissive of the idea that America is rushing headlong towards a kind of dumbed-down religious state. He's aware that the most distrusted group in the US is the legal profession – but his books remind us that there are good eggs in with the bad. It's not that easy to virtually hijack a genre, but the crown prince of the sharply written legal thriller may no longer be **John Grisham** (since his born-again Christianity has crept into his work and vitiated it) but Turow. In his *Reversible Errors* (2001) we find gritty and plausible legal detail and a cold-eyed, dispassionate examination of human behaviour. Tackling once again the collision of ordinary human existence and the exigencies of the legal apparatus, Turow vividly brings to life not just the beleaguered attorney who is his protagonist, but also the hate-filled characters that populate this heady narrative. You may be tired of legal thrillers – but here's one to remind you why this genre got so damned popular.

Presumed Innocent
dir. Alan J. Pakula, 1978

The presence of **Harrison Ford**, then at the peak of his career, ensured the massive box-office success of this smooth and professional job, with an adaptation of a hot novel being the other ingredient in a recipe for success. Though it's undoubtedly true that director Pakula produced more personal work in less commercial projects, he turns in a professional job here. Good support from such reliable character actors as Brian Dennehy and Raul Julia, and the deliciously scheming Greta Scacchi, makes up for the fact that the complexity of the plotting has been somewhat smoothed out.

Amateurs

Journalists and innocent bystanders

Although many crime novels fit more or less comfortably into a clearly defined category – private eye, police procedural or whatever – the genre has many books which resist easy characterization. As in much classic literary fiction, a crime in these novels is committed, and the lives of the characters are irrevocably changed. Also like literary fiction, these non-category novels can explore with more penetrating analysis the murkier reaches of the human psyche, not being tied down to the exigencies of the professional or private cop working his way through a list of suspects. But the books in this section do occasionally have protagonists from other professions: journalists, art experts, jockeys, priests, modern Robin Hoods… and, of course, victims.

Be My Enemy 2004

Christopher Brookmyre

Abacus

Edgy, uncomfortable crime fiction with its finger on the *zeitgeist* is the trademark of the talented Christopher Brookmyre – and (like the earlier *Quite Ugly One Morning*, 1996, or *Boiling a Frog*, 2000) *Be My Enemy* is characteristic stuff. There was a time when Brookmyre was filed under the generic heading of 'tartan *noir*', and certainly his books deliver the gritty diversions that such a label suggests. But Brookmyre was always keen to stretch the possibilities of the crime genre – and his Scottishness was a long way from that of his crime-writing confrère **Ian Rankin**. Brookmyre has always been more than ready to tread on the toes of the politically correct while outraging those of a conservative bent, but his ideas are never pushed in our faces at the expense of the narrative. *Be My Enemy* has many of the familiar Brookmyre fingerprints: sardonic wit, danger – but it is also an attempt to do something new, such as examining the fascist leanings that even the best of us can harbour. Jack Parlabane, Brookmyre's regular protagonist, is obliged to participate in a few days of corporate team-building in a secluded (and well-appointed) hotel. But some very dangerous things are to happen in conjunction with the team-building activities, and Jack is soon in trouble again. Using the isolated setting as a chemical mixing pot for some of the most extreme views and attitudes in society acts (as often in Brookmyre) as a metaphor for larger issues – is the hotel Britain? But the author is just as happy to offend those on the left as on the right – and it's this even-handedness (as well as the cutting wit) that makes *Be My Enemy* so diverting.

The Innocence of Father Brown 1911

G.K. Chesterton

The affection with which the **Father Brown** books are held has slipped somewhat in recent years (possibly a result of a more secular age), but anyone prepared to sample the Chestertonian delights will not regret the experiment. Chesterton was, of course, a remarkable figure in his day. After a stellar career in journalism, he became (like **Graham Greene**) a Roman Catholic in middle life, and from this grew his creation of the deceptively unassuming priest and detective Father Brown. This ecclesiastical descendant of **Sherlock Holmes** first appeared in *The Innocence of Father Brown*, and the standard of the stories rarely

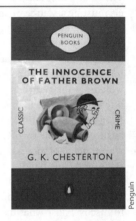

Penguin

faltered thereafter. The Brown tales are a bright and idiosyncratic picture of their era, with as bizarre a selection of problems as the denizen of 221b Baker Street ever had to face. While the solutions to the mysteries are often (it has to be said) a little strained, their ingenuity always wins the reader over. And possibly the real achievement for the modern reader is the way in which Chesterton avoids making the inevitably 'good' Father Brown insufferably pious – no easy task. This may be due to the tongue-in-cheek humour which is never far away from Chesterton's writing.

The Graft 2004
Martina Cole

The unarguable success of Martina Cole's sizable tally of crime novels must be a source of envy to other practitioners. Almost from the beginning, she has gleaned praise for her gritty and pungent fiction. And while other authors like **Stephen King** gave birth to a slew of imitators in the same genre, Cole virtually created a new genre: the tough East-end crime novel with a single-minded (if damaged) woman at the centre, usually sexually involved with dangerous (but often attractive) villains. Since the success of such Cole novels as *Dangerous Lady* (1992) and *The Know* (2003), every publisher now has to have their own Cole-lite author, ploughing the same furrow with much less success. In *The Graft*, a male character is put centre-stage, and Cole handles the narrative with her usual assurance. Nick Leary is having difficulties with both his business life and his wife and family. One night, he hears the sound of a break-in, and is forced to discover just what his limits are when protecting his family and property – a decision with major consequences. The moral crises of Cole's characters are not subtly handled – that's not her thing – but the sheer power of her storytelling know-how makes it very easy to understand her massive following.

Dead Cert 1971
Dick Francis

The classic Dick Francis thriller *Dead Cert* has rarely been out of print in more than three decades. But is it a representative of an era that has passed? Whatever ones feelings about the Turf – Francis's chosen territory – the book itself has not aged a day. Jockey Bill Davidson, riding on the favourite Admiral, has been murdered. Another jockey, Alan York, takes on the mantle of detective to track down a group of

> **Dead Cert**
> dir. Tony Richardson, 1974
>
> Tony Richardson, director of such seminal British new wave films as *The Entertainer* and *A Taste of Honey*, might seem a curious choice for a straight-forward thriller like this, but by this stage of his career, the late Richardson had been choosing some very unsuitable projects. That proved to be the case here, but this tale of Grand National shenanigans has a strongly realized racing background, with all the horsey elements securely in place. A strong cast (including **Judi Dench**, before she became a national treasure) make the most of their characters.

savage criminals. His investigations get him nowhere, until he finds himself waylaid by a group of heavies. And then the answers to the problem suddenly start to come thick and fast until Alan York loses his memory. The first-person narration still leaps off the page, and it really doesn't matter whether or not the reader is interested in the world of racing: the vividly drawn background is so idiomatic that it ensures the thriller mechanics move with a total assurance. Many current thriller writers could pick this up and learn a trick or two. The very same qualities that made Francis such an immediate winner back in the 1960s hold true today: the machine-tooled plotting, the insider's knowledge of the racing world, and the elementary but sharply drawn characterizations, qualities amply demonstrated by 2000's *Shattered*.

Spend Game 1980
Jonathan Gash (pseudonym of John Grant)

The character of **Lovejoy**, the ducking and diving antiques dealer (and sometime detective) is inextricably linked in most people's minds with the actor **Ian McShane**, who incarnated him in a long-running TV series. But for the real Lovejoy, it's necessary to go back to the novels of Jonathan Gash. The books are sardonic, clever and always full of needle-sharp plotting. In *Spend Game*, an old friend of Lovejoy's who has also become an antiques dealer is killed, while Lovejoy watches. He is constrained from talking to the police because of complications involving a woman he is having an affair with, which forces him to bring the murderer to justice himself, and find out what was behind the killing. As ever, Lovejoy is a wonderful creation: comic, resourceful and only just this side of the law. But he remains the perfect guide for the reader through the fascinating world of antiques dealing and the many suspicious characters that swim in its deeper waters.

Dying to Tell 2001
Robert Goddard

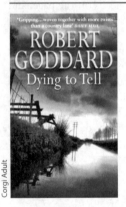

Storytelling ability is enjoying a comeback (after a period of unfashionability) and Robert Goddard's work remains the *sine qua non* of this kind of writing – it must amuse him to observe the vagaries of such trends, particularly as his faithful readers largely ignore such things and continue to return to his books. They're hardly cutting edge in terms of modern fiction, but who cares? *Dying to Tell* is a key entry in an illustrious line of Goddard winners. His less-than-energetic hero here is Lance Bradley, stewing in Somerset when he receives a request to trace an old friend, who has cut his relatives adrift financially. Calling on the shipping firm Rupert worked for, it seems clear that he has been involved in a large-scale fraud. And other people are looking for Rupert… Goddard fans will know what to expect – polished writing and plotting that puts most writers to shame.

No Laughing Matter 1997
Peter Guttridge

The tag-line for Peter Guttridge's debut comic novel, *No Laughing Matter*, was: 'Comedy is a serious business – some people just die laughing.' And that pretty much sums up the book's absurdist blend of laugh-out-loud comic incidents and ugly deaths. Nick Madrid – Guttridge's yoga-obsessed, lousy-in-bed journalist protagonist – witnesses the suspicious death of one of the performers at the 'Just For Laughs', the biggest comedy festival in the world, where ambitious performers would kill to get that movie or TV deal. Nick turns gumshoe to find out whether the death was accidental or intended. He is helped in his quest by Bridget Frost, the Bitch of the Broadsheets, whose pushy and tacky exterior conceals – well, a pushy and tacky interior. Madrid and Frost quickly discover that there is no rest from the witty – except when they start getting killed off. As the trail leads first to the mean streets of Edinburgh during the Festival and then to Los Angeles, where the truth lurks among the dark secrets of some of Hollywood's biggest movie stars, Guttridge takes satirical swipes at performers, movie stars, showbiz in general and, of course, journalism, that being his trade.

Tokyo 2002
Mo Hayder

The sheer energy and invention of Mo Hayder's writing virtually obliterates any less than felicitous passages in her work, and the disapproval that greeted the violence of her books (such as *Birdman*, 2000, and *The Treatment*, 2001) has been sidelined of late (perhaps because there are so many women around these days travelling in the same bloodstained territory – **Tess Gerritsen**, for one). But another reason that Hayder shows signs of having writing longevity is her reluctance to continue to tread paths she has trod before – as the ambitious *Tokyo* most satisfyingly proves. The central character here is a woman, trawling Tokyo trying to find a missing piece of film revealing unpalatable truths about the Nanking Massacre in 1937. Grey, Hayder's vulnerable heroine, tackles a job as a hostess in a nightclub and greatly increases the danger she is facing – then finds a lead to the missing film, an academic who lived through the massacre. As the foregoing might attest, Hayder is painting on a large canvas here: it's audacious work, sometimes ill-focused, but always restlessly involving.

Angels of the Flood 2004
Joanna Hines

A strong sense of place and an unusual take on the crime genre are two characteristics of the novels of Joanna Hines. *Angels of the Flood* is set in Florence, but it is a Florence few tourists have ever seen, and a Florence that no one will ever have the chance to see again. In November 1966 the city was devastated by a freak flood with catastrophic results for buildings, manuscripts and art, as well as for the Florentines themselves. The eponymous 'Angels of the Flood' were the young people who flocked to the city to help with the clean-up. Kate Holland, naive and full of enthusiasm, joins the volunteers. So too does Francesca Bertoni, an enigmatic Italian-American who is secretive about her reasons for hiding from her family. She is tracked down by Mario Bassano, the ambitious doctor who claims to be her fiancé. Tensions come to a head at a weekend party at the Villa Beatrice which belongs to Francesca's uncle. Kate falls in love; Francesca dies in a hideous accident. Thirty years later, Kate has become a respected conservator. She is sent two paintings which have been crudely tampered with; the alterations contain coded references to events which hardly anyone would recognize, apart from

Kate and the long-dead Francesca. The real strength of the novel is its vivid evocation of Florence during the disastrous floods and the very different Italy of the present day. Hines knows her locales, and her writing is as good as a holiday under Mediterranean skies.

Dark Horse 2002

Tami Hoag

Elena is a woman who likes to live life at the edge. Her recklessness has cost her a job in the Miami P.D. and (more torment-ingly) the life of a colleague. She goes to ground in Florida, surrounds herself with horses, and attempts to regain her equilibrium. But her new-found peace isn't to last. A friend, the elderly Molly Seabright, is convinced that something has happened to her young stepsister, a groom at the stables that Elena uses, and soon the troubled ex-policewoman finds herself drawn into danger again, with the

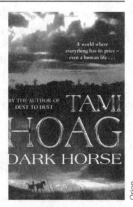

high rollers of the hyper-rich world around her quite as lethal as the scum of Miami. Hoag has carved out a career for herself as one of the most pungent and vivid of American crime writers, and *Dark Horse* is very much a calling-card book, with its troubled heroine, powerfully drawn locales and intricate plotting all well up to par. For those who have not read her, this is a good entry point, even though it's darker than most of her other work (after all, she began her writing career back in 1998 with romance novels). And whether or not you're interested in horses, the show season in South Florida is an atmospheric backdrop to the skulduggery on offer.

Chapter 7

Sleeping Cruelty 2000
Lynda La Plante

Although the TV incarnation of her *Prime Suspect* remains Lynda La Plante's calling card (due as much to **Helen Mirren**'s memorable incarnation of Jane Tennison as any writing skills of the author), other La Plante books such as *The Legacy* (1987) demonstrate the range of her achievements. Her other TV series, *Widows*, utilizes her trademark 'tough woman' motif, not a million miles from similar territory mined by **Martina Cole**. But (also like Cole), La Plante clearly wanted to demonstrate that she could forge an equally strong male protagonist – and that's just what she does in *Sleeping Cruelty* with the ambiguously characterized Benedict, about whom the reader is invited to change their mind several times. Sir William Benedict has secured all the baubles that success can offer, including property in the Caribbean, and has been financially supporting and mentoring the younger, gay Andrew Maynard. But when Maynard takes his own life, a juggernaut is set in motion that looks set to destroy Benedict. He isn't going to take it lying down, though… All of this is writ large in trademark La Plante fashion, but the poster-coloured writing is absolutely apposite, with the dramatic effects pulled off spectacularly.

Rum Punch 1992
Elmore Leonard

Of course, most crooks are amateurs too, and the greatest chronicler of the kinds of clowns that make life a misery for the rest of us is Elmore Leonard. *Rum Punch* is one of his Florida novels, featuring an array of classic Leonard types such as Max Cherry, a bail bondsman, and Ordell Robbie, an ambitious psycho who has the Mercedes and attitude and wants more, but is unlikely to achieve

Elmore
Leonard
RUM PUNCH

Filmed as Jackie Brown
by QUENTIN TARANTINO

Phoenix Press

it with his posse of loser, weed-smoking ex-cons. Enter Jackie Burke, glamorous but getting-on air hostess who is supplementing her income by doing a bit of smuggling for Robbie. When she is caught red-handed by a couple of shady cops, Max Cherry raises her bail, and falls in love with her at the same time. His problem is how to get her out of her dilemma, whilst not crossing the cops, or Ordell Robbie. The usual sly plotting, narrative pace, matter-of-fact offhand violence and sharp street dialogue make for a Leonard classic, but the portraits of the dumber-than-he-thinks Robbie and his risible henchmen are what finally sticks.

Jackie Brown
dir. Quentin Tarantino, 1997

Hollywood *enfant terrible* **Quentin Tarantino** was born to direct Leonard's novels. He has called the writer his 'mentor', and although Leonard has frequently been let down on the screen, this movie was a match made in heaven, restraining Tarantino's imaginative verve to a taut plotline, and with surprisingly little upfront violence. With his usual quirky eye for casting, Tarantino used 1960s blaxploitation star **Pam Grier** as the subtly renamed sky smuggler, and the suitably world-weary B-movie actor **Robert Forster** as Cherry. But his *coup* was casting **Samuel L. Jackson** as a charmingly scary Robbie, **Robert de Niro** as his plug-dumb sidekick, **Bridget Fonda** as their doped-up nympho squeeze, and **Michael Keaton** as a corrupt cop. As always there are great Tarantino set-pieces, none better than the multi-viewpoint bag-switch in a shopping mall, reminiscent of Kurosawa or even Jacques Rivette.

The Executioners 1957
John D. MacDonald

This is a novel of extremely dark menace, which plays on many lawyers' or witnesses' fears about what might happen when a villain they send down finishes his sentence. Retired Defense Attorney Sam Bowden is seeking a new, quiet life with his young family in the picturesque resort of Cape Fear, North Carolina. Then one Max Cady turns up, an illiterate rapist Bowden had unsuccessfully defended in a case 14 years earlier. Blaming Bowden for a flawed defence, and clued up having spent his time profitably in the prison library, he is out for revenge. Firstly the family dog is poisoned, then Bowden's daughter is threatened, but Cady is careful to appear on the right side of the law. Then, in classic 'For God's sake don't do that!' mode, Bowden decides to retreat with his family to their remote boathouse, providing the perfect scenario for Cady to exact his planned vengeance, by assaulting Bowden's wife. Will family man Bowden be up to vanquishing his nemesis?

Cape Fear
dir. J. Lee Thompson, 1961

Mauled by the UK censors upon release, this stunning exercise in really nasty suspense benefited enormously from having **Gregory Peck** as the weak lawyer and a supremely threatening **Robert Mitchum**, reprising something of his *Night of the Hunter* role, as Cady. Thompson wasn't a great director, but the balance between the bright daytime scenes of sunny small-town America and the night scenes as Cady's increasingly violent plan unravels works wonderfully. **Martin Scorsese** is a great director, but his 1991 remake raised questions, the main one being 'Why?' With **Nick Nolte** as Bowden and **Robert de Niro** at his most disturbing as Cady, Scorsese ups the suspense quota considerably (especially when Cady stalks Bowden's daughter in her deserted school), not to mention the explicitly sexual drive of the original novel. Mitchum, Peck and **Martin Balsam** (who had also featured in the 1961 movie) were given cameo roles.

The Portrait 2005
Iain Pears

The literary crime novel is a rarified form, always in danger of losing the primal compulsion of books in the wider crime arena by paying too much attention to carefully honed prose, and prissily scorning the melodramatic effects in which less ambitious fare customarily revels. Some writers, however, are able to strike a judicious balance between the populist and the sophisticated – and Iain Pears is firmly in their number. He made his name with *An Instance of the Fingerpost* (1997), utilizing the world of fine art which was to become his favoured milieu. *The Portrait* is another finely drawn exercise in malice, with Pears setting himself a difficult task: how to ensure that a restricted cast of characters can compel the reader's involvement. The setting is an isolated island, where the painter McAlpine has marooned himself, clinging to his seclusion. There he is visited by a figure from his past, the influential (and often destructive) art critic William Nasmyth. Is Nasmyth there (as he claims) for a portrait sitting? Or for other clandestine reasons? What ensues is a sinister and lethal struggle of wills, delivered in Pears' understated (but cutting) style.

Adam and Eve and Pinch Me 2001
Ruth Rendell

One of Ruth Rendell's most quirkily titled books, this is also one of her most individual, utilizing a real-life event – the Paddington train disaster – in a fashion that is audacious, but not meretricious. It seemed that Jock Lewis was one of the victims, and his girlfriend Minty has a double cross to bear – sadness at his death, and the fact that Jock was holding all her money, which has disappeared (along with him) in the accident. Rendell introduces another character, a woman called Zilla, who has been notified by British Rail that she is a widow. But then Minty sights someone – is it the supposedly dead Jock, alive and well and up to something sinister? Rendell is always at her best dealing with the less comfortable fringes of psychopathology, and that's what she's up to here, balancing the disparate story strands with consummate skill.

Ruth Rendell (b.1930)

For many years, there were two women at the top of the crime writing tree in the UK: P.D. James and Ruth Rendell (though a host of claimants for their dual crown have appeared recently). It's invidious to claim that either author has the greater talent, particularly as their similarities are matched by very different ambitions. Rendell's novels featuring her doughty detective **Wexford** utilize the tropes of the classic English detective novel, with the characterization of Wexford and his supportive wife subordinate to the truly ingenious plotting. But Rendell admirers usually claim that her best work lies in her non-series novels such as *A Judgement in Stone* (1977) – where she addresses some of the darkest reaches of human behaviour and the lonely alienation of modern urban life. The characterization of such books is much more complex and ambitious than in those featuring her long-serving copper. When Rendell initiated a second writing career as **Barbara Vine**, sceptics who felt that she might overextend herself were quickly routed when it became clear that the Vine books were even more multi-faceted and astringent. *Asta's Book* (1993) is a study in betrayal, personal identity and, of course, murder. Like all the Vine novels (as well as the best of the non-series Rendell titles), this is psychological crime writing of the most fastidious kind, always idiosyncratic in its treatment of character. And her short stories – a difficult discipline all of its own – are outstanding.

The Smile of a Ghost 2005
Phil Rickman

Phil Rickman's highly unusual protagonist Merrily Watkins, parish priest and single mother, is working in Ludlow with a new diocesan advisory panel, alongside less-than-congenial colleagues when a teenage boy falls from ruins to his death. Two more deaths quickly follow, and the resourceful Merrily must tread the mean medieval streets to uncover a lurking evil. Phil Rickman's smoothly turned narratives always scrupulously avoid the tweeness that his heroine could so easily lend herself to, and remain tough-minded, atmospheric mystery narratives, with particularly sharp scene-setting.

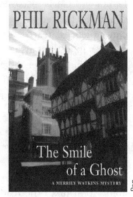

The Predator 2001
Michael Ridpath

Michael Ridpath made his mark in high finance, and like many of his fellow financiers moved from the financial market into the book market, parleying the expertise from his earlier profession into several novels that gleaned speedy acclaim. These distinctive and strongly written thrillers owed little to his writing peers (with *Free to Trade*, 1994, being the most individual). *Final Venture* (2000) concentrated more firmly on a powerful linear narrative, and (while less immediately striking than his earlier work) was probably his best-written novel. Until, that is, the appearance of *The Predator*, which is a quantum leap over the author's earlier books. The novel is in two parts – a brief first part, and a more ambitious second section. The deal-making training in the world of investment banks counsels that participants should take no prisoners, as colleagues Lenka and Chris discover. But a pleasure trip by boat results in the death of a trainee – and the covering up of the death has disastrous consequences. Years later, Chris is horrified to see Lenka die before his eyes in a street assault in the Czech Republic – and it is down to him to nail the killer. As a legacy of his earlier career, Ridpath knows all about greed and its consequences, and he weaves a moral strand into his page-turning narrative.

Derailed 2003
James Siegel

Siegel manages to match finely tuned plotting with a storytelling ability that takes the reader instantly by the throat. Admittedly, he starts with a surefire premise: the ordinary man torn from a boring, quotidian existence and plunged into a nightmare. This scenario has served many artists well (think **John Buchan**'s *The Thirty-Nine Steps* or **Hitchcock**'s *North by Northwest*), but this is one of the most assured treatments of the theme. Charles Schine is on his way to work, conscious that his life moves along well-oiled tracks. But then he encounters the beautiful and enigmatic Lucinda Harris, and his association with her not only pulls apart the well-ordered fabric of his day-to-day routine, but threatens his very life. Charles has to learn (and very quickly) some basic survival tactics, not to mention the niceties of dealing with some very dangerous people. And it's in the latter area that Siegel really shines: his villains (from petty thugs to more urbane and dangerous *éminences grises*) are drawn with a very varied and imaginative skill, with street language rendered quite as plausibly as the exchanges involving top-level corruption. The first-person narrative is a particularly nice touch, making it very easy for the reader to identify with the hapless Charles. Siegel is good, too, at the various set-pieces that maintain the interest, and as Charles is catapulted from one dangerous situation to another, we find ourselves forced to make exactly the same tough decisions as he does.

Friends, Lovers, Chocolate 2005
Alexander McCall Smith

McCall Smith was not content to rest upon his laurels with his *No.1 Ladies' Detective Agency* series (see p.73), and in *The Sunday Philosophy Club* (2004), he inaugurated a new crime series with amateur sleuth Isabel Dalhousie, located in Inspector Rebus' Edinburgh – although Isabel could not be further from that other prober of Scotland's darker side. Isabel is a philosopher who uses her calling to crack 'unsolvable' mysteries, and also hosts the 'Sunday Philosophy Club' at her house. In that novel, the plotting had all the quirky inventiveness of the Botswana-set series. But both that book and the second, *Friends, Lovers, Chocolate*, can't, of course, call on the more exotic backgrounds of the foreign novels – although McCall Smith invokes the highways and byways of Edinburgh with as much vividness as he can muster. Isabel, too, is a very different character from Precious, her philosophical discourses being much more sophisticated than the homespun charm of the Botswana sleuth. Here, McCall Smith presents his second heroine with some moral challenges more complex than those she faces in her professional life. She finds herself reluctantly reviewing her feelings for a younger man, Jamie, who was to marry her niece, Cat. Her attempts to maintain a philosophical distance crumble in the face of a more physical response to the attractive young man. But her troubles have only just begun: Cat is on vacation in Italy, and has asked Isabel to run her delicatessen. One of the customers, a recent recipient of a heart transplant, is disturbed by memories that he feels are not his own.

Needless to say, Isabel investigates, and once again finds herself in far more dangerous territory than that of her philosophy classroom. While some will be keen for McCall Smith to get back to more sultry climes, this is actually rather seductive stuff. In the course of the book, there are all kinds of beguiling asides on everything from the messiness of relationships to the difficulties of resisting temptation (whether that be chocolate or handsome Italians).

Cardiff Dead 2000
John Williams

'The most un-decaffeinated voice since Dylan Thomas.'
Kinky Friedman

CARDIFF DEAD

JOHN WILLIAMS

Bloomsbury

This, the second part of John Williams' celebrated Cardiff Trilogy, is the most individual of the three books (the first was *Five Pubs, Two Bars and a Nightclub*, 1999, and the third *The Prince of Wales*, 2003) – which is no mean praise, given the sharpness of the writing on offer in all of them. Set partly in 1999 and partly in the early 1980s, the book follows the stories of journeyman rock guitar player Mazz and sometime bassplayer turned single mother Tyra as they cautiously attempt to rekindle their love affair. There's also a (possible) murder and a surprising amount of discursiveness for a work of concentrated urban *noir*. John Williams' prose may be caviar to the general, but those open to the universe he so strikingly creates will find rich rewards.

All in the mind

Matters psychological

Literary critics now take crime fiction seriously as a form for discussing the human condition – a relatively new situation. Like another once-despised popular genre, science fiction, crime novels were routinely dismissed as a medium for superficial thrills – even though both genres (from their very inceptions) had been exploited by ambitious writers for many a pertinent commentary on the darker byways of psychopathology. Crime fiction, in particular, has long specialized in an unsparing examination of extreme states of mind – and the psychology of crime. In the 19th century, **Dostoyevsky**'s tale of murder and detection *Crime and Punishment* (the blueprint for many a later novel, with its dogged policeman wearing down a guilt-ridden killer) demonstrated that the genre could be infinitely more powerful and penetrating than more genteel fictional forms.

The books discussed below all foreground the psychology of their characters *in extremis* – but never at the expense of page-turning narratives of crime.

Forest of Souls 2005
Carla Banks (pseudonym of Danuta Reah)

HarperCollins

Banks comes from a family of academics and writers, and expresses a strong interest in language. Her father was an East European military officer who came to the UK as a refugee during World War II. This is a commanding and persuasive piece of work, in which the heroine is taken to the furthest extremes of human behaviour and forced to confront the darkness at the heart of the psyche. Helen Kovacs has been researching the Nazi occupation of Eastern Europe, though she has chosen to keep her research from her close friend Faith Lange. But then Helen is killed, much to Faith's horror. At first, she believes that the police have found the murderer, but Faith begins to suspect that the man in custody is not the man who killed her friend. At the same time, a journalist, Jake Denbigh, has also been led to believe that there is more to Helen's murder than meets the eye; he has discovered that among the supposed concentration camp victims who have escaped from Minsk were several disguised war criminals. It would appear that Faith's much-loved grandfather Merek may be one of these. But who is responsible for Helen's death? Someone from this dark past, or a totally unexpected (and well-hidden) source? What makes Banks's novel so forceful in its appeal is the strength of its dual narrative. Faith delves into the secrets of her own family; Jake travels to the mass graves in the Kurapty Forest in Minsk, on a related – but even more dangerous – quest. This is psychological thriller writing of a rare order; both Faith and Jake are fully rounded figures, and we are thoroughly involved in the danger.

The Wasp Factory 1984
Iain Banks

Who could have suspected from this remarkable (and disturbing) debut novel the many and varied directions that Iain Banks's subsequent literary career would take? He has written thrillers, political suspense, social commentary and is, of course, as Iain M. Banks, a giant in the sci-fi genre. *The Wasp Factory*, however, clearly marked out the dark territory that was to be his domain. Frank Cauldhame is, to put it mildly, a young man with troubles. He is a disturbed adolescent, living in an isolated Scottish household with two other invalid males: his disabled father and his psychopathic elder brother, Eric. Of all the members of this dysfunctional family, Frank is the most tragic case. And told in the first person, his autobiography is particularly chilling. His life began with a crime: the minor one of not having his birth registered. But more significant crimes lie in his future. Apart from his utter alienation from society and its norms, he has particular disapproval for the female sex, who he regards as weak and subservient. Much of this he blames on his mother, who he sees as responsible for his accidental castration. As a young boy, he was playing with the family dog while his mother was giving birth, and the dog bit off his genitals. As the above conveys, this is not comfortable reading, and as the narrative traces its shadowy trajectory, with more and more horrific details emerging about Frank's psyche, squeamish readers will fall away. They will be doing themselves a disservice, for as well as the wholly original first-person narrative voice here, there are some jawdropping revelations to be found in this study of the corruption of the sexual impulse.

Chapter 8

The Eye of the Beholder 1980
Marc Behm

This is often called the private eye novel to end all private eye novels, but it is much more than a gumshoe narrative. *The Eye of the Beholder* is quite unique in combining a fascinatingly baffling puzzle and a wonderfully realized love story with a highly subjective metaphorical descent into the underworld. In just 200-odd pages, Behm covers 40 years and a massive body count as his private eye (a disturbed and sociopathic figure) relentlessly tracks down a bisexual serial murderess whose speciality is disguise. As his protagonist (always referred to as 'The Eye') follows the killer as she murders her way through a series of moneyed partners, we are taken on a nightmare odyssey through every state in the US to a grim and disturbing climax. One thing is certain: the reader is quite unlikely to encounter anything like this again. This is unquestionably a dazzling one-off. Or it would be if Behm hadn't written the similarly unnerving *Afraid to Death* (1991).

Eye of the Beholder
dir. Stephan Elliott, 1999

The cinematic qualities of Behm's novel are unsurprising – he has extensive experience writing screenplays (including Stanley Donen's often underrated 1963 thriller *Charade* and, rather strangely, Richard Lester's 1965 Beatles film *Help!*). And this novel in fact began life as a screenplay for Philip Yordan. However, it was hardly done a service by Elliott's misfiring adaptation that sidelines the psychological observation of the book and transforms the obsessiveness of the plot into a simple chase scenario. **Ewan McGregor**, displaying little charisma, is on the trail of **Ashley Judd**'s ruthless assassin. The globetrotting is flatly handled, and it's interesting to speculate whether Elliott was ever aware that the novel he was adapting was far richer than anything shoehorned into his rather dull movie. However, it is worth tracking down *Mortelle Randonnée* (directed by Claude Millar in 1983), with the delicious Isabelle Adjani as the black widow.

The Murmur of Stones 2005
Thomas H. Cook

The American writer Thomas H. Cook has rapidly become a must-read author. He bagged an Edgar award for *The Chatham School Affair* (1996) and has been short-listed for the award a further six times, most recently with *Red Leaves* (2005), his breakthrough book in the UK. Family life as a source of psychopathological damage is the subject of *The Murmur of Stones*, a satisfyingly convoluted tale of which Peter Straub noted: 'With this book the crime novel had moved firmly into literature.'

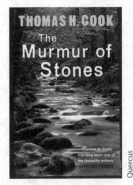

Cook's protagonist Diana has grown up caring for her schizophrenic father, and when her own son, Jason, is discovered to be similarly afflicted, Diana stoically accepts her responsibility. But her son will always be different – a fact that Mark, Diana's husband, cannot handle. When Diana leaves her son in the care of his father for a short time, she returns to discover her son has drowned, and she cannot accept the 'accidental' verdict the case is granted. She begins to construct a case against her husband – and soon destabilizing forces of madness and death are unleashed. The late **Ross Macdonald** wrote many unsettling novels in which the family was the sum of its various cupboarded skeletons – Cook concentrates the notion to a more deeply unnerving degree.

Chapter 8

Land of the Living 2003
Nicci French

Nicci French is actually a husband-and-wife team consisting of writer **Sean French** and journalist **Nicci Gerrard**. *Land of the Living* is part of their sequence of impressive psychological thrillers, beginning with *The Memory Game* (1996) and *The Safe House* (1998), that marry detailed plotting with masterful characterization – particularly the off-kilter side of human behaviour. And, as in such books as *Beneath the Skin* (2000) and *The Red Room* (2001), the basic situation in this book is immediately compelling. Waking up to find herself hooded and bound, Abbey Devereux has no conception of how she arrived in this frightening state. She finds herself looked after by a man whom she never sees, but who does speak to her, and what he says compounds her terror: he promises that she will eventually be killed 'like the others'. Abbey finds that her very identity is at threat along with her life, and aspects of both her career and a failing relationship come under her mental spotlight. She has a dual problem: she must fight to retain both her sanity and her life in the face of an impossible situation. If the basic premise is reminiscent of **John Fowles**' 1963 debut *The Collector*, *Land of the Living* is far more than a reworking of the theme. The authors are fully aware that the best thrillers take us deep into the minds of their protagonists, a theme they extended into a memorable psychological battle of wits in *Secret Smile* (2004). The tension and suspense are ratcheted up with total assurance, and as the narrative moves towards its conclusion, readers will have to force themselves not to rush the pages. Forget that terrible film of *Killing Me Softly* (directed by Kaige Chen, 2002): as a literary phenomenon, judge the work of this dual-identity author on their books.

Seeking Sanctuary 2003
Frances Fyfield (pseudonym of Frances Hegarty)

Such writers as Frances Fyfield and Minette Walters have found their way into the upper echelons by dint of sharp psychological observation and stylish, elegant writing. The accumulated suspense of Fyfield's books in particular is hard to resist. Her novels featuring Crown Prosecutor Helen West and D.C.S. Geoffrey Bailey have built up a steady following since they first appeared in *A Question of Guilt* (1988), and draw on the author's experience as a criminal lawyer. But *Seeking Sanctuary* is something else; Fyfield's customary delving into the more astringent aspects of the human mind is here taken to a new level of intensity. At the reading of the will of Theodore Calvert, it becomes apparent that this strangely worded document has been calculated to perpetrate revenge on the dead man's former wife, whose pietistic homilies destroyed the marriage. The beneficiaries of Calvert's will are his daughters Therese and Anna (his fastidiously religious wife Isabelle has died), and Therese has followed her mother's unceasing injunctions to piety by becoming a nun. When an enigmatic young boy named Francis appears, he quickly makes himself invaluable at Therese's convent. But soon the lives of Anna and Therese are to be changed irrevocably by the handsome Francis, who is not everything he appears to be; violent emotions may only be suppressed, Fyfield warns, for a limited time. The relationship between the three central characters is trenchantly created, and the rigorous constraints of religion add a further level of repression that mirrors the secrets at the heart of this idiosyncratic narrative. Vividly written and exuberantly entertaining, this is one of Fyfield's best books. Other titles such as *Staring at the Light* (1999) mine the same vein of psychological acuity and dark menace as **Patricia Highsmith**, and *Undercurrents* (2000) is worth checking out for the same reason. The intense quality of her prose illuminates narratives that both celebrate traditional storytelling values and explode them. *Undercurrents* displays some of her most disturbing work.

Strangers on a Train 1950
Patricia Highsmith
(pseudonym of Mary Patricia Plangman)

Penguin

What a debut novel! Looking back on Highsmith's career as one of the most disturbing practitioners of the psychological crime novel, it's astonishing to see how she virtually arrived fully formed with this classic of the genre. Readers are now, of course, obliged to disentangle the original novel from **Hitchcock**'s celebrated adaptation, but the effort is worthwhile – particularly as censorship restrictions of the day forced the director to soften one key element in the narrative. Two men meet on a train.

Guy Haynes is the reader's surrogate: relatively normal, locked in a loveless marriage with the unpleasant Miriam. But Charles Bruno is a psychopath, and when he offers to swap murders with Guy (Bruno will dispose of Miriam, if Guy will murder Bruno's inconvenient father), Guy doesn't take the proposal too seriously – until Miriam is killed. Soon, Bruno is asking Guy to complete his part of the bargain, and commit murder himself. This, of course, is the point at which novel and film diverge. Hitchcock, in the cinema of the early 1950s, could not have his hero behaving in such a fashion, whereas Guy is forced by the unremitting assault of the mad Bruno to do just that. Nor could he dwell on the homosexual undercurrent of the two protagonists' relationship. This is the first example in Highsmith's work of the dark moral equivocation that became her stock in trade – and

Patricia Highsmith (1921–95)

Patricia Highsmith is an unlikely heir to **Henry James**, but like her celebrated predecessor, Highsmith was an unromantic American writer of rarefied sensibility, living in Europe and treating her characters with a cool, Olympian detachment. Highsmith was born Mary Patricia Plangman in Fort Worth, Texas, in 1921, and inaugurated her career with the remarkable *Strangers on a Train* in 1950, instantly setting a benchmark she often had to struggle to maintain. Her books have garnered such celebrated admirers as **Graham Greene**, who particularly admired her perfectly formed short stories (posthumous collections of her work in this form showed that she had to struggle to attain this crystalline perfection). In such books as *This Sweet Sickness* (1960) and *A Suspension of Mercy* (1965, aka *The Story-teller*), Highsmith mapped out a terrain that was very much her own. Eschewing detectives as protagonists, she takes the reader inside the sensibilities of characters whose carefully constructed lives are often torn apart by the violent disruptions which (she hints) are not too far beneath the surface of most people's quotidian existence. Often bloody murder lies at the heart of her plots (*The Blunderer*, 1954, for instance), but as often as not nothing much seems to be happening, although a feeling of intense disquiet beneath the veneer of her prose can be sensed, quite viscerally (try *A Tremor of Forgery*, 1969).

Her admirers are most fond of the books featuring the totally amoral conman **Tom Ripley** (see p.181) and splendid though these are, the author's unquestioning sympathy for her murderous character is often dismaying (Highsmith bridled at the suggestion that Tom Ripley was a psychopath, and her manner as an interviewee was often fearsome). But her body of work established a yardstick for edgy psychological crime writing which most of her successors can only aspire to.

The top five Highsmith books (excluding Ripley)

▶ *Strangers on a Train* (1950)
▶ *This Sweet Sickness* (1960)
▶ *A Suspension of Mercy* (1965)
▶ *A Dog's Ransom* (1972)
▶ *Edith's Diary* (1977)

the reader's changing attitude towards the apparently normal Guy is actually the kernel of the book. Bruno may have a hideous mother (who may be partly responsible for what he is), but how much can they identify with Guy, either before or after he commits murder?

Confessions of a Romantic Pornographer 2004
Maxim Jakubowski

As well as being one of the most respected editors in the crime genre (bringing back into print many neglected names) and proprietor of the London mecca of crime enthusiasts, Murder One in Charing Cross Road, Jakubowski is one of the most fascinating and idiosyncratic writers of fiction at work today. His phantasmagorical novels synthesize a variety of elements into a heady brew indeed: hardboiled idioms, skewed psychology and the unabashedly erotic. It's the author's controversial treatment of the latter that has earned him the sobriquet 'King of the Erotic Thriller', but this understates the literary qualities of his work, with many clever postmodern concepts informing the always vivid and unsettling narratives. A good introduction is *Skin in Darkness* (2006), a blistering anthology collecting three of the author's most arresting tales in a mélange of unbuttoned sexuality and *noir* sensibility. The protagonist of *Confessions...* is Cornelia, a woman who has earned a living as a stripper, but is also an adroit assassin. She is commissioned to track down the last, incomplete manuscript of the dead writer Conrad Korzeniowski (the literary reference is not accidental). This writer turns out to have had certain things in common with Jakubowski himself: he wrote erotic crime, and spoke at book conferences on crime fiction (in which he is expert). As Cornelia encounters the women who had encounters with Conrad, we are vouchsafed chapters from the enigmatic book by the late author, with each having as its focus an act of extreme sexuality. Some of these paragraphs are, needless to say, not for the narrow-minded – Jakubowski has always been comfortable moving in the more radical areas of literary experience. As the book progresses, the heroine's consciousness is drawn deeper and deeper into the recesses of the human soul, and Cornelia begins to feel a sense of second-hand violation by the dead author.

Half Broken Things 2003
Morag Joss

Morag Joss bagged the Crime Writers' Association Dagger Award for this striking book. It's a novel that built on the achievement of such earlier Joss winners as *Funeral Music* (1999) and *Fearful Symmetry* (2000). *Puccini's Ghosts* (2005) combined the same narrative assurance with unblinking psychological insight. And like *Puccini's Ghosts*, *Half Broken Things* is concerned with the lies we tell ourselves to conceal unpalatable truths. The protagonist Jean is a housesitter, living a pointless life as her grey years approach. But in Walden Manor, her current housesitting assignment, she has access to the sealed cabinets and cupboards – which also gives her, she finds, access to proprietorship of the house. As she settles into her new role, she acquires a couple of unsuccessful individuals like herself, and a semblance of happiness seems possible in this damaged group. But the past erupts into the present, wreaking destruction. Joss aficionados will have an inkling of the dark treats in store here: the elegance and penetration of her prose probes the loamy ground of the darkest human behaviour.

Flesh and Blood 2001
Jonathan Kellerman

Jonathan Kellerman's Alex Delaware thrillers have amassed a devoted following, and the reasons for this are readily apparent. Kellerman (in such books as his debut *When the Bough Breaks*, 1985, and *Over the Edge*, 1987) had used his background as a paediatric psychologist to create a profession for his hero (who is a crack practitioner) of total verisimilitude. Kellerman also writes textbooks on clinical psychology. In fact the Kellerman clan, including wife Faye and son Jesse, seem almost to have cornered the market in psychiatrically based tomes, building up a catalogue of harrowing case studies of the disturbed. In the first Delaware books, Alex, though officially retired, took on cases referred to him by Milo Sturgis of the LAPD, and a recurrent theme was that of damaged children, suffering from emotional or physical abandonment by parents – and that is (to some degree) the theme of *Flesh and Blood*. When Alex first sees Lauren, she is a teenager with all the usual problems – moody, uncommunicative, resentful of her parents. But years later, at a bachelor party, Alex finds himself watching two strippers go through a graphic display – and one of them is the unhappy Lauren. Then she disappears – and we're off into familiar Delaware territory, delivered with all the aplomb we expect from the reliable Kellerman. In earlier books, Alex was occasionally portrayed as being a little too prescient, but Kellerman has given his hero a satisfyingly conflicted emotional life, and his personal involvement here gives *Flesh and Blood* a strong underpinning of drama that counterpoints the central mystery and sharpens it at every point. Only Kellerman's earlier *Billy Straight* (1999) displayed the same degree of penetrating psychological insight and unvarnished view of human nature – here, the plotting is even more assured and trenchant.

The Monsters of Gramercy Park 2005

Danny Leigh

Danny Leigh's striking first novel *The Greatest Gift* (2004) suggested that he possessed formidable gifts, and this impressive successor confirms that even if he were never to write another word, his legacy for these novels would be assured. Readers sometimes experience a lowering of the spirit when they encounter yet another central character in a novel who is a writer – it's a device that has passed so far beyond cliché that something very special is required to re-energize the concept. But Leigh has

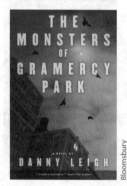

managed to do just that. American crime writer Lizabeth Greene is stinging under the negative press she's been having, and undertakes to write about the life of a psychopathic killer, thereby (she hopes) putting her back at the top of the tree (echoing similar moves by **Norman Mailer**). Wilson Velez seems to have regarded prison as merely a blip in his criminal career, and his organization of crimes on the outside continues unabated from within his cell. But the most surprising thing about him (Lizabeth finds) is the children's book he's writing (the eponymous *The Monsters of Gramercy Park*). When Lizabeth is persuaded by the sinister Velez to help with this book, she finds her participation has terrifying results. In artfully constructed prose, Leigh takes us on a frightening journey with his out-of-her-depth protagonist.

Candyland 2001
Ed McBain/Evan Hunter
(pseudonyms of Salvatore Albert Lombino)

Orion

As Ed McBain, he created the groundbreaking **87th Precinct** series, whose innovations were much plundered by TV series such as *Hill Street Blues* and crime writers such as **Patricia Cornwell**. As Evan Hunter, he wrote such indelible 1950s novels as *The Blackboard Jungle* (1954) and the screenplay for **Hitchcock**'s *The Birds* (1963, adapting a **Daphne du Maurier** piece). But with *Candyland* both pseudonyms appear on the cover (is this a publishing first?) to produce a compelling piece of work. Architect Benjamin Thorpe has an obsession: unknown to his family, he wanders the New York streets in the wee small hours looking for dangerous female companionship, and has a confrontation in a seedy brothel that will change his life. A teenage prostitute known as Heidi has crossed paths with him, but ends up strangled and viciously mutilated in an alleyway. Thorpe is the obvious suspect… but is he too obvious? McBain had stated that he felt many readers had forgotten who Evan Hunter was. He decided to give this persona another spin, but the portmanteau writing credit was actually something of a marketing ploy. This is a crime novel of some considerable psychological power, and actually reads like neither of the 'two' authors' previous books.

Dancing with an Uninvited Guest 2002
Julia Wallis Martin

This bracing crime novel from the highly acclaimed Julia Wallis Martin returns the reader to the psychological suspense of her first, *A Likeness in Stone* (1997). Lyndle Hall, a medieval manor house, lies in the heart of Northumbria's national park. It is from here that an 18-year-old girl disappears – along with Lyndle Hall's owner, Francis Herrol. First assumptions are that the two ran off together, but evidence indicates otherwise, and when D.I. Tate encounters Herrol's tormented son, his fears for the girl's fate deepen. Parapsychologist Audrah Sidow is convinced there is nothing on earth for which there is no rational explanation. But she knows there is more to the collection of fractured people gathered at Lyndle than is apparent, and, as the search for a living girl becomes a hunt for a dead body, she must discover what lies at Lyndle Hall's dark heart. Julia Wallis Martin, as ever, knows her stuff (a former commissioning editor for Hodder & Stoughton, South Africa, witness to a fatal shooting, attempted suicidee, she's been through a lot) – and this is nigh-unputdownable.

I Was Dora Suarez 1990
Derek Raymond
(pseudonym of Robert Arthur William Cook)

Of all Derek Raymond's highly impressive Factory novels (including *He Died with his Eyes Open*, 1984, and *The Devil's Home on Leave*, 1985), *I Was Dora Suarez* is one of the most strikingly original. The Factory books were narrated by the unnamed Sergeant, and set in the Metropolitan Police's 'Department of Unexplained Deaths', codenamed A14. In his autobiography, the author chose this book as the pinnacle of his career, and pointed out the unpleasant effect the writing of this frequently painful book had on his psyche. The raw materials of the novel are unsettling indeed: necrophilia, extreme and graphic violence, and various other extremes of sexual behaviour (including a felching club) coexist in these bitter pages, but the final effect is cathartic: a genuine purging of evil through confronting its furthest reaches. The murderer in *Dora Suarez* is a psychotic, and decapitates his luckless victims before arranging them in bizarre tableaux to facilitate his black rituals of mutilation. Astonishingly, Raymond is able to take us inside the mind of a monster and, if not sympathize, perhaps understand.

Ghost of a Flea 2001
James Sallis

Walker & co.

In this disorientating novel, the reader is forever being cast adrift by one of the American Grand Masters of the genre. Questions of memory and the past are handled with the allusiveness of Proust, though Sallis is a considerably more plot-focused writer. The central character is black writer-cum-detective Lew Griffin (who first appeared in *The Long-Legged Fly*, 1992 – the series all feature insects in the title). As the novel starts, Lew has given up the craft of novel writing and is living an off-the-grid existence in New Orleans as a part-time journalist. A friend in the police force has been shot during a holdup, and at the same time, his relationship with the intriguing Deborah has collapsed. Only engagement with criminal activity and the darker side of the human psyche can kickstart Lew's life and propel him from his torpor. While Sallis never forgets the imperatives of the crime narrative, this is a far more deeply philosophical book than most people will be used to encountering in the genre – and some will find it forbidding. Literary references abound, and those seeking a straightforward, uncomplicated narrative should look elsewhere. For fans of the more ambitious writing in the genre, Sallis is key reading. In fact, this jazz-loving polymath has also written a critical work on pulp writers, *Difficult Lives* (1993), and a biography of pioneering black crime-writer **Chester Himes** (2000).

Disordered Minds 2003
Minette Walters

With nary a false step, Minette Walters has been burnishing her reputation as one of the most powerful yet nuanced practitioners of the psychological thriller. Actually, Walters' winning streak has been continuing for an unfeasibly long time, with each succeeding book slightly more ambitious than its predecessor. Walters has been building a total picture of modern Britain that cuts across all social strata, while still using the apparatus of the crime novel. Since pocketing the Creasey Award for her debut novel, *The Ice House*, in 1992, such books as *Acid Row* (2001) have demonstrated Walters' assurance with a variety of social groups, while *Disordered Minds* reached into darker areas of the human psyche. And now the unthinkable is being quietly whispered: has Minette Walters hijacked the title of Britain's crime queen from long-time joint holders **Ruth Rendell** and **P.D. James**? *Disordered Minds* is solid fuel for this argument – not least because Walters has tackled a more ambitious agenda than before. Howard Stamp was an educationally subnormal man who died in prison by his own hand in the 1970s, after (apparently) murdering a relative. But after his death, anthropologist Jonathan Hughes looks into the case again, not persuaded of Stamp's guilt. He meets a man convinced of the dead man's innocence – but as the move towards

Minette Walters (b.1949)

As a crime writer, Minette Walters began at the top and has stayed there for the succeeding years of her creativity in the genre. Her first book, *The Ice House* (1992), won the John Creasey Best First Crime Novel Award, and her subsequent books, such as *The Sculptress* (1993) and *The Scold's Bridle* (1994), similarly gleaned prizes. This critical acclaim has been matched by an enthusiastic following among readers, possibly because she disregarded advice given to her when setting out: she had been told to avoid 'one-offs'. Walters was assured that **Ruth Rendell** could only do it because she was so well known, and she still had to use the Barbara Vine alter ego to get away with it. But even early in her career, Walters was very reluctant to write a series. When *The Sculptress* won the American Edgar Award, and *The Scold's Bridle* won the Gold Dagger, she felt that her 'right to be different' was confirmed. Her sales are pretty phenomenal – which suggests that many readers respond to the deeper psychological profile she can give to characters that only appear in one novel – along with the closure. *The Shape of Snakes* (2000) is a good example of Walters' interest in incorporating social issues into her novels – the plot is set in motion by the death of a black woman, living on the edge of society. By having a woman from a different social background take an interest in the death (which no one else believes to have been a murder), Walters is able to tackle issues of commitment and white middle-class guilt, while avoiding making her protagonist a noble doer of good deeds.

the truth begins, the real murderer is keen to retain the status quo – violently. All of this couldn't be further from the cosy Home Counties mystery that gently comforts the reader; Walters is in the business of disturbing us, but not merely out of a desire to shock. As ever, truthful characterization is paramount (fully rounded, conflicted characters with whom it's impossible not to identify), and there are truths spoken here about society; Walters' readiness to tackle larger themes than her more parochial English peers remains her most salient attribute.

Hello Bunny Alice 2003
Laura Wilson

Laura Wilson has never been happy staying within the parameters of the conventional crime novel. In *My Best Friend* (2001) she brilliantly deployed a device in which the novel was narrated by three strongly delineated protagonists. Her succeeding book, *Hello Bunny Alice*, returns to the single narrative voice. Alice Jones has displayed her wares as a Bunny girl, and has been engaged to the celebrated comedian Lenny Maxted. The novel opens with her receiving an anonymous clipping concerning a corpse discovered in an English lake. Slowly (and tantalizingly) Alice discovers that her involvement in this mystery will change her life. The other cleverly realized plot strand involves the ex-partner of Maxted, Jack Flowers. After Maxted commits suicide, Flowers finds himself cut adrift and unable to make it on his own. The fashion in which Wilson ties together the various storylines is masterly, though some patience may be required – Wilson is not interested in providing a popcorn read. But the demands made on the reader are more than repaid.

Rear Window 1942
Cornell Woolrich

Woolrich, one of the great workhorses of the pulp era, turning out an immense body of work for minimal rewards, is a writer whose name conjures up psychosis, threatening cityscapes and plots of tortured complexity, and there are few of his many books that are not worth attention. Having said that, it's easier to appreciate his work as a totality, rather than via the assessment of individual books. *Rear Window*, however, is a good entry point, and exemplifies many of the pulp writers' interest in psychology and aberrant behaviour. Photographer L.B. Jeffries is virtually imprisoned in his apartment after he breaks his leg, and begins to clandestinely observe his neighbours from his window. Slowly, he becomes convinced that one of his neighbours has murdered his wife, and his attempts to prove this turn out to be very dangerous indeed. While **Hitchcock** made much more of the voyeuristic elements of the scenario, Woolrich's novel can also be read as a metaphor for the way in which fiction writers construct scenarios from observing the traits and sometimes intriguing activities of people around them. Woolrich is no stranger to the quirkier elements of human behaviour, and it's that as much as the adroit plotting which makes this short piece work so well.

Rear Window
dir. Alfred Hitchcock, 1954

Undoubtedly one of Hitchcock's greatest films, *Rear Window* investigates the very process of watching in a voyeuristic fashion (much as the audience itself is doing). The celebrated 'transference of guilt' theme has its richest exploration here, with **James Stewart** exemplary as the troubled, housebound hero. But more so than in the book is the nagging suspicion that the supposed crime is purely a figment of the frustrated voyeur's imagination, adding a further psychological twist. Interestingly, the studio settings actually enhance the claustrophobic feel of the movie, and only Michael Powell's notorious *Peeping Tom* (1960) approximates to Hitchcock's examination of the dark pleasures of voyeurism.

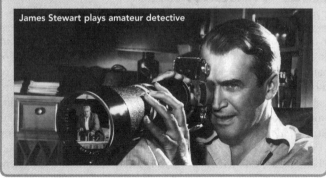

James Stewart plays amateur detective

The killer
inside me

Serial killers

Bestselling American crime writer **Patricia Cornwell** was clearly bemused when her attempts to prove that the great English painter Walter Sickert was, in fact, **Jack the Ripper** were met by massive scepticism and scorn in the UK. After all, Cornwell had spent jaw-dropping amounts on research (buying – and forensically examining – Sickert paintings, hiring experts, etc), and it can hardly have been a ploy to sell her book on this nigh-obsessive quest (after all, Cornwell is top of the tree, and needed no massaging for her sales figures). So – she wondered – why the UK hostility? Actually, the answer is straightforward: Jack the Ripper is not only claimed as the first serial killer in history, but he was British – and a national icon (however bloodstained and psychopathic). Jack the Knife was not (Brits felt) up for grabs by an American interloper. But the US need hardly worry – after all, the sales of serial killer novels (which still obliterate all others in the crime field) were virtually created by an American – and one of prodigious skills at that. But **Thomas Harris** is by no means the only proponent of this most modern of literary forms, nor indeed the inventor of the genre – and for every cynical **Hannibal Lecter** imitation, there are a dozen writers forging new innovations (such as the phenomenally successful **Mark Billingham**) in a field that is now becoming over-crowded… time for a cull, maybe?

Hour Game 2004
David Baldacci

After the floodgates were opened for the serial killer genre by **Thomas Harris** and his cannibalistic aesthete Hannibal Lecter, this book may have you groaning 'not another serial killer thriller!' But if this is your response to *Hour Game*, you're not reckoning on the fact that this one is written by David Baldacci, a man who would rather give up writing than repeat himself – or, for that matter, copy other writers. Yes, a lot of the territory here has been traversed before, but this isn't Thomas Harris-lite – readers may be battle-weary from the avalanche of entries in the genre, but *Hour Game* bristles with a bushel of innovations that obliterate any sense of over-familiarity, even if the grisly opening chapters come perilously close to things we've read about often before. Ex-Secret Service duo Michelle Maxwell and Sean King, having inaugurated a partnership that best combines their individual skills in *Split Second* (2003), look into the disappearance of some highly confidential papers owned by the well-placed Battle family. The decomposed body of a young woman is found, arranged in a bizarre position, and two teenagers are bloodily slaughtered while having sex in a car. It seems a serial killer is at work – and King and Maxwell soon learn that the Battle family is (needless to say) in things up to their necks. So what's new here? Baldacci has come up with something we haven't encountered before: a murderer who mimics the methods of a series of famous serial killers, such as the highly intelligent psychopath **Ted Bundy** and several other real-life monsters. And it goes without saying that the horrific narrative is dispatched with maximum effectiveness by the author. But the question now is: what else can he do to re-invigorate the serial killer genre? No need to worry, Baldacci's considerable strengths are not limited to multiple murderer sagas.

Lifeless 2005
Mark Billingham

Billingham's breakthrough was inevitable: he made a considerable impression with the first two books in the Tom Thorne series, *Sleepyhead* (2001) and *Scaredy Cat* (2002), novels that instantly marked him out as one of the most impressive writers on the overcrowded British crime scene. Subsequently, *Lazy Bones* (2003) showed the author's willingness to tackle uncomfortable themes, dealing as it did with convicted rapists being savagely killed after their release from prison. And it has to be

Little, Brown

said that Billingham's novels take no prisoners in terms of extreme violence – he will never be a favourite read among those who want polite mayhem amidst the tea-cosies, as 2004's *The Burning Girl* amply proved. *Lifeless* added more lustre to Billingham's achievement – not least for the element of social critique folded into it. D.I. Tom Thorne is aware of the downward trajectory of his career. Finding it difficult to cope with the recent death of his father, Thorne is also smarting under bitter criticism of his professional life (he broke all the rules on his last case), and he finds that, against his wishes, he's forced to take gardening leave. But this enforced inactivity isn't to last. Homeless people on the streets of the capital have been savagely kicked to death, their corpses discovered with a £20 note pinned to their chests. Random killings of alcoholics and junkies – or more targeted? Thorne finds himself back at the sharp end, as he takes dangerous journeys into the clandestine byways of the underclass, with their inflexible codes and strictures. *Lifeless* is not a comfortable read – Billingham never is, despite or perhaps because of his alternative career as a stand-up comedian – but many have become addicted to the stronger fare that the author offers.

Bad Men 2003
John Connolly

Irish-born Connolly's treatment of the ethics of human degradation and retribution has quickly established him as one of the most provocative writers in the UK; utterly unafraid to alienate his readers, his books are a plunge into a dark world where nothing is safe, nothing is secure. *Bad Men* synthesizes two of the writer's favourite themes: the devastating effects of crime as performed by men of zero morality, and a dark vision of the supernatural. Sanctuary was once the name of what is now known as Dutch Island, near the coast of Connecticut. In the novel's prologue, massive bloodletting in the 17th century establishes it as a very black place indeed, but now the area has been tamed, and is a placid village whose one lawman, the outsized Joe Dupree, finds it hardly a challenge to his abilities. But Joe senses that the ghosts of the area are stirring. And things will soon change with the arrival of a man called Moloch, an immensely cruel criminal who has been doing time, while his wife (who escaped from his malign influence with their son) has settled on Dutch Island. When Moloch's team of killers spring him from jail, things become very hard for his wife. Joe Dupree and his rookie female colleague soon have to deal with both the living and the dead. As always with Connolly, this is pulse-racing stuff. His series of books featuring the detective Charlie 'Bird' Parker (which kicked off in 1998 with *Every Dead Thing*) will remain his calling cards for most readers, but this headlong dive into macabre crime is the perfect test for readers uncertain as to whether or not they can stand the course of a Connolly novel.

American Psycho 1991
Bret Easton Ellis

This biting black comedy was certainly never conceived as a 'crime' novel in the genre sense, but rather as a satire on the Wall Street 'preppy' generation for which brand names were all-important, and anything, but anything, could be acquired. Patrick Bateman is the archetype: he has everything – good job, fat salary, Brooks Bros. clothes, charm, and intelligence. It seems he is also a psychopath, treating his 'hardbody' one-night stands with increasing disdain, until he discovers the simple delights of killing them after, or preferably during, sex.

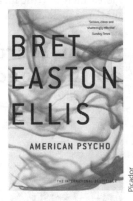

And, as the novel progresses (with wonderful discursive passages on brand names, clothes, the quality of one's business card, etc) the more dangerous the situation, the more exciting Bateman finds it. What makes it truly disturbing (and very controversial) is the first-person narration, which not only absolves the author from any moralizing judgements, but indeed reverses the position, with Bateman as narrator treating the escalating body count (and increasingly horrific means of achieving it) as matter-of-factly as a shopping spree on Fifth Avenue.

Silent Terror/Killer on the Road 1986
James Ellroy

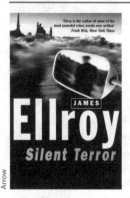

Arrow

If **Thomas Harris** hadn't pipped him at the post, this little-known early Ellroy masterwork would be regarded as *the* seminal modern serial killer text. Probably inspired by the high-profile activities of real-life serial murderers **Ted Bundy** and **David Berkowitz** ('The Son of Sam'), the novel intelligently penetrates the mind of an apparently motiveless mass-murderer on the move. Known as the 'Sexecutioner', Martin Michael Plunkett takes deep personal pride in his job. And we know this because of Ellroy's chilling use of a first-person narrative. As often with this author, we almost find ourselves in sympathy with his protagonist as he wreaks his awful revenge on the demons that torment him and the uncompassionate universe he sees around him. Until, that is, he teams up with a like-minded serial killer, in a twist which at the time seemed unlikely, but which increasingly seems not far from the mark.

The Silence of the Lambs 1988
Thomas Harris

In crime writing terms, *The Silence of the Lambs* took the serial killer and profiler phenomenon which Harris established in *Red Dragon* (1981) onto a whole new level. Clarice Starling is a trainee FBI agent, working hard to discipline mind and body. She is sent by her boss, Section Chief Jack Crawford, to interview the serial killer **Hannibal Lecter**, kept in the very tightest security, to see if he's prepared to

---

🎬 The Silence of the Lambs
dir. Jonathan Demme, 1981

Given the phenomenal success of his novel, Harris could certainly have survived a maladroit cinema adaptation when the inevitable movie was made. In fact, Harris was lucky: Jonathan Demme got everything right, orchestrating the tension with the skill of a latter-day Hitchcock. The real success of the movie, however, lies in the casting: **Jodie Foster**, impeccably incarnating the out-of-her-depth Clarice against **Anthony Hopkins**, masterly as the urbane Lecter (even sidestepping the Hollywood cliché of casting all well-spoken intelligent villains as Englishmen by developing an indiscernible but distinct American accent). Above all the film (like the novel) is intelligent, a sharp contrast to most dumbed-down slasher Hollywood fare.

The masterly Hopkins as Hannibal Lecter

Chapter 9

There can hardly be a crime or thriller writer in the world who does not wish that he had **Thomas Harris**'s bank balance – not to mention a little of his unparalleled storytelling abilities. Harris has long since gone beyond being merely a top-flight writer: he is now a brand, and his sanguinary serial killer novels are the defining works of the genre. His name is routinely (and mostly vainly) invoked for every new writer who attempts to cover the same territory. But there is only one Thomas Harris, and each novel (and inevitable film adaptation) featuring the super-intelligent monster aesthete **Hannibal Lecter** is an event, nothing less.

Harris's first novel, *Black Sunday* (1975), about a terrorist attack at a sports venue, went almost unnoticed (although it was successfully filmed by John Frankenheimer in 1976) but, in the wake of the Oklahoma bombing and 9/11, seems now amazingly prescient. It was *Red Dragon* (1981) which first introduced the cultivated serial killer Lecter. Really he was a bit-part player, an incarcerated cannibalistic monster whom FBI Special Agent Will Graham has to consult to solve a series of particularly unpleasant slayings, perpetrated by a loner with an obsession with the English proto-Romantic painter/poet/visionary William Blake. Graham is assigned to such cases because of his ability to place himself in the mind of monsters – an early example of 'profiling' – and the plot of the novel was very swiftly imitated. Many consider it superior to its successor, *The Silence of the Lambs* (1988). But it was *Lambs* which, in one bound, established Harris's credentials, vaulting him to the top of the crime league.

help in the case of a killer using a bizarre *modus operandi*. But the inexperienced Clarice is no match for the Machiavellian Lecter, and he begins to play highly sophisticated mind games with her – while the other monster, the unincarcerated one, known as 'Buffalo Bill', continues to ply his bloody trade, chopping up women and skinning them. It's not hard to see why this book achieved such acclaim: it is, quite simply, a *tour de force*. And while Lecter may not be like any serial killer who ever walked the earth (most are dull, stupid men with predictably abused or damaged childhoods, and from a less privileged social class than Lecter) he remains the most iconic über-criminal in modern fiction.

Harris – notably shy of PR and interviews and appearing in publicity shots as an avuncular, scholarly-looking cove – seems to have realized that he had created a Shelley-like Frankenstein monster, in danger of eclipsing his creator. While the crime-reading world were kept in suspense for years, waiting for the next publication, Harris was busy building an increasingly baroque character and elaborate series of scenarios. *Hannibal* (1999) saw Lecter at full pitch, enmired with such monstrous types that he himself seemed almost normal, if not heroic. And despite – or perhaps because of – outrageous scenes involving flayed living corpses, conger eels, specially bred man-eating swine and the epicurean devouring of a living human brain, the most shocking element was FBI agent Clarice Starling disappearing off for a romantic future with Lecter at the finale.

Meanwhile, movies had swelled the Harris/Lecter franchise. While many argue that Brian Cox's low-key Lecter in Michael Mann's underrated version of *Red Dragon* (*Manhunter*, 1986) was superior to Anthony Hopkins' rather mannered interpretation in Demme's *Lambs*, in retrospect it was inevitable that Hollywood high-flier Ridley Scott would run away with Lecter's histrionics (and Hopkins) in *Hannibal* (2001), and a remake of *Red Dragon* (2002). In 2006's *Hannibal Rising* (and another Scott/Hopkins movie within weeks of publication) the various earlier exploits of Lecter, oft hinted at in the previous novels, were explored; but the book seemed perfunctory and carelessly written, a response to a hungry publisher's demands rather than one which would slake the public's appetite for dining at Lecter's high table, fava beans, Chianti, sweetbreads and all.

The Treatment 2002
Mo Hayder

The success of her debut novel *Birdman* (2000) was something of a double-edged sword for Mo Hayder: the book enjoyed astonishing success, but called down a fearsome wrath on the author for unflinchingly entering the blood-boltered territory of Thomas Harris' Hannibal books. Part of the fuss was clearly to do with the fact that a woman writer had handled scenes of horror and violence so authoritatively, and *The Treatment* provoked a similar furore. Actually, it's a remarkably vivid and meticulously detailed shocker:

less compelling than its predecessor, perhaps, but still a world away from the cosy reassurance of most current crime fiction. In a shady south London residential street, a husband and wife are found tied up, the man near death. Both have been beaten and are suffering from acute dehydration. D.I. Jack Caffery of the Met's murder squad, AMIP, is told to investigate the disappearance of the couple's son, and as he uncovers a series of dark parallels with his own life, he finds it more and more difficult to make the tough decisions necessary to crack a chilling case. As in *Birdman*, Caffery is characterized with particular skill, and Hayder is able (for the most part) to make us forget the very familiar cloth he's cut from. The personal involvement of a copper in a grim case is an over-familiar theme, but it's rarely been dispatched with the panache and vividness on display here.

A Cold Mind 1983
David Lindsey

It is an unrecognized fact that Lindsey was among the first crime genre writers to focus on serial killing and the motivations behind such behaviour, not least its frequent links with sexuality. This novel was the first in a short series featuring Houston cop Stuart Haydon, who has a way with multiple murderers. In it, Haydon is on the trail of a serial killer who has been targeting the city's call girls. The novel was rapidly followed by *Heat from Another Sun* (1984). Quite why Lindsey didn't capture the public's attention in the way that Harris was to do is a mystery, and it would be several years before *Mercy* (1990) really established his reputation. Nevertheless, he is a powerful writer, whose ability to create a tense narrative which balances the problem confronting the cop with the many problems motivating the murderer remains remarkable.

Faithless 2005
Karin Slaughter

Karin Slaughter is a woman unafraid of dealing with unspeakable violence in her books. Her focus is not so much on the fashion in which the social contract is shattered, but on the reasons why. That's not to say that she doesn't deal, unblinkingly, with the consequences of violence, and her name (appropriately enough) has become a byword for the toughest and most unrelenting of crime thrillers. She is much concerned with the factors that sanction the ruthless taking of life, but such things as the nature vs. nurture debate are always embedded in narratives that are as well-crafted as they are blood-curdling. Her familiar protagonists (police chief Jeffrey Tolliver and medical examiner Sara Linton, who first appeared in *Blindsighted*, 2001) are two of the strongest characters in the genre, with a beautifully detailed relationship – and *Faithless* is as good an entry point for Karin Slaughter as anything she has written. The duo discovers a body in the woods, and it is revealed that the girl's death is the result of extreme terror. Aided by detective Lena Adams, the pair initiate an investigation in a nearby county, where a closed community offers little help in their search. All of this is handled with the assurance we expect from Slaughter, but perhaps the best thing here is the worm in the bud that Slaughter introduces into her investigating team: Lena's disturbingly erratic behaviour is as much a threat to the group as the implacable killer. Irresistible stuff.

Four Blind Mice 2002
James Patterson

Short chapters. Very short chapters. That's James Patterson's sure-fire recipe – perhaps a tad over-used – for retaining his grip on a reader's attention span. His other calling card is the use of nursery

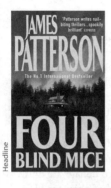

Headline

rhyme titles in his extensive Alex Cross series, which debuted with *Along Came a Spider* back in 1992. But his phenomenal sales – on both sides of the Atlantic – rout all criticism. The author knows precisely how to manipulate his readers, and the finely honed, utilitarian prose gets the job done. In *Four Blind Mice*, Cross is recovering from a savage duel with a murderous psychopath, and finding consolation in a new relationship. But he agrees to tackle a fresh assignment: a man is accused of a double murder at an army base, and Alex soon comes to feel that this is a fix, with the real killer still on the loose. This is tense, pared-down stuff, authoritatively handled. But good detective series invariably have the deathwatch beetle chewing away at the central concept, so that authors from **Conan Doyle** to **Colin Dexter** have tried to kill off their sleuth (Dexter succeeded, Doyle didn't). Patterson's Alex Cross series was definitely showing signs of slipping into autopilot, perhaps because Patterson set himself the task of maintaining a protagonist who wasn't (for instance) dealing with a broken marriage (a principal cliché of the genre). The first novel in a new, non-Cross series, *1st to Die* (2001), clearly had a galvanizing effect on the author, with Lindsay Boxer, the only woman homicide inspector in San Francisco, making for a well-rounded and engaging heroine.

The Rottweiler 2003
Ruth Rendell

Rendell has turned out a body of work notable for both teasing ingenuity and seamless literary style. She is the British writer who is closest to her American predecessor **Patricia Highsmith** in dealing

The remarkable Mr Ripley

Can a calculating killer be cool? Well, some 30 years before 'Hannibal the Cannibal' was projected onto our collective consciousness as a cultural icon, **Patricia Highsmith** wrote a remarkable book, *The Talented Mr Ripley* (1955), which follows a feckless Ivy League 'preppy', **Tom Ripley**, as he conceives a plot to ensure a pleasant expat future life in Europe. His plot exploits his enormous capacity for duplicity, guile, deceit – and killing. And even worse, Ripley reappears regularly but infrequently through Ms Highsmith's remarkable *oeuvre*, and such is her talent that we readers share her concern for him.

Following his first appearance, Ripley is comfortably ensconced in France, busy collecting paintings, has a beautiful partner, but is occasionally in need of extra funds. Who would stoop so low as to convince a vulnerable man that he has a terminal disease in order to get him to carry out a crime for you, to ensure his *post-partum* family's future (*Ripley's Game*, 1974)? Who would connive to encourage an innocent child to be a killer (*The Boy Who Followed Ripley*, 1980)? Actually this is of course the fascination of Ripley, a fascination played out in the handful of films (all great) based on Highsmith's character, with an interesting array of portrayals of this most ambiguous anti-heroes: **Alain Delon** in René Clement's version of *The Talented...*, titled *Plein Soleil* (1959); **Dennis Hopper** in Wim Wenders' *Der Amerikanische Freund* (*The American Friend*, 1977, based on *Ripley's Game*); and **Matt Damon** in *The Talented Mr Ripley* (dir. Anthony Minghella, 1999).

The Ripley books

▶ *The Talented Mr Ripley* (1955)
▶ *Ripley Under Ground* (1970)
▶ *Ripley's Game* (1974)
▶ *The Boy Who Followed Ripley* (1980)
▶ *Ripley Under Water* (1991)

with the darker corners of human psychology, and that's very much the case in *The Rottweiler*. London is at the mercy of a vicious serial killer, dubbed 'The Rottweiler' after bite marks are found on the neck of his first victim. When a second murder takes place near a London antiques shop, the narrative focuses on the owner of the store, Inez Ferry, and her neighbours, a rich gallery of character portraits. Inez herself is wasting her life, forlornly watching videos of her dead actor husband, while the Asian woman who works for her, Zeinab, enjoys a versatile sex life, having liaisons with two separate men while living with a third. Then there is the solitary Jeremy, and the educationally subnormal Will who lives in an unhealthy relationship with his aunt. But this is not standard whodunnit territory, with a hidden killer and a tenacious detective; as before in Rendell, the mystery is almost casually thrown away with the killer's identity dispensed relatively early. What concerns her is the insidious progress of evil in the human soul. **P.D. James** may be the writer with the more religious sensibility, but Rendell has the bleaker vision, with the murderous possibilities of human behaviour given full rein in her dark world. A blackmailer, too, is stirred into this heady brew, and this character is a mirror image of both the killer's evil and the less savoury aspects of the other protagonists. With the minutely observed portraits of Inez and her neighbours counterpointed by the horror of a seemingly psychopathic killer, we're in safe hands with Rendell.

The Killer Inside Me 1952
Jim Thompson

Orion

Stanley Kubrick was one of the famous admirers of this remarkable novel, and its terrifying picture of a psychopathic consciousness conveyed in the first person has not dated, and is still a truly disturbing read. Lou Ford is the Deputy Sheriff of his modest Texas town, and is well thought of by the small populace. The general view of him is that he is efficient but unexciting – but Lou has a very dark secret, which he describes as his

> **The Killer Inside Me**
> dir. Burt Kennedy, 1976
>
> While Burt Kennedy was an efficient director of no-nonsense Westerns, he was signally out of his depth in this misguided adaptation of Thompson's classic; but then Elmore Leonard's books often play like films in the reader's head, although it takes a Tarantino to make them work on the screen as well as they do on the page (see *Rum Punch/Jackie Brown*, p.141). This is a shame, as the actor playing the tormented Lou was the excellent **Stacey Keach**, a man more than able to deal with troubled inner states when the right director could channel such things; on this occasion, Burt Kennedy wasn't that director, and made a travesty of Thompson's novel.

'sickness'. His adopted brother was blamed for an act of violence that Lou committed when he was younger, but this twisted part of his psyche is on the point of emerging again, and the consequences for Lou this time can't be shrugged off onto others. In some ways, Thompson's technique here echoes that of the existentialist novelists **Albert Camus** and **Jean-Paul Sartre**, with the cruel, affectless prose conveying intense inner turmoil through indirect impressions. Once read, *The Killer Inside Me* is not easily forgotten.

Dead Calm 1963
Charles Williams

Williams, like **Charles Willeford** (see p.111), is an unsung hero of the US post-pulp mystery thriller, and can often be found sidling alongside him on the bookstore shelves. His career started with Jim Thompson-style smalltown 'erotic' thrillers such as *Hill Girl* (1951) and *The Diamond Bikini* (1956), and his *Hell Hath No Fury* (filmed impressively as *The Hot Spot* by no less than Dennis Hopper in 1990) bears comparison with his mentor. This novel is one of several sailing thrillers which Williams produced – the author committed suicide by drowning off his yacht. Newlyweds John and Rae

Chapter 9

Ingram are cruising in the Pacific, an idyllic dream come true until, becalmed in the doldrums, they drift across a sinking hulk. They rescue the lone passenger, but not before the experienced navigator John senses something is seriously wrong. The young survivor claims that his wife and another couple on the vessel died of lead poisoning. In a dramatic reversal of roles John Ingram is left on the sinking death vessel, while the clearly psychopathic survivor makes off with his wife on the honeymooners' yacht. A tense slow-motion chase ensues, with Rae doing her best to outwit her unwelcome sailing companion, while John uses all his maritime skills to come to her rescue. Genuinely spine-chilling and enormously suspenseful, despite the lack of wind this is a breath of fresh air in the mystery genre.

> ### Dead Calm
> dir. Phillip Noyce, 1988
>
> Australian 'new wave' director Noyce introduced a family tragedy as the reason for the Ingrams' cruise, giving a certain edge to the relationship between John (**Sam Neill**) and his young wife (introducing... **Nicole Kidman**). The photography and pace is superb, as is **Billy Zane** as the unhinged killer, and Noyce wrings every drop of suspense he can out of a small cast and beautifully placid oceanic setting.

In the belly of the beast

Criminal protagonists

While – theoretically – most readers of crime fiction don't actually commit the bloody murders or ambitious thefts they enjoy reading about, there's no denying the *frisson* produced when we put ourselves inside the consciousnesses of these ruthless protagonists. In the cinema, **Alfred Hitchcock** seduced us into feeling how exhilarating it was to identify with a criminal – and feel suspense over whether or not they'll be caught. And we fell for this strategy every time (however impeccably law-abiding our instincts). This moral equivalence had long been the principal stock-in-trade of the best crime writers. Some authors moved exclusively in this dark universe – **Patricia Highsmith**, for instance, with her murderous *dramatis personae*. And admirers of **Ruth Rendell** (beyond her books featuring the doughty Inspector Wexford) often feel her best work lies in her books *sans* detective – where the central characters perform terrible, destructive deeds. Such books are usually more disorienting than the crimefighter-led novel, where we feel the compass of universal order will rest at the correct point by the final page; it's a more unsettling experience to be dropped into the psyche of a murderer or a thief – individuals who (more often than not) have a tragic destiny. There is, however, a fragile sense of morality at work here, however off-kilter: if we're ever tempted by the world of crime, such writers as **Elmore Leonard** (with his luckless protagonists) will quickly disabuse us of the notion that this is a glamorous life. Here's a batch of top-notch writers who (despite our ordered, non-transgressive lives) put us into the heads of individuals who live life at the very edge…

The Killing of the Saints 1991
Alex Abella

Truth, as we now all know in an open-access age, is definitely stranger than fiction. And religious truths have now become a frightening reality. With a 'born-again' president in the White House, there has not, as yet, been a great novel dealing with the confusing mess of international Islamic *jihad* which he may have brought down on our heads. But we can nevertheless look back to the equally confusing horror scenarios played out at Jonestown (over 600 suicides) and in the woefully mishandled FBI siege of David Koresh's 'temple' at Waco to see just how uncomfortable religious fundamentalism (or fervour) can become. And it is interesting to note that key US pulse-feeler **Elmore Leonard** wrote a signally non-crime novel about the incipient dangers of messianic, charismatic religion in *Touch* (1987). With a US population built on the 'boiling-pot' foundations of mixed race, mixed religion and mixed culture, a novel like Alex Abella's *Killing of the Saints* is at least instructive. Two crack-head losers plan a jewellery-shop robbery, which goes horribly wrong, resulting in mass, unmotivated slaughter. What makes this book so disconcerting is not the drug use, but the influence of Santeria religious ideas on the killers, where effectively all responsibility for their actions can be placed on a deity, and the cult which exists behind it. Conceived by the Cuban-born author surely as an examination of one of the many sub-cultures which constitute modern America, this powerfully written book nevertheless has a prescient feel in a post-9/11 world.

The Burglar on the Prowl 2002
Lawrence Block

This tenth appearance of Lawrence Block's sophisticated crook Bernie Rhodenbarr is an exuberant delight. Bernie sells rare first editions for his day job, but spends evenings engaged in larceny. In the course of the series, Block very cleverly pulled off (after the fashion of **Patricia Highsmith**) a tricky task: making us root for a criminal, via the accommodation of sharp dialogue and some masterful plotting. Sometimes the series was a little hit and miss, but when Block is on top form (as here), he demon-

No Exit Press

strates why he enjoys such a loyal following as a writer. Bernie's friend Marty has commissioned him to get his hands on some money in the apartment of a plastic surgeon. This money is undeclared, but Bernie isn't exactly suffering any moral qualms in any case. As so often in the past, things go wrong: Bernie makes a mistake by checking out other apartments in the doctor's neighbourhood, and evades capture by hiding under a woman's bed, when he realizes that the woman is being raped by yet another intruder in her flat. His moral code may be flexible when it comes to robbery, but this outrage inspires him to get on the trail of the brutal attacker. Needless to say, everything goes pear-shaped, and soon the body count is rising. While Block's plotting sometimes causes the eyes to widen at its sheer audacity, largely speaking he makes the reader buy into some of the more outrageous developments on offer here.

No Beast So Fierce 1973
Eddie Bunker

Eddie Bunker is the real thing. 'Mr Blue' in Tarantino's signature 1991 film *Reservoir Dogs*, Bunker is an ex-con who knows all too well the inside of a penitentiary. His writing has both the raw energy and dark poetry of writers with a more heavyweight though shady-side literary reputation, such as **Jean Genet**, **William Burroughs** and **Charles Bukowski**. In the small cadre of American prison writers, Bunker is *numero uno*: he has lived the life, and this bleak and gripping novel about an ex-con's fraught attempt to deal with the depressing prospect of going straight after a lengthy spell inside is both mercilessly unsentimental and utterly gripping. As Bunker's anti-hero begins the slow and inevitable slide back towards crime, the reader's guts are twisted in quite as painful fashion as they are reading the novels of other great lowlife chroniclers such as **Nelson Algren** (with whose *Never Come Morning*, 1942, this book shows some similarities). Intriguingly, Bunker makes the prospect of a straight, crime-free existence for his born-under-a-bad-sign protagonist more terrifying than the exhilarating return to lawbreaking, however disastrous the prospects of the latter option. Bunker spent some 30 years of his life in and out of prison, and his writing (with its echoes of a broken home and an alcoholic father) is never reassuring. But it is always trenchant and coolly observed.

> **Straight Time**
> dir. Ulu Grosbard, 1978
>
> For a commercial Hollywood movie, Ulu Grosbard's adaptation of Bunker's novel is truly audacious in its complete refusal to request sympathy for its ill-fated ex-con protagonist as he moves through a bleak and unyielding universe. **Dustin Hoffman** underlines this decision in an uningratiating performance that is both understated and powerful, even if the final effect of the film is dispiriting.

Maura's Game 2002
Martina Cole

When her debut thriller *Dangerous Lady* appeared in 1992, Martina Cole immediately established herself as a cutting-edge voice in crime fiction. That book introduced us to her tough and canny protagonist Maura Ryan, Queen of the Underworld. The amazing success of all Cole's crime novels must be a source of despair to those writers who have struggled for years. Right from the start, she has enjoyed unqualified approval for her distinctive, no-nonsense fiction. Even the workaday TV adaptations of *Dangerous Lady* and *The Jump* (1995) merely brought more kudos her way (she's been less lucky than **Colin Dexter** in her transfer to the screen – but she shouldn't worry). *Maura's Game* signals the return of Cole's resilient heroine, bent on going straight now that she's salted enough away from her crime days to be comfortable. Needless to say, all her good intentions go up in smoke when she finds that she can't leave her old life behind – her old associates won't let her. In prose that is always blunt and trenchant, Cole weaves her spell throughout this scabrous narrative. Maura is an exuberantly characterized heroine, and the supporting cast enjoys equally gritty handling from the author.

Chapter 10

The Final Country 2001
James Crumley

Among current practitioners of the American hardboiled crime genre, few would deny that James Crumley is in the upper echelons. His hard-edged, racy prose, his dangerous, quirkily drawn characters and (most of all) his exuberant narrative skills have pretty comprehensively seen off all the competition, although he is surprisingly little known outside the US. But such supremacy brings a price: reader expectations for each new novel are higher than ever, so Crumley has to top himself with each successive outing. Has he done so with *The Final Country*? The first chapter, featuring a dangerous head-to-head with a shotgun in a redneck bar, instantly makes it clear that we're in for vintage Crumley, every bit as grimly diverting as such earlier winners as *Bordersnakes* (1996, see p.204) and *The Mexican Tree Duck* (1993). Enos, Crumley's tough anti-hero, is out of jail and on the track of the partners in crime who set him up. But a drug dealer pulls a gun on Enos and ends up dead, so the police are set to add murder to Enos' charge sheet. The one person who can save him from a death sentence is Crumley's long-term protagonist, low-rent, 50-something private investigator Milo Milodragovitch – but Milo is struggling (as so often before) with corrupt politicians, heavy-duty crime bosses and two women keen to get him into bed, despite his bad back. Crumley once called himself 'the bastard son of Raymond Chandler', but *The Final Country* is a reminder that he's very much his own man: the plotting here is as outrageously inventive as ever, while a very dangerous Montana is evoked with great vividness. The resourceful Milo is established even more firmly as one of the most strongly realized characters in current crime fiction. As always with Crumley, the heady cocktail of drugs, violence and dark humour makes for an irresistible read.

The Day of the Jackal 1971
Frederick Forsyth

The problem for an author who creates a groundbreaking, highly distinctive book early in his career is the singular one of following it up, and it has to be said that nothing Frederick Forsyth has written since *The Day of the Jackal* has matched this remarkable thriller. But that's not to say that Forsyth's subsequent career is not studded with some remarkable successes. *Jackal* is, of course, a book with one of the most striking premises in all crime/thriller fiction – a notion that would be described (in Hollywood parlance) as 'high concept'. An anonymous Englishman is hired (in the early 1960s) by the Operations Chief of the OAS to assassinate the French president, General Charles de Gaulle, and thereby alter the political landscape irrevocably. With this premise, Forsyth set himself an intriguing task: the reader knows that de Gaulle was not assassinated, so how can suspense be maintained throughout the novel when we know that the mission is doomed to failure? As in **Geoffrey Household**'s *Rogue Male* (see p.26) this is, of course, the audacity of the novel: Forsyth makes the tradecraft of an assassin's work utterly fascinating. With every stage of the planning

---

The Day of the Jackal
dir. Fred Zinnemann, 1973

The considerable success of Zinnemann's film consolidated that of the novel, with the honours evenly divided between the director's cool and efficient approach to this material, a clever and fastidious script by Kenneth Ross, and (notably) the charismatic performance by **Edward Fox** as the super-efficient assassin. The most surprising thing about the success of the film is that it did not turn Fox into an international star, though he has subsequently enjoyed a strong career as a character actor. The novel was filmed again in 1997 as *The Jackal*, with **Bruce Willis** as the eponymous assassin. While Willis turns in a credible performance, almost everything that made the earlier movie memorable is jettisoned by director Michael Caton-Jones.

and execution assiduously detailed, we suspend our knowledge of the inevitable outcome – or, more precisely, begin to wonder how such a professional killer will fail to change the course of history. The methodical detail of the book has been copied many times since (and Forsyth's own attempts to reproduce the formula have been less successful, although books such as 1972's *The Odessa File* still exert a powerful grip), but another, less acknowledged triumph of the book is the way in which we are involved in the activities of a protagonist whose humanity is ruthlessly suppressed.

Brighton Rock 1938
Graham Greene

Even in the 21st century, this remains one of the most blistering and galvanic pictures of urban crime in all British literature. When not wrestling with the problems of guilt (Catholic or otherwise), Greene remains fascinated by the extremes of human behaviour, and his teenage gangster Pinkie, cutting a violent swathe through the seaside underworld of Brighton, is one of the great monsters of fiction, wrestling in an inarticulate fashion with the faith which is merely a source of negativity and retribution to him as he attempts to jockey for position against what prove to be insuperable odds. The details of gang war in Brighton are brilliantly delineated, with Pinkie's violent killing of a man in the early chapters marking him out as a young man not to be trifled with. But set against the terrifying Pinkie is the figure of Ida Arnold, blowsy but sympathetic, and determined to bring about revenge for the death of a man she knew but briefly. Ida could easily have been a sentimental figure. But Greene is, of course, much too good a writer for that and creates a fully rounded, confused but positive character who acts as the perfect counterweight to the teenage hoodlum. The celebrity of the novel is fully justified, and the conflicting moral qualms of all the characters (even the most irredeem-

> **Brighton Rock**
> dir. John Boulting, 1947
>
> Even today, the razor-wielding violence of John Boulting's seminal British gangster film has a considerable impact. It's intriguing, therefore, to muse on the fact that we are only familiar with a censored version of the film, softened after the moral guardians of the day threw up their hands in horror. But while Boulting does sterling work (working from Greene's own script of his novel), it's **Richard Attenborough**'s truly unpleasant – but fascinating – Pinkie that remains in the mind, a British gangster to set alongside the memorable portrayals of Cagney and co. No accident, then, that Attenborough went on to play other memorable monsters in Bryan Forbes' *Séance on a Wet Afternoon* (1964) and Richard Fleischer's *10 Rillington Place* (1970).

able) are marshalled with immense skill. Many non-religious readers are often put off by the concept of Catholicism in Greene's books, but there is never a sense of evangelism: for Greene, belief merely alters the quality of misery of those who possess it. He was pleased with the fact that he was not considered a good advertisement for the Catholic Church, and lost his faith towards the end of his life.

Sick Puppy 2000
Carl Hiaasen

It's always fascinating to watch a thriller writer progress from being the esoteric favourite of a small minority to being a highly influential, much-read success on a far grander scale. It happened with **Elmore Leonard**, and it can certainly be said to have happened to the wonderful Carl Hiaasen. This novel sports all the usual Hiaasen fingerprints: Florida setting, lurking environmental issues, quirky, offbeat humour, bizarre but totally plausible characterization, plotting whose crazy ingenuity leaves the reader reeling, and characters who seem to be unaware that laws exist. It's a tradition that he established in *Tourist Season* (1986), *Double Whammy* (1987) and *Strip Tease* (1993), and continued with *Skinny Dip* (2004). As a thriller writer, Hiaasen is on his own, and if *Sick Puppy* broke no new ground, admirers did not complain. His protagonist Palmer Stoat is worried by a black pick-up truck following him, and is convinced that his beloved Range Rover is about to be carjacked. But the man tailing him is vengeance-bent. Twilly is hardly your average criminal: wealthy and pathologically idealistic, he is on a crusade to save Florida land from despoliation. And Stoat's trail of fast-food litter is the curtain-raiser to a weird and wonderful narrative in which this highway encounter leads to a much larger-scale bout of political fisticuffs. From phoney big-game hunters to prostitutes who will only service Republicans, the cast of characters is as wonderful as only Hiaasen can create.

Night and the City 1938
Gerald Kersh

Unquestionably the key book by the dizzyingly prolific British pulpmeister Gerald Kersh, *Night and the City* is a rich delight. Kersh had beavered away in a variety of genres for many years, pleasing an army of pulp readers, before he attracted critical attention. But when it came, there was a definite sense of a wrong being righted: despite the very mixed nature of his achievement, at his best, Kersh was a considerable writer. This is his best book, needing no recommendation these days. Harry Fabian lives life at the very edge, ducking and diving through a grittily realized London, playing both ends against the middle as he tries to make his mark as the leading wrestling promoter in the city. But Harry needs money – just a hundred pounds, but scams and blackmail aren't paying off for him. Can he squeeze the dosh out of a corrupt nightclub owner and his predatory wife? As Harry's enemies close in and his options narrow, he begins to assume a genuinely tragic status. If you only ever read one novel by Gerald Kersh – guess which one it should be.

> ### Night and the City
> dir. Jules Dassin, 1950
>
> First published in 1938, *Night and the City* has inspired two films, the classic 1950 *film noir* starring **Richard Widmark** and **Gene Tierney**, filmed in London by blacklisted American director Jules Dassin, and Irwin Winkler's 1992 workaday remake set in New York and starring **Robert De Niro** and **Jessica Lange**. Dassin's phantasmagoric film still completely eclipses the indifferent remake, with Richard Widmark's nervy, career-defining performance unassailable.

Swag 1976
Elmore Leonard

The best entry point for Leonard remains his mid-period work (1970s–1980s), and such books as *52 Pickup* will demonstrate to any reader why Leonard is thought of so highly. In *Swag*, a highly entertaining outing by Leonard, two bottom-feeding crooks, Frank and Stick, are taking a crash-course in armed robbery and trying to gain the necessary experience while knocking over liquor marts and other small joints. They have coined the '10 Golden Rules for Armed Robbery', but when they start to bend these rules themselves, trouble is in store. This is as lean and efficient a book as the ever-reliable Leonard can deliver: just reading it is in itself a crash-course in how to write the very best modern crime fiction. Leonard is particularly good on the banality of crime and its practitioners: no criminal masterminds here, just none-too-efficient low-level types trying to behave in a vaguely coherent fashion.

Phoenix Press

195

Chapter 10

The Sins of their Fathers 2002
Gilda O'Neill

Gilda O'Neill is a woman of multiple skills, and her variety of endeavours as a writer (novelist, social commentator, historian) dovetailed together very satisfyingly to produce *The Sins of their Fathers*, a vivid, flint-edged picture of London's East End in the 1960s, which leaps off the page with its richly idiomatic dialogue and sharply realized characters. Her protagonists, the O'Donnells, are living the life of Reilly. Their brief includes prostitution, protection rackets and gambling, and their very name inspires respect and fear. But Harold Kessler, long-time nemesis of Gabriel O'Donnell, head of the clan, has decided to bring his family back to the East End, and a bloody confrontation is inevitable. While the plotting here is quite as adroit as one could wish, it is the realization of some less-than-admirable characters that is O'Neill's trump card. The author allows the reader to make his or her judgements on the characters and resists any kind of moralizing authorial voice – and this refusal to dispense judgements may disconcert readers looking for pointers – something O'Neill is aware that we all search for. But her resistance to conventional novelistic ploys such as these pays dividends – and treating the reader with intelligence is not a bad move for most writers. You won't like many of the people you encounter here, but you'll find it very difficult indeed to put this one down. Gabriel O'Donnell is one of the most powerfully drawn protagonists in the British crime genre for quite some time – a memorable piece of characterization.

The Crust on its Uppers 1962
Derek Raymond (pseudonym of Robin Cook)

A quite extraordinary book, and as extraordinary as its author (see profile overleaf). It is one of the few novels which actually has a glossary of terms (at the beginning), and in fact most readers would be lost without it. Written entirely in an odd argot of Cockney rhyming slang and London underworld *spiel* from the post-World War II period, this book is a form of confession, and reveals as much about the author's shady life as it does about England

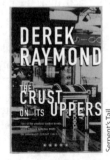

Serpent's Tail

Chapter 10

half a century ago. It describes a world in which chancing and criminal activity is the norm, and one by no means exclusively inhabited by social underdogs. Everyone, from the ex-Eton author sideways, is on the make, whether it's rigging horse races, recycling stolen vehicles or simply blagging and poncing (literally) on the backstreets of Soho. The late Raymond, frequently out of print, but never forgotten, can unfortunately be blamed for the hypnotically jokey style of recent London gangster films such as *Lock, Stock and Two Smoking Barrels* (dir. Guy Ritchie, 1998) and *Sexy Beast* (dir. Jonathan Glazer, 2000). But Raymond was a considerable cut above this sort of stuff. A masterpiece of unexplored social history.

Clubland 2001
Kevin Sampson

Why do we read thrillers? Part of the fascination of the genre is that we know we will be taken into a different and dangerous world, where the rules that govern our existence count for little. With Kevin Sampson's *Clubland*, that world is a particularly unsettling one, and at no point can the reader feel comfortable. But we don't read thrillers to be comfortable, do we? Sampson's protagonist Ged Brennan combines his expertise in violence with a strongly moral streak. He has absolutely no intention of becoming involved in seedy clubs, drugs and topless bars. But then he receives an offer to assume control of the clubland empire of an executed gangster. He gives the opportunity to his cousin Moby (a man obsessively addicted to sex). This proves to be a disastrous move. Samson's other principal character, Margot, has ambitions in the property development field, but discovers that her signature project, a media village, is to be summarily taken away from her. She is not happy – and then the council's regeneration committee appoints Ged Brennan to handle the final stages of Margot's development. Conflict between the two is inevitable, and is handled with considerable skill by Sampson (whose *Outlaws*, 2001, was also a critical success). But the real appeal of this rugged thriller lies not so much in the Machiavellian intrigues as in the dark, lurid (and occasionally surrealistic) world the characters negotiate. This is often very funny, always hard-hitting.

Answers from the Grave 2003
Mark Timlin

In his Nick Sharman thrillers, London writer Mark Timlin performed a very clever sleight-of-hand: while giving every impression of gritty urban reality and the life of a cynical London private eye,

Chapter 10

the actual narratives functioned on an almost hyper-real level, with plausibility less important than sheer narrative momentum. *Answers from the Grave* shows the rebarbative Timlin taking his writing to a whole new level, with its notions of dreaming built into a customarily hard-edged narrative. Marcus Farrow's father was a criminal who moved to the other side of the law, and died at the hands of the brutal Jimmy Hunter in a 1960s bank robbery that goes wrong. Marcus has been patiently waiting for Jimmy to serve his lengthy prison sentence to exact an appropriate revenge. At the same time, Sean Pearse, the criminal's alienated son, has become a cop. When this incendiary cast of characters get together, it's inevitable that there will be fireworks. Timlin's long-term protagonist Sharman makes a cameo appearance, but this is a more ambitious crime novel than most of the author's other works, and represents a considerable achievement.

Organized crime

Wiseguys and godfathers

If, as the Prussian theorist Carl von Clausewitz claimed, warfare is 'diplomacy conducted by other means' then organized crime is free-market capitalism on the same 'other means' basis. J. Edgar Hoover's Federal Bureau of Investigation refused to acknowledge that organized crime existed in the US, until a cascade of cases from the 1960s onwards – often the result of squealers like Joe Valachi and Henry Hill, or deep-cover cops like 'Donnie Brasco' – made it all too clear that criminal activity on an industrial scale was endemic in America, and had infiltrated not just the police force but possibly the corridors of political power too. After all, J.F.K.'s father (and America's World War II ambassador in London), Joe Kennedy, had made a fortune running illicit liquor across the Great Lakes during the Prohibition years. Organizations like the (Sicilian) Black Hand, Jewish gangsters,

Triads, Japanese Yakuza and Irish republican support groups had existed in localized ethnic enclaves, richly documented by journalist Herbert Asbury's excellent series of books on 19th-century US crime, most notably *The Gangs of New York* (1928), filmed rather disappointingly by Martin Scorsese in 2002. But it was the Volstead Act, instituting alcohol prohibition in 1919, that not only immediately turned many American citizens who liked a highball in the evening into criminals by default, but also provided the impetus for the growth of industrialized crime. And when the Act was repealed in 1932, like any other corporation, the big guys, notably the immigrant southern Italian *mafiosi* families, needed to find new products and new markets. Prostitution, extortion and, above all, gambling and narcotics, became their turf. But the turf was becoming overpopulated. While, in truth, British organized criminals were pretty amateur (the activities of the Kray brothers and the Richardson gang have been glamorized out of all proportion), traditional and historical high-rollers like the Chinese Triads and Tongs and the Japanese Yakuza saw international, global opportunities opening up. And now, since *perestroika*, a new and menacing breed of organized criminals emanating from Russia and Central Asia are rewriting the rulebook – if there ever was one.

The Long Firm 1999
Jake Arnott

As a picture of the London underworld in the 1960s, Arnott's brutal and impressive novel is social history with impeccable thick-ear credentials. As in Kurosawa's classic *Rashomon*, different characters give us different perspectives on one thing. In this case, it's Harry Stark, a brutal gangster. But as the reader learns more about Harry, we realize that there is more to him than simple bone-crunching violence. Arnott presents Harry through the prism of East End proletarian

> ▥ **The Long Firm**
> dir. Billie Eltrigham, TVM, 2004
>
> This TV adaptation of Jake Arnott's blistering novel created a considerable stir, not least for its canny casting of **Mark Strong** in the role of the charismatic anti-hero. While the screenplay inevitably simplified the more intriguing aspects of the novel (often reducing it to a straightforward tale of lowlife brutality), the impressive sheen of the production often did full service to Arnott's prose. Strong casting of other parts, too, backed up Mark Strong's memorable central turn.

gangland subculture, as seen through the eyes of a sociologist who is involved with him. Harry combines charm with ruthlessness, and his intelligence wins over the reluctant, appalled reader. The characters he interacts with (seductive blondes, Marxist writers) are drawn with the same vividness, and the surprising analyses of cultural behaviour (not least from the mouth of Harry himself) are as entertaining as the more visceral elements.

Little Caesar 1929
W.R. Burnett

Perhaps best remembered these days as the source for **Edward G. Robinson**'s career-forging performance as the ruthless gangster making his fatal way to the top of the heap as a Capone-style mobster (while repressing a secretly gay nature), Burnett's novel reads as caustically as when it was written, its flinty prose as bluntly effective as ever. *Little Caesar* was Burnett's first novel, and is often described as the first gangster novel. Cesare Rico Bandello is a small-time hood who claws his way to an all-too-brief period as King of the Mobs, before a fatal flaw in his character destroys him (conforming to the trajectory described in Robert Warhow's famous essay 'The Gangster as Tragic Hero'). The novel is played out mostly in dialogue, but it's perhaps difficult for the modern reader not to see (and hear)

Robinson's strutting protagonist – particularly as Burnett keeps the reader at some distance from Rico, and our post-Robinson perceptions are wont to creep in. For those unfamiliar with the Mervyn le Roy film, though, the lack of any stylistic flourishes – once criticized as a failing – can now seem like a rather modern virtue.

Bordersnakes 1996
James Crumley

Crumley's world is (like that of **Cormac McCarthy** and **Sam Peckinpah**) the arid zone of the American Southwest, where moral borders are as invisible as the now all but dried up Rio Grande. It is a world of deserts, tumbleweeds, and local crime barons – on either side of the river – who sweat pesos and dollars out of illegal immigrants, migrant workers and drug-running mules who are aiming for the rich pastures of 'El Norte', LA and its environs. Although wryly humorous, Crumley paints a picture of an updated, but

Collins Crime

still lawless, Wild West, where anything goes, and nothing is that predictable. To not carry a Savage double-ought pump-action scattergun in your car, let alone a handgun in your waistband, would be a sign of severe vulnerability, and as Crumley's protagonists play a dangerous criss-cross game of chance, he paints a portrait of a frontier of America where organized criminal activity is more normal than white picket-fence 'normality'. And as with the landscapes painted by Cormac McCarthy, this cruel region is dominated by lawbreakers rather than law-enforcers.

Get Carter/Jack's Return Home 1970

Ted Lewis

There's no doubt that Mike Hodges' film adaptation was the primary factor in granting this novel cult status (Lewis had initially done himself no favours with one of the most clunky titles in crime fiction). But as our image of the vengeful Jack Carter is forever stamped with **Michael Caine**'s indelible performance, how does the original novel read in the 21st century, viewed in its own right? While (in all honesty), Hodges undoubtedly added layers to the original, there's still much to commend, notably the brilliantly drawn Doncaster locales. As Carter takes leave from his Kray-like employers to return to his home town to arrange the burial of his estranged brother, he quickly realizes that the circumstances of the death are suspicious. Soon, Carter is cutting a brutal swathe though the local hoods (gambling, prostitution, blue movies, corporate corruption), trying to find out why his brother died. Lewis's speciality is the pithy evocation of place, and few novels (even those of such northern lit-

---

Get Carter
dir. Mike Hodges, 1970

There's no getting away from it – this is a film that really does fully justify its cult reputation. Quite simply, Mike Hodges' version of Ted Lewis's remarkable novel about organized crime in the provinces (he relocated the action to Newcastle) is the best British gangster movie ever made, and a career-best for just about everyone associated with it. **Guy Ritchie** and other current genre specialists can only wistfully dream that they could create something as hard-edged and brilliant as this (but then Hodges himself was never able to top this film, despite the critical success of later work, such as *Croupier*, 1997). As the brutal, affectless Jack, Michael Caine has never been better, and playwright/actor **John Osborne** as the local crime baron is utterly convincing.

erary specialists as John Braine) place the reader so securely in this territory. The grim industrial vistas, the down-at-heel private clubs and porn cinemas – all are as vividly painted as the amoral cast of characters.

And Then You Die 2002
Michael Dibdin

Despite Michael Dibdin's efforts, Reichenbach Falls-style, to do away with his series protagonist, we all knew **Aurelio Zen** wasn't dead – it would take more than an exploding car to finish off that tenacious Italian copper. In *And Then You Die*, the star detective of Rome's elite Criminalpol is back, recovered from the bomb attack and lying low under a false name at a beach resort on the Tuscan coast. Using the fact that many think he's dead, Zen is waiting to testify in an imminent anti-Mafia trial. His brief is straightforward: enjoy the Italian sun and seafood, and do nothing else. But a mild flirtation with the attractive woman under the next beach umbrella doesn't (needless to stay) stop Zen from becoming restless, particularly as people are dropping dead around him. And how long before the Mafia realizes that it didn't finish the job it started on that secluded Sicilian road? It's a cliché to remark that an author and his work need no introduction, but it's the phrase that is most apposite here. Dibdin has no peers in this kind of elegantly written, brilliantly plotted crime writing, and the Italian locales are evoked as vividly as ever.

American Tabloid 1995
James Ellroy

American Tabloid is an authentic American masterpiece. Whilst the Updikes, Mailers, Fords and De Lillos mud-wrestled for the trophy of 'The Great American Novel', wild-man Ellroy crept up, pulled the carpet from under them, and stole the prize. *Tabloid* takes the defining era of post-World War II America, J.F.K.'s Camelot, head-on, no-holds-barred. Using the technique he had honed in the *Hollywood Quartet* (see *LA Confidential*, p.86), Ellroy mixes real-life characters such as the President, his brother Bobby, FBI supremo J. Edgar Hoover,

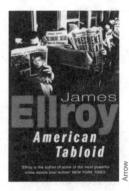

Teamsters boss Jimmy Hoffer and mobsters like Vito Genovese and Traficante with fictional (but entirely credible) shadowy fixers to create a heady cocktail of political and criminal intrigue in which all moral margins are shaken, stirred and then served over ice. The novel concentrates on both the Bay of Pigs fiasco and the Kennedy assassination, although Ellroy interestingly stops minutes short of the day in Dallas which everyone remembers. The next novel in the cycle, *The Cold Six Thousand* (2001), begins in November 1963: Wayne Tedrow Jr, a young Vegas cop, arrives in Dallas as the American Dream explodes in Deeley Plaza. As Dallas and the nation mourns, his assignment to track down drug-dealing pimp Wendell Durfee is eclipsed, and Tedrow is drawn into the cover-ups and murders that follow. As in *American Tabloid*, fact and fiction rub shoulders, and the Ellroy style is as perfectly honed as ever – though many found the prose of this follow-up (short sentences, minimal punctuation) mannered and irritating.

Chapter 11

Get Shorty (1990)
Elmore Leonard

Once he abandoned writing very good Westerns to the benefit of crime enthusiasts in the late 1960s, Leonard's novels took place mainly in one of two geographical locales: Miami and his home town of Detroit. This highly enjoyable novel takes us further afield, to Hollywood, and reflects something of Leonard's jaded view of the place, where he was courted as a scriptwriter. Chili Palmer is a debt collector for Miami gangsters, who follows a defaulting client to Hollywood. Chili takes a surprising decision to abandon his enforcing work and get into the moviemaking business. This is absolutely wonderful stuff, with such strongly drawn characters as Chili's defaulting customer Leo, who has faked his own death in an air-crash and absconded with the $300,000 his wife received from the airline company. And then there's the thick-headed Mafia cruiser Ray Bones, who has no love for Chili since the latter shot him in the head. Sublime.

> **Get Shorty**
> dir. Barry Sonnenfeld, 1995
>
> Casting is the key to the success of this sharp and witty adaptation of Elmore Leonard's unsparing picture of Hollywood and organized crime. **John Travolta**'s turn as Chili has the superficial appearance of some of his lazier work, but is actually spot-on in conveying the ambiguities of a quintessential Leonard character. And with **Gene Hackman** as a sleazy producer (not to mention **Danny DeVito** and The Sopranos' **James Gandolfini** in the cast), the excellent Barry Sonnenfeld has great material to work with. Talk about biting the hand that feeds you, though.

The Godfather 1978
Mario Puzo

The novel that put the Mafia on the map has had an inestimable influence, and the ripples from Mario Puzo's massive blockbuster (not to mention its various film adaptations) continue to spread to this day. Deploying the hyper-detailed format perfected by **Frederick Forsyth** in *Day of the Jackal*, Puzo relates in exhaustive detail the day-to-day dealings of an influential Italian family in America – who just happened to be ruthless *mafiosi*. Other writers had dealt before with the acrimonious meetings

between heads of families (and the often bloody business that followed), but Puzo was the first to render these as nigh-operatic set pieces. In fact, all the criminal business is essentially a backdrop for what is a violent version of a classic Shakespearian theme: the education and corruption of a young man. Michael Corleone, back from a stint in the army, is slowly and steadily prepared for accession to the throne vacated by his father, the patrician Don Corleone, who dispenses wisdom and summary justice in the manner of a Renaissance Pope. Puzo's prose is a tad penny-plain, and the characterization is lacking in any deep psychological insights, but while other books by the author (*The Sicilian*, 1984, *The Last Don*, 1996) may seem to support this more jaundiced view of his career, there is no denying that *The Godfather* touched a nerve (and not just with the reading public; Puzo was directly intimidated by a number of the New York 'families' who felt this was a *roman à clef* cut too close to the bone). It is one of the most important novels in the crime genre. Essential reading, in fact.

> ### 🎬 The Godfather
> dir. Francis Ford Coppola, 1972
>
> Generally speaking, it goes without saying that Hollywood adaptations of celebrated books usually simplify and dilute the essence of the originals, but Coppola's famous adaptation of Mario Puzo's novel is the exception: with its top-drawer cast (**Marlon Brando**, **Al Pacino**, **Robert Duvall**, **James Caan**) and cool measured pace (punctuated by moments of bloody violence), it is a richer and more intricate experience than Puzo's original, with a career-restoring performance by Brando, effortlessly charismatic – and sinister – as Don Corleone. Coppola went on to make a follow-up which was even better in *The Godfather Part II* (1974), examining both Michael's developing career and his father's early life (a unique prequel and sequel formula), and completed the trilogy with *The Godfather Part III* (1990), in which his star Al Pacino had sufficiently aged to play the role of the Don facing eternity. And there's that haunting Nino Rota score…

Point Blank/The Hunter 1962
Richard Stark (pseudonym of Donald E. Westlake)

While Donald Westlake's achievement as a crime writer is legendary, many aficionados have a sneaking regard for the cold, spare Parker novels he wrote under the pseudonym of Richard Stark. Rarely was a *nom de plume* so well chosen: the Parker books (with a ruthless, largely unemotional mob hitman as a central character) are truly existential enterprises, with everything stripped away that does not facilitate the fast-moving plot. In *The Hunter* (now better known by the title given to its celebrated film adaptation, *Point Blank*), Parker is shot and left for dead by his associate Reese. Later, bent on revenge, he cuts a bloody swathe through 'the Organization', in which Reese is now a senior player. And, as Parker gets ever closer to the money he feels is his, he also tracks down the source of his betrayal: his own wife, who has had an affair with the treacherous Reese. All of this is delivered in uncluttered, affectless prose that allows the reader to make up his own mind about the characters.

Organized crime

> **Point Blank**
> dir. John Boorman, 1967
>
> John Boorman claimed never to have read Richard Stark's original novel, while Stark claimed never to have seen the film. Whether or not we buy either of these highly dubious statements, it's the perfect match, with British director Boorman marrying the disorienting time shifts of the arthouse movie ('Antonioni with a bullet') to the thick-ear exigencies of Stark's no-nonsense plot. And casting the ultimate icon of dangerous cool, **Lee Marvin**, as the hunter (unnecessarily renamed Walker) is the icing on the cake.

A certain sleight of hand is evident on Westlake/Stark's part: every so often an innocent bystander will have the misfortune to get in Parker's path, as the author tries to remind us that it's not just gangster scum who get hurt by people like his anti-hero. But readers will forgive this piece of sophistry, so fast moving and involving are the always-compact Parker novels.

The Getaway 1959
Jim Thompson

A late entry in Thompson's extraordinary canon, this remains outstanding. The novel opens with Doc McCoy being sprung from prison as a result of his girlfriend sleeping with an influential local politician and crime boss. Little did she know that the real reason was that Doc was needed for a heist. Doc, ever professional, pulls off the score, but with back-up not of his choosing. The robbery results in bloody mayhem, but Doc, proceeds of the job in hand, wants to settle old scores. In doing so, he makes

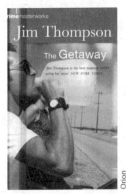

211

enemies of the local Mob and is forced to flee with his girl. Using insider contacts, he is introduced to a bizarre Mexican resort for past-their-sell-by-date villains on the run. As usual with Thompson, there is a very unpleasant and off-the-wall twist in the end of the tale but, until then, the story of Doc and his girl, the heist, and their getaway over the border is prime pulp crime writing at its best.

The Getaway
dir. Sam Peckinpah, 1972

Sam Peckinpah shared more with Thompson than did **Stanley Kubrick**, the writer's most noted cinematic collaborator/patron. A dyed-in-the-wool Westerner, a loner, an alcoholic gambler regarded as a pariah within his industry, and yet capable of moments of sustained genius, Peckinpah's film of *The Getaway* remains high in his canon, focusing on the characters of Doc (**Steve McQueen**) and his girlfriend (**Ali McGraw**), and the mechanics of the heist and its bloody aftermath. The set-piece, high-calibre shoot-out at a dingy Southwest motel is cinematically outstanding, and Peckinpah's abbreviated ending (Doc and his girl escaping in a garbage truck, then being ferried across the Rio Grande by another Peckinpah stalwart, Slim Pickens), although disliked by Thompson, is a great example of Peckinpah's less surreal and more refined sense of irony. A pointless remake (1994) by Roger Donaldson with Alec Baldwin and Kim Basinger merely glamorized the 'crucified heroes' of the Thompson/Peckinpah source material, and the action sequences only served to emphasize Peckinpah's mastery in this area.

Crime and society

Class, race and politics

The best crime writing has always addressed key issues affecting society – often with more forcefulness than more self-consciously 'literary' fiction. **Chandler**'s Philip Marlowe moved between the various strata of LA society – from the dispossessed underclass to the luxurious homes of the rich – and a detailed canvas of an American class structure emerged. Forensic examinations of American society continue with such remarkable writers as **James Ellroy** and **James Lee Burke**, with a broader political dimension than was ever tackled by Hammett or Chandler. The massively talented **Robert Stone** has used the apparatus of the thriller to paint a picture of post-Vietnam America that seems ever more relevant in the light of current US overseas interventions. And **George Pelecanos** and **Walter Mosely** tackle issues of race quite as trenchantly as writers (such as James Baldwin) who wrote exclusively about such concerns. In the UK, the class system, of course, remains a pertinent factor in crime fiction – and when the *doyenne* of British crime writers **P.D. James** suggested that the well-educated middle classes were more often confronted with moral choices than those living in the impoverished inner cities (where crime was a fact of life), a furore erupted in the crime-writing fraternity. The bitter division that appeared, however, was not always along predictable class lines: many of the 'Young Turks' who took issue with James were notably middle class (and not, for that matter, particularly young). British writers such as **Minette Walters** continue to anatomize such societal divisions (including sexual politics) with great acuity, while the multi-faceted **Ruth Rendell** still manages to turn over unpredictable stones to examine the horrors lurking beneath the veneer of modern England. The other factor forging change in society is, of course, science – and many writers (such as **Michael Crichton** in the US and **Michael Marshall** in the UK) brilliantly synthesize the imperatives of crime and thriller fiction with the seismic changes science has wrought on all our lives.

Acid Casuals 1995

Nicholas Blincoe

Serpent's Tail

Nicholas Blincoe is a writer of cutting-edge skills who cannily negotiates the parameters between flashy, fashionable writing and genuine literary brio. In *Acid Casuals*, the reader is taken into a variety of bizarre underworlds within the city of Manchester, the beat that Blincoe has made his own. This is the sometimes dangerous world of the Manchester club scene, with its plentiful drugs and (running things behind the putative managers) some pretty nasty criminals. The protagonist is a young man at the edges of this scene – and who also has another identity: a Brazilian transsexual, no less. He's back to settle a score by putting an end to his old boss, a deeply unpleasant club owner. This is by no means standard gangster fare – that's not Blincoe's territory – the outrageous trappings (along with the sharply observed Mancunian locales) are the things that give real pleasure here. While Blincoe has also written more serious, politically engaged books, most people will find this a more diverting entry point.

Gagged & Bound 2005
Natasha Cooper

Although Cooper's great strengths are her characterization and the way she sets her London-based novels in well-realized, credible backgrounds, she also boldly explores ideas of responsibility – parental, professional and emotional. Her series character, first appearing in 1998's *Creeping Ivy*, is Trish Maguire, a 30-something barrister whose career began in family law but who now works mainly with commercial cases. Her involvement with the crimes of each novel comes out of her rage at any kind of injustice and her inability to refuse help to those who

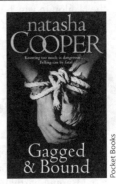

need it. The crimes she solves have none of the perverse glamour of serial killers. Whether the people she interacts with are successful professionals or denizens of inner-city estates, such as Mikey and his loan-sharking grandmother in *Out of the Dark* (2002) or retired soldier Daniel Crossman from *Keep Me Alive* (2004), they are absolutely credible. Cooper gives the impression that she writes to ease her own nightmares. In *Gagged & Bound* she tackles various ways of silencing people who know too much: the legal, by means of a libel case; the emotional, by rubbishing a would-be whistle-blower; and the physical, in a horrific 'bag-and-gag' killing. The plot involves Trish with a 30-year-old terrorist outrage, when a bus-load of children are bombed outside a pharmaceutical factory, a possible case of police corruption, and a family of rich south-London villains who make outrageous profits from drugs, people-smuggling and identity theft. Trish's activities put her young half-brother at risk and threaten her relationship with her long-standing partner, George. The wickedness and double-dealing she encounters make her question her own values and fight to hold on to what matters. *A Greater Evil* (1997) is more truthful, penetrating fare from Cooper, who is always aware of the fashion in which various institutions, ostensibly at the service of the public, can distort or maim lives. The legal profession, the prison system: in Cooper's books, these monolithic systems can wreak quite as much harm as they do good – even though Cooper's protagonists toil within them, trying to do the best they can.

State of Fear 2004
Michael Crichton

As far back as his prescient movie *Westworld* (1973), filmmaker and writer Michael Crichton was the finest practitioner (and, some would argue, virtual creator) of a particular genre of thriller: the science-based novel of adventure. The premise is usually this: take a highly plausible scientific thesis, put it into practice in a cloistered environment… and let things go horribly wrong, with much ensuing bloodshed. *Prey* (2002), concerning micro-robots, is a prime example. The formula has worked triumphantly well for many years, and readers always know that Crichton will deliver the requisite amount of intelligent thrills; he may not be a writer who will win any literary

Ethnic crime writing

Crime fiction as a lens through which society can be examined in harsh relief is exemplified by those writers who have focused on particular ethnic communities. But defining the limits of such work can be tricky. Are **Harry Kemelman**'s books (such as *Friday the Rabbi Slept Late*, 1964), in which Rabbi Small solves crimes by Talmudic reasoning, to be considered 'ethnic'? But there are a number of crime writers who have not just focused on remote or different parts of the world, but have dug deep into the peoples and cultures therein.

Arthur Upfield's novels reflect the characters among whom he lived and worked in rural Australia. Although he was English in origin, he had a passion for the country and its landscape, which is almost like a character in several of his books such as *Death of a Lake* (1954). Upfield's detective, Napoleon Bonaparte, is half aboriginal and half white. Although in some ways the books (from 1936 to 1964) are dated and now seem non-PC, there can be no doubt that Upfield's 'Bony', who dares not fail, because then it will be said that aborigines always fail, was making a point about the terrible wasted potential of so many native Australians. Similarly, he points up the cruelty and social imprudence of forcing them away from the life they understood to probable degradation on the fringes of white society, for example in *Murder Must Wait* (1953). Upfield's novels were very popular in both England and the US, but not in Australia, no doubt in part because an aboriginal hero was unacceptable, but also because for the Australians the background was too familiar and boring; it lacked the nostalgic exoticism of the English country-house thriller.

Canada and America can offer a number of examples of internal ethnic detective stories, some written by people with an excellent knowledge of the people they have used for their setting. The very popular series of modern novels by **Tony Hillerman**, featuring the Navajo tribal policemen Joe Leapham and Jim Chee, provide a large amount of background information on the Navajo and Hopi Indians and, in using the men's different personalities, explore their attitudes to majority culture and interaction with it. Much less known are the two novels by the Canadian sports journalist **Scott Young**, *Murder in a Cold Climate* (1988) and *The Shaman's Knife* (1996), both set in the Arctic Circle and featuring an Inuit detective. A relative newcomer is **Daniel Woodrell**. He is by no means exclusively a crime writer, but his 'Ozark *noir*' novels, notably *Winter's Bone* (2006), describe a modern American backwoods society in which crime is a way of survival, with the old trope of bootlegging replaced by illicit crystal meth outhouse factories, and guns (and using them) as commonplace as in-breeding.

prizes, but he is one of the most reliable practitioners of popular fiction at work. So, have you been lying awake at night worrying about global warming? Relax – according to Michael Crichton, it just ain't so. In fact, the bestselling writer's highly controversial pronouncements on such issues have done something that has no doubt made his publishers very happy indeed – he's been projected from newspaper book review pages onto the news pages, where his position (basically, that much global warming speculation is unnecessarily alarmist) is hotly debated. And why should he care if he's taken some very heavy criticism for his unfashionable stance? Even before Spielberg filmed the novel *Jurassic Park* in 1993 Crichton was an 'A'-list author, a writer who married considerable narrative skill with a knack for technology-based plotting. This winning combination stormed the bestselling lists time after time. And accusations that his position on global warming comes across as the kind of complacency that led George Bush to spurn the Kyoto Agreement did absolutely nothing to hurt the sales of *State of Fear*, which built a highly compelling plot around his contentious ideas. There's little doubt that this novel makes some less-promising-than-usual material quite as dynamic as his earlier books. Several disparate events around the world are forming a curious pattern: an experiment in a French laboratory causes the death of a physicist; clandestine purchases in a Malaysian jungle are made by a powerful unidentified purchaser with extensive excavation in mind; and in Canada, a midget sub is hired for 'research' in the Pacific. As attorney Peter Evans finds that his work for rich businessman George Morton has very dangerous implications, a South Pacific island initiates a million-dollar lawsuit against American interests, while ecology-minded terrorists inaugurate a fantastic scheme: they will create earthquakes and subterranean tremors with a view to persuading the world that global warming is responsible.

9tail Fox 2005

Jon Courtenay Grimwood

Combining alternative North African history with a crime sensibility, Jon Courtenay Grimwood came to critical notice with his three *Arabesk* mysteries (2001–2003), finely detailed crime novels set in the city of El Iskandryia and featuring Ashraf Bey, ex-US prisoner and half-Berber detective. These were followed by *Stamping Butterflies* (2004), a novel hung around the attempted murder of the US president and an investigation into a killing in 1970s Marrakesh. As always with Grimwood, magic realist elements combined with sly humour and straight police detection to produce a novel that can be read on many levels. *9tail Fox* begins with the murder of his main character and then, instead of working backward to explain the killing, moves forward to allow the victim to investigate his own death. Having failed as a father, husband and SFPD officer, Sergeant Bobby Zha finds himself at his own funeral, unable to recognize the glowing description of the officer being honoured. A flashback to the siege in Stalingrad during World War II ties Bobby Zha's murder to medical research carried out on the orders of Stalin and lets the reader begin to tie this research to the current situation in Russia. Set in San Francisco's Chinatown and drawing on Chinese myth, genetic manipulation and the rise of the Russian Oligarchs, *9tail Fox* displays Grimwood's habitual obsession with finely detailed location, narrative twists and sudden outbreaks of violence. As in all his novels, the hero's need for redemption ties to wider questions about identity and what actually constitutes justice.

Chapter 12

Ash & Bone 2005
John Harvey

There were many who felt that John Harvey was robbed when his novel *Flesh & Blood* (2004) failed to bag the prestigious Crime Writers' Association Dagger Award (the American **Sara Paretsky** pipped him to the post). Ms Paretsky used her acceptance speech to rail (by proxy) against the iniquities of George Bush's government, but Harvey casts quite as cold an eye on the UK as his American colleague does on the US, though his understated social criticism sports a British patina that is more quietly effective than Paretsky's in-your-face rant. Harvey's world-weary detective Frank Elder has what seem like insuperable problems with his ex-wife and daughter. But – wait a minute – is Elder the principal character here? While he handles the police procedural business, he doesn't appear until Chapter 4, and the sympathetic and vulnerable female copper Maddy Birch launches the book centre-stage, eyeing herself in the mirror and snapping her ponytail tight before fastening the Velcro on her protective vest and setting out on an armed raid to bring down a north London Mr Big. Things go bloodily wrong: the gangster is shot by another policeman who appears to plant a weapon near the dead man. Meanwhile, Frank Elder is finding himself unable to cope with his daughter's hostility, and welcomes the opportunity to get back into harness, investigating the murder of a female colleague with whom he had a one-off sexual encounter. The picture of Britain which Harvey paints as his backdrop is a dark and minatory place: everywhere from London's Crouch End (whose disused railway line is the site of a murder) to a Lincolnshire in which crumbling houses have been the site of sadistic sexual murders. Harvey's UK is seemingly at the mercy of an army of barely socialized council-estate kids, their small-scale crimes mirroring the more serious mayhem committed by their elders.

Cotton Comes to Harlem 1965
Chester Himes

The best-known book by one of the most celebrated of black crime writers, this idiosyncratic and engaging thriller features Himes's classic characters, Coffin Ed Johnson and Grave Digger Jones, New York City cops with good reputations (despite their unorthodox methods) assigned to Harlem. Using their carefully maintained network of informers, the duo are looking into the murky background of the 'Back to Africa' movement, inaugurated by ex-con Deke O'Malley. Deke has skimmed nearly $90,000 from trusting families to buy berths to the Motherland on ocean liners (which don't happen to exist). The money is stolen by white thugs, who hide it in a bale of cotton which ends up with the exotic dancer Belle at the Cotton Club. And all the time, the body count is rising. The knowing Himes has great fun at the expense of racism (the stress on cotton, classic byproduct of slavery, is no accident), and the rich gallery of eccentrics encountered by the two dogged black coppers are matched in interest by the duo themselves. Dialogue, as ever with Himes, positively leaps off the page and demands to be spoken aloud (whatever your ethnic background).

Missouri-born Himes has certainly not been afraid of confronting issues; his first novel *If He Hollers Let Him Go* (1945) was a striking

---

Cotton Comes to Harlem
dir. Ossie Davis, 1970

Directed by the talented black actor Ossie Davis, the strength of this sometimes hit-or-miss adaptation of Chester Himes's novel lies largely in the judicious casting, with **Godfrey Cambridge** and **Raymond St Jacques** essaying larger-than-life (but highly entertaining) versions of Himes's bickering protagonists. The quirky talent on offer raises this above the more standard blaxploitation movies of the period.

book dealing with a crew of black workers in a Los Angeles shipyard in the 1940s. As an examination of the social strictures placed on black Americans in this era, this was cold-eyed and intense fare, but the author's anger is always kept in proportion to the narrative he is creating: Himes always wrote a solid novel above all else, never a piece of agitprop. Recognized and admired in France, Himes migrated there (like contemporary black novelist **James Baldwin**, and numerous jazz musicians), finding the European temperament more congenial than a racially segregated US.

The Constant Gardener 2001
John le Carré
(pseudonym of David John Moore Cornwell)

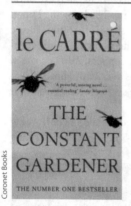

The Spy Who Came In From The Cold was the book with which John le Carré set the world of espionage thrillers on its ear back in 1963. That coruscating, unflinching picture of Cold War betrayal obliterated all le Carré's rivals and marked him out as the pre-eminent writer in the field – a position he's held (with some hiccups) ever since. After the end of the Cold War, le Carré (like his talented contemporary **Len Deighton**) seemed adrift for a while, until he found a way to address the new issues threatening our world. *The Constant Gardener* took on the unfettered power of the great pharmaceutical concerns, and delivered the author's most resounding success in years. Justin Quayle is in the Diplomatic Corps, with a position in the British High Commission in Nairobi. His wife, as socially engaged as he is complaisant, changes his life as he tries to accommodate to her anti-establishment views (an embarrassment to him in his job). But she is murdered, and Justin finds himself on a nigh-obsessive quest to find the reason for her death. Justin is in the line of British expats in dangerous countries most memorably created by **Graham Greene**, but le Carré's concerns and targets are very much his own. This ex-civil servant's anti-establishment fury makes rebels from the underclass seem mere dilettantes – and that is the engine for this brilliantly sustained novel.

White Devils 2004
Paul McAuley

We live in a dangerous world. What is it that's going to finally do for us all? Once it might have been rat-borne plagues, but we've learned to be wary of many more things: sexually transmitted diseases, sneezes from the Far East, salmon sandwiches, bird-borne influenza. And, of course, genetic engineering. The current furore about this grey area of science springs from its many possibilities. McAuley's chilling *White Devils* plays cannily on our fears of unrestricted experimentation in such areas (it's not giving too much away to say that the 'Devils' of the title are the grotesque product of GE experiments), but this is only one of the many elements the author mixes into a particularly heady brew. It's a biotech thriller, certainly, but McAuley's consummate skills extend into the areas of characterization and sociological observation quite as much as the all-too-plausible scientific underpinnings. Nicholas Hyde is doing volunteer work with a humanitarian charity in a strife-torn Africa when he is caught up in a scene of carnage in the dense Congo forests. His team is suddenly under attack – but from what? The things that lay siege to Nick and his crew are bizarre ape-like creatures, pale in colour and possessing enormous strength. Only Nick and a government observer escape the bloody slaughter with their lives – and Nick finds that the truth about the encounter does not chime with the government-approved view of events. The team was, apparently, attacked by 'rebel troops in body paint'. But who is behind the government cover-up? All of this is handled with panache by McAuley, and (as one would expect with this author) the science is handled with total assurance. McAuley (a professional research scientist) built a reputation as a purveyor of meta-fictions that defy category, and since 2001's *Whole Wide World* really established his reputation, his books transmute futuristic tropes into bizarre artefacts that illuminate darker areas of psychology. But he's best at vividly realized alternative societies that refract the more arcane aspects of our own.

Exile 2001
Denise Mina

Bantam

Mina won the John Creasey Best First Crime Novel prize for her remarkable *Garnethill* (1998). But high reader expectations can be a heavy cross to bear, and more than one writer has come to grief attempting to recreate earlier triumphs. *Exile*, however, proved that Mina was a writer up for the long haul. The Glasgow setting of this piece is rendered with a gritty authority that anchors the narrative in a strongly realized universe. Mina's central character is Maureen O'Donnell, who is used to encountering damaged women at the Glasgow Women's Shelter where she works, but one particularly badly treated woman, Anne, affects her – not least as Anne is battling drink along with the myriad other things wrong in her life. To Maureen's horror, she later learns that a body dumped in the Thames is the luckless Anne. Her corpse has been treated appallingly, and she is wrapped in bedding. Maureen has reasons of her own for leaving Glasgow, and a trip to London results in her looking into the death of her charge. But any feelings that she has seen the worst of life in terms of drugs and abuse in Glasgow are soon set side when she sees the dark underbelly of London – and tries to track down Anne's killer. The social issues addressed by the book are as cogently handled as the satisfying plotting.

Walking the Dog 2001
Walter Mosely

Walter Mosely has long been one of the most respected names in the black crime-writing fraternity. His Easy Rawlins series, which launched in 1990 with *Devil in a Blue Dress*, is a firm favourite of aficionados, including **Bill Clinton**, but his non-crime novels such as *Blue Light* (1998) demonstrate the same mastery of atmosphere and idiom, and *The Man in My Basement* (2005) was a powerful study of prejudice and the nature of identity. In *Walking the Dog*, Socrates Fortlow (who first appeared in 1997's *Always Outnumbered, Always Outgunned*) is struggling to come to terms with life after prison. He's living in a dingy two-room shack in Watts, maintaining (against the odds) a relationship and even holding down a job. But, as so often in this kind of narrative, the past won't leave him alone, and Socrates has to risk everything he's achieved to bring down some savage enemies. Ghetto life has rarely been delivered with such dark-edged panache, and Socrates is a character readers cannot help but identify with, for all his (plentiful) misjudgements.

The Dispossessed 2004
Margaret Murphy

When *The Dispossessed* was published, Margaret Murphy was already the author of seven highly acclaimed crime novels. She writes with a textual immediacy, creating complex plots peopled by sensitively drawn, flawed and believable characters. Her trademark is compassion for the victim, and she never lets you forget that there are devastating consequences to violent crime, but judicious splashes of humour lighten the darker aspects of the narrative in all her work. *The Dispossessed* began a Liverpool-based series, featuring D.C.I. Jeff Rickman and D.S. Foster. Rickman's investigation into an Afghan refugee's sordid death leads first to the heart of a community who can't – or won't – talk to him, and then home to his own private life. As the body count starts rising he is framed for a crime he didn't commit. A murderer is trying to make things personal. Is he on the trail of a serial killer? Or something even more sinister? In this challenging novel, Murphy presents a clear-eyed exploration of the dual themes of voicelessness and the exploitation of the disenfranchised, within the context of the vile underworld of migration scams, racism and prostitution in Liverpool. She writes so evocatively of her native city, of its beauty and its ugliness, that you can almost taste the salt tang of the Mersey estuary on your tongue and feel the undercurrent of tension in its lively and sometimes dangerous streets. *The Dispossessed* evokes the gritty reality of crime in one of Britain's most vibrant and brutal cities.

Gene 2004
Stel Pavlou

Stel Pavlou's *Gene* really is something different. As *Decipher* (2001) and his treatment for the movie *51st State* in the same year resoundingly demonstrated, Pavlou is an author capable of marrying the glossy surface of the (slightly) futuristic thriller with steel-hard plotting. This second novel adds a layer of sophisticated characterization, as the protagonist struggles to cope with some jaw-dropping revelations about his own past. Detective James North is handed a difficult assignment, having to deal with a mentally disturbed young man holding a child hostage at the Metropolitan Museum of Art in New York. The hostage taker has been asking for North by name, even though the detective has never met him. When the hostage situation ends badly, North is injected with a preparation that plunges him into a hallucinogenic state, with nightmarish manifestations and fragments of memory that are not his own. As North ransacks the city for his assailant, he finds himself mentally impelled to destroy a man called 'Gene'. And when he does, a bizarre secret about his own past manifests itself – one with a 3000-year legacy. This involves the unknown Greek warrior Cyclades, a combatant in the Trojan Wars who was destined by the gods to be reincarnated many times. When so much crime and thriller fiction these days is thin, recycled material, this one is amazingly ambitious, with a canvas conceived on the broadest possible scale, studded with brilliantly orchestrated set pieces. Gene should be catnip to those seeking the unusual.

Nineteen Seventy Seven 2000
David Peace

Is it possible to create a new genre in crime fiction? Amazingly, the answer seems to be yes: David Peace produced what can only be called Yorkshire *noir*. The caustic delights of his earlier *Nineteen Seventy Four* (1999), a breathtaking and violent Yorkshire-set thriller, were to be found again in this equally powerful and visceral piece. It's the year of the title – the year of punk and the year of the Silver Jubilee. And the **Yorkshire Ripper** is plying his bloody trade. This is the dark world into which beleaguered copper Bob Fraser and over-the-hill journalist Jack Whitehead are drawn in their sympathy for the prostitutes of Chapeltown. And as Peace's narrative treads inexorably towards the bonfires of Queen Elizabeth's Silver Jubilee night and more grisly deaths, the two men come to the grim conclusion that there may be more than one killer at large. This is tricky work that Peace has undertaken: weaving a real-life tragedy into a work of fiction. But such is his way with idiosyncratic characterization and remorseless plotting, the result is a totally convincing novel that is also, thankfully, highly responsible. The book formed the second of the Riding Quartet, completed by *Nineteen Eighty* (2001) and *Nineteen Eighty Three* (2002). As crime fiction chases its tail and vainly attempts to create innovation in an overcrowded genre, Peace seems able to effortlessly render everything anew in his lacerating and compelling novels. His journo hero Whitehead is a particularly sharp creation, and comparable at times to the anti-heroes of **Graham Greene**.

Drama City 2005
George Pelecanos

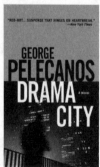

"RED-HOT...SUSPENSE THAT HINGES ON HEARTBREAK."
—*New York Times*

GEORGE PELECANOS
DRAMA CITY
A Novel

Little, Brown

Lorenzo Brown has left his criminal background behind, and is struggling to scratch a humble living as a dog warden. His parole officer, Rachel Lopez, finds that Lorenzo, despite his good intentions, is turning out to be her biggest problem. As the dangerous problems of George Pelecanos' beleaguered characters proliferate, the world they move in is realized with the kind of casual skill that we expect from this outstanding writer. Here, the blue-collar ambience has a grittiness and plausibility that bespeaks the author's sympathy for those making their way far from middle-class comforts – and once again Pelecanos freights a subtle social commentary into his narrative in a fashion that always foregrounds the narrative imperatives.

A Masculine Ending 1994
Joan Smith

This is the first of Joan Smith's detective novels featuring her academic-detective, Loretta Lawson. She arrives in Paris after a fraught journey to stay at an apartment on the Left Bank that she has borrowed from a friend. To her dismay, Lawson finds a stranger asleep there; creeping into another bedroom, she spends an uncomfortable night and leaves early the next morning to give a paper at a symposium organized by a feminist literary journal. Returning to the flat that night, she finds the stranger gone – and a tangle of bloody sheets on the bed. Her reluctance to go to the authorities runs deep: like many people on the left, she has been distrustful of the State since the British miners' strike of 1984–85. Returning to England without contacting the French police, she decides to investigate herself, with the assistance of her journalist ex-husband. Her inquiries lead her to Oxford University, and a mystery involving a missing don, his estranged wife and one of his most talented students. *A Masculine Ending* cannily plays with the conventions of the traditional British crime novel, presenting Lawson as an intelligent woman who is an outsider on account of her politics and her feminism. It offers a perspective deliberately at odds with that of Golden Age writers such as Christie, especially in its scepticism about the idea of resolution. This is most evident in its ending, which enraged some readers (especially in the US) but is in keeping with the ambivalence evident throughout the novel. The fourth Lawson book, *What Men Say* (1993), takes its title from Catullus's poem about Theseus and Ariadne, signalling

> 🎬 **A Masculine Ending**
> dir. Antonia Bird, TVM, 1992
>
> Intelligent direction from Antonia Bird, and a strong cast of some of the most interesting British performers (**Janet McTeer**, **Imelda Staunton**, **Bill Nighy**): all of this guarantees a creditable stab at Joan Smith's intriguing novel, but one that irons out the complexities – as so often, there is no substitute for the richer texture of a book over its adaptation, however sympathetic.

its concern with loyalty and the darker side of relationships between men and women, Smith's constant theme.

Wolves Eat Dogs 2005
Martin Cruz Smith (b. Martin William Smith)

You've heard it before. 'It's Martin Cruz Smith's best book since *Gorky Park*!' But surely each outing since that first Renko novel of 1981 (see p.109) has been impressive? Well, up to a point; all have been imaginative, making full capital out of the novelty of having a Russian detective in strikingly realized Russian settings (even when the novelty was no more). But until *Wolves Eat Dogs* only one, *Polar Star* in 1989, had had the same power as that first book. *Wolves* is a reminder of just how good the Renko books are – and there are several new elements added to this one. First of all, this is Russia today – not the antediluvian Russia that Renko moved in when *Gorky Park* appeared. This is Vladimir Putin's Russia (Putin himself is described as always looking like he's 'sucking on a sore tooth') – a country half in the modern age of mobile phones, home cinema and sushi bars, and half mired in the timeworn government double-dealing that has beset the country since Dostoyevsky's day. Complex inter-relations with Western big business are now a part of the scene, and this forms part of the plot here: the death of a businessman (after a plunge from a high window) can't be seen as murder, Renko is told – suicide won't frighten away foreign business from a country still nervously perceived as in thrall to organized crime. But apart from the virtuoso realization of his locales, Smith has deepened the characterization of his hero: Renko is now facing the scrap heap, dealing wryly with daily humiliation, and shoring up the emptiness of his life by acting as friend and visitor to a silent, sociopathic boy (who he takes at weekends to an amusement centre at Gorky Park, no less). As Renko tries to ferret out the truth behind the suspicious death, he encounters the usual stonewalling and (often violent) interference, and the solution has ramifications that reach to the most privileged echelons of Russian society.

Dog Soldiers 1973
Robert Stone

Other writers may earn higher advances, but Robert Stone is considered by many to be the finest American novelist at work today, with a body of work (most of which utilizes the thriller format) far more accomplished than many better-known names. This novel is so much more than a tale of drug dealing that goes wrong: one of the premiere American novelists of the Vietnam era (and beyond), Stone may exploit the tropes and conventions of crime fiction, but he always has a much bigger fish to fry. The story is

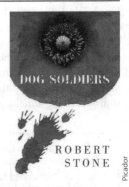

set in Saigon, during the final months of the war in Vietnam. John Converse has decided that his future fortune will result from one large-scale drugs deal. But back in the States, divided loyalties and double-dealing ensure that things quickly go wrong. The 3kg of heroin that Converse has smuggled from war-scarred Southeast Asia to the streets of San Francisco plunges him and his colleagues into a nightmare trip through the deserts of California. Hot on their heels are both the drug-dealing thugs on whose patch they've encroached and some very nasty bent cops. While Stone is unquestionably a literary novelist, with a lambent prose that brilliantly delineates his characters and a cool sensibility that informs his narratives with a real sociological edge, he nevertheless deals with the violence and menace of his plots with the assurance of **Hemingway**. While the tough accoutrements of *Dog Soldiers* allow the novel to function on a straightforward thriller level, its formidable achievements lift it several notches above most American novels written in the 1970s. And Stone has continued, if sporadically, to hit the right nails. *Outerbridge Reach* (1992) tackled ambition, celebrity and self-defeat in a circumnavigation race, while *Damascus Gate* (1998) is an outstanding analysis of the conflicts of interests centred on the Israel/Palestine issue. The stripped-down *Bay of Souls* (2003), with a naive academic unexpectedly embroiled in third-world corruption, threatening local drug dealers and duplicitous expats, allows him once again to explore notions of redemption of the soul and crises of conscience stirred into a particularly rich goulash. As ever, the author shares with another of his heroes, **Joseph Conrad**, a startling skill at creating a mélange of the poetic and the horrific: the sudden

---

Dog Soldiers/Who'll Stop the Rain?
dir. Karel Reisz, 1978

What a glorious period for truly individual cinema the 1970s were! Karel Reisz may have drifted since his early success with films like *Saturday Night and Sunday Morning* (1960) and *Night Must Fall* (1964), but he was very firmly back on form with this sure-footed adaptation of Stone's blistering novel. As a picture of the post-Vietnam *zeitgeist*, it's full of insight – and as an edgy thriller, it's equally engaging. Strong performances from **Nick Nolte** and **Tuesday Weld**.

surfacing of the bloated corpse of a drowned pilot, looking like some fabulous sea monster with an attendant host of beautiful but flesh-consuming fish, genuinely chills the blood. But *Dog Soldiers* should remain your entry point to this fascinating writer's work.

Acid Row 2001
Minette Walters

'Acid Row' is the ironic name given to their home by the luckless inhabitants of a sink estate. Disenfranchised, dangerous youths roam the streets and into this no man's land of one-parent families comes Sophie Morrison, a young doctor visiting a patient. But she is unaware that she is entering the home of a paedophile known to the police. The first pages of *Acid Row* clearly mark the book out as a further step in the author's move into the kind of crime novel in which social significance is every bit as important as the page-turning imperatives of a thriller. Once again, Walters is just as interested in the psychology of the characters and the problems of modern life as in the dictates of the classic crime novel. The use of the young Sophie as the protagonist is a brilliant stroke. When reports circulate that a disturbed child called Amy has disappeared, Sophie finds herself caught between dangerous vigilantes and a man she dislikes intensely. As in 2002's outstanding *Fox Evil*, Walters keeps the cutting-edge aspects of her narratives to the fore, cleverly wrong-footing the reader at every turn: although we think we have decided how we feel about the endangered paedophile and the vigilantes, she never allows these aspects to overwhelm the nagging, disturbing power of her narrative. At heart, *Acid Row* is still a mystery. Is Amy, the supposed victim, really missing?

Chapter 12

The Prince of Wales 2003
John Williams

In Cardiff, local paper features editor Pete Duke, 40, has split up from his wife and is looking to have some fun. He meets Kim, 28, who works for the BBC. Bobby, 36, is a lesbian pimp who sees her world coming to an end as the demolition of the Custom House nears. Pete and Kim go to the last night of the Custom House. They meet Bobby and her prostitute girlfriend Maria and shoplifter/failed pimp Mikey, and all get drunk and go for a joyride. A complex web of intrigues and messy relationship shifts ensue in Williams' scabrous picture of life in Wales's capital city as the millennium approaches. In earlier books (such as *Cardiff Dead*), Williams had staked out his claim to be the definitive, cold-eyed chronicler of his home town, and he has been refining his unforgiving canvas ever since. The black-economy Cardiff Trilogy (see p.148), of which *The Prince of Wales* is the culmination, has proved to be writing of both ambition and idiosyncratic skill; the bid by Cardiff to forge an identity as the city's appearance and economy undergo seismic changes is matched by the rich *smorgasbord* of relationships and characters in this novel.

Espionage

Spies, spooks and supercriminals

It looked for a while as if the literary espionage genre was on the ropes. The field that had produced some of the most sophisticated and profound writing (as well as some of the most suspenseful) in what is loosely called the crime/thriller genre was dealt a body blow by the end of the Cold War, and two of the most acclaimed contemporary practitioners, **John le Carré** and **Len Deighton**, showed signs of being cast adrift by international events. But both writers (to different degrees) adjusted to this new landscape with its new threats, and found fresh challenges for their protagonists. **Le Carré** turned his attention both to the nefarious modern-day activities of multinational corporations in *The Constant Gardener* (2001) and to sniffy criticism of Anglo-US unilateralism in *Absolute Friends* (2003). It's still a dangerous world, after all, and newer writers have found great mileage in such areas as fundamentalist terrorism and ruthless big-business exploitation of the third world. Meanwhile, **Henry Porter**

Chapter 13

Stirred but never shaken

The phenomenon of **Ian Fleming**'s 007 continues to amaze. Few fictional heroes concocted in the early 1950s remain in public view, or indeed in print. But the **James Bond** franchise, whether on the page, at the cinema, in graphic novels, in computer games or simply in the popular imagination, seems impervious to age or the vagaries of fashion.

When Fleming (1908–64) settled down to pen his first 'entertainment', which appeared as *Casino Royale* in 1953, he conceived a remarkable formula: a secret agent whose 'license to kill' on behalf of Her Majesty's government meant that he could be unleashed both as a counter-espionage operative (in the Cold War novels such as *From Russia With Love*, 1957) and in the fight against organized crime (*Live and Let Die*, 1954, and *Diamonds Are Forever*, 1956). Bond was also charged with taking on a range of megalomaniac supercriminals, often members of the sinister SPECTRE organization, such as the eponymous villains of *Dr No* (1958) and *Goldfinger* (1959), *Thunderball*'s Emilio Largo (1961), or Bond's arch-enemy, Ernst Stavro Blofeld (*You Only Live Twice*, 1964).

In truth, Fleming's writing now seems slightly turgid, and the novels betray their age, but the continuing reinvention of Bond on the screen (in a range of increasingly outlandish 'adaptations') has provided the only agent who is also a brand of remarkable longevity. And, unlike most brands (which carefully protect their trademarks and personae), Bond on screen has now been portrayed by six very different actors, and in print by Kingsley Amis, John Gardner and Charles Higson, among others. Nevertheless, it is Fleming, with his Eton and the Guards pedigree, background as a dirty tricks planner in Naval Intelligence during World War II, and subsequent work as a journalist for *The Sunday Times*, who retains ownership of the concept, some 40 years after his death. Bond's classless snobbery, sadism and rampant libido remain a beacon of political incorrectness in an insane world.

The top five Bond books

▶ *Live and Let Die* (1954)
▶ *From Russia with Love* (1957)
▶ *Dr No* (1958)
▶ *Goldfinger* (1959)
▶ *On Her Majesty's Secret Service* (1963)

and **Robert Wilson** have woven new fabrics out of the legacy of Nazi and Soviet ambitions, often spanning parallel historical and contemporary plotlines.

Of course the genre enjoyed a magnificent birth with such works as **Joseph Conrad**'s 1907 masterpiece *The Secret Agent*, whose vision of fanatical terrorist mentalities is (soberingly) as relevant as ever a century later. Inaugurating the action-driven narrative, **Sapper**'s Bulldog Drummond stories (despite their now-questionable ideology) had great exuberance, and adumbrated the resourceful espionage hero that would be burnished to perfection in **John Buchan**'s Richard Hannay in such classics as *The Thirty-Nine Steps*, the prototype for the modern thriller. Clubland hero Hannay's direct descendant was, of course, **Ian Fleming**'s James Bond, who interpolated more exhilarating sex, violence and gracious living into the bone-crunching action. The image of espionage as a corollary of the dark reaches of the soul had previously been explored by **Somerset Maugham** in his *Ashenden* stories. But the right-wing assumptions of such classic spy fiction were yet to be challenged by **Eric Ambler**.

Journey into Fear 1940
Eric Ambler

There are many neglected authors in the crime and thriller pantheon, but the most shamefully neglected is undoubtedly Eric Ambler. In any poll of the best dozen or so thrillers ever written, Ambler's pioneering and wonderfully atmospheric novel *The Mask of Demetrios* (aka *A Coffin for Demetrios*, 1939) would certainly figure. In this and other titles, including *Epitaph for a Spy* (1938) and *The Nightcomers* (1956), the author could be said to have inaugurated the modern spy thriller. Considered by such masters as **Graham Greene** and **John le Carré** to be the greatest of all English thriller writers, his fall from grace (at least in so far as most of his books are out of print) is astonishing. Some of his finest books are finding their way back into print, embellished with the glowing imprimatur of many modern practitioners, still in debt to Ambler. His most striking innovation was, of course, to remove the thriller from its right-wing clubland milieux and create protagonists with a more left-of-centre political viewpoint; the norm now, but groundbreaking in Ambler's day. In this novel, the engineer Graham, an Englishman undertaking a terrifying flight across wartime Europe, is the archetypal Ambler hero, an ordinary man attempting to survive in extraordinary circumstances of massive danger and corruption. The modern spy story begins here, with all the comfortable right-wing certainties of an earlier generation of thriller writers seeming remote and implausible.

Eric Ambler (1909–98)

At the time of the publication of his last book, Eric Ambler's publishers lamented the fact that the venerable writer had to be 'sold' to younger booksellers almost as a new name: the writer who forged the style later adopted in the espionage novels of **Graham Greene** and **John le Carré** was almost a forgotten man – at least to a new generation of readers. The situation is a little better these days, with sporadic reissue programmes making such masterworks as *Journey into Fear* (1940) available again – and it's to be hoped that new readers will be drawn to this most gifted of writers. Ambler sampled a variety of careers (comedian, playwright, advertising copywriter) before publishing his seminal thriller *The Mask of Demetrios* in 1939. The journalist Latimer is the first of Ambler's ordinary men caught up in dangerous situations in threatening, sultry foreign climates, and it is a masterpiece of the mystery genre. While Ambler enjoyed a very successful second career as a screenwriter, he continued to produce brilliantly written, carefully crafted novels such as *The Light of Day* (1964), several of which were filmed. His greatest innovation was probably the shift of political balance in the genre: the right-wing certainties of **le Queux**, **John Buchan** and **Sapper** were replaced by a marked left-wing bias, in which Establishment figures were no longer to be trusted, and there was little perceptible moral difference between different countries' espionage services and methodologies. Ambler was able to accommodate the modern world in such books as *The Levanter* (1972), though the wattage of his talent burnt less brightly in later years.

> ### 🎬 Journey into Fear
> dir. Norman Foster, 1942
>
> Eric Ambler was particularly lucky in this adaptation of one of his best novels, but the force of the film is not down to the credited director, Norman Foster. This was, in fact, **Orson Welles'** third film as a director (uncredited): as well as etching a memorable portrayal as the creepy Colonel Haki, Welles handled most of the direction, as well as working on the screenplay with principal star **Joseph Cotten**. While the storytelling is, at times, a touch muddled, the atmospheric *mise-en-scène* contains many pre-echoes of Welles' later *noir* masterpiece *Touch of Evil* (1958).

There's no denying that certain elements of Ambler's narratives have dated a trifle, but that shouldn't deter those who've not yet treated themselves to his consummately well-written thrillers.

Running Blind 1970
Desmond Bagley

The opening lines of Bagley's most impressive thriller immediately arrest the attention: 'To be encumbered with a corpse is to be in a difficult position, especially when the corpse is without benefit of a death certificate.' The reader is then launched into what is essentially a breathless chase through a stunningly realized Iceland, as vividly drawn as any locale in crime and mystery fiction. Bagley had a long and distinguished career in the field, but most of his books (even such impressive pieces as *The Spoilers* and *High Citadel*) have fallen from favour these days. If there is any justice, his work should regain its former lustre, and *Running Blind* is his most ingenious and pacy novel. Alan Stewart is told by his employers that he is to be just a messenger boy, a carrier of unimportant materials. But before long, he finds himself on a deserted road in Iceland, with a corpse at his feet. Is the parcel he is carrying more important than he has been led to believe? And who are the people who are following him, seeking his death? Stewart's increasingly desperate flight for life (encumbered with a girlfriend) through inhospitable territory is brilliantly detailed. All of this is conveyed in breathless but literate prose, and Bagley's knowledgeable authorial voice ensures an irresistible read.

Red Rabbit 2002

Tom Clancy

It's often difficult to locate the precise point at which an author becomes the most celebrated name in his or her field. And while his work is not as consistent as some of his predecessors, few would deny that Tom Clancy is now the world's number one thriller writer. Certainly, his sales (and royalty advances) indicate that readers have voted with their wallets and put him at the top. Clancy's novels featuring ace CIA operative (and later politician) Jack Ryan were initially promoted as anti-**James Bond** thrillers, but this is something of a smokescreen. Certainly Ryan is more of a family man than Fleming's creation (less given to serial promiscuity), and 007 never achieved (or wanted to achieve) high office, but both protagonists are usually the key players in high-octane action in which a combination of their wits and brawn often brings the world back from the brink of catastrophe. While Ryan has been incarnated on film by several different actors, the literary version remains distinctly different from the celluloid versions. This is particularly true of *Red Rabbit*, which is an innovative Clancy entry, satisfyingly sketching in details of Ryan's early life. The author can still be counted on to deliver the expected Clancy trademarks: this one is full of well-researched detail, and studded with the adroitly staged action set-pieces we have come to expect. Working on the bottom rungs of the CIA's analysis departments, Jack Ryan is given the unenviable mission of debriefing a key Soviet defector. He discovers a dark secret: there is a plot afoot to murder Pope John Paul II. Of course, this is only one aspect of a massively complex skein of skulduggery, and as Jack penetrates to the heart of the mystery (with less assurance than usual – he is younger, after all), Clancy admirers will definitely feel all the right areas are being massaged.

A Spy by Nature 2001
Charles Cumming

It's a slim body of work – but within the space of just a handful of books, Charles Cumming has established an enviable reputation as one of the most adroit practitioners of the modern spy novel – as skilled and accomplished as **John le Carré** and **Len Deighton** in their heyday (giving the lie to those who said that there would be no modern-day successors to these titans). But with *A Spy by Nature* (and, to a similar degree, *The Hidden Man*), Cumming has triumphantly established that the literary spy novel is still a genre that has much to

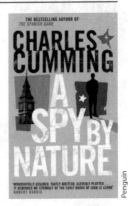

Penguin

offer. Both novels deal in the betrayals and dissemblings that are the *sine qua non* of the field – and the characterization has the richness of an early generation of writers, notably Greene and Ambler. This is a disquieting study of Alec (the name is clearly a nod to le Carré's ill-fated Alec Leamas in *The Spy Who Came In From The Cold*, see p.246), a young MI6 operative who finds himself caught between two masters. *The Hidden Man* deals with difficult relations between fathers and sons (a recurrent theme, of course, in le Carré), and sports a vividly drawn canvas stretching from London to Moscow and Afghanistan. Plotting in both books is exemplary – and if you haven't investigated Charles Cumming yet, now's the time.

The Ipcress File 1962

Len Deighton

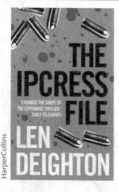

HarperCollins

It's hard to realize today what an impact Len Deighton's remarkable spy novel had on its first appearance in the 1960s. Like **John le Carré**, Deighton was reacting against the glossy, unrealistic depiction of espionage in the novels of **Ian Fleming** (a certain Puritanism was a factor at the time, less *à propos* these days, now that Fleming's considerable virtues have been recognized). But certainly *The Ipcress File*, with its insolent working-class hero and low-key treatment of all the quotidian details of a spy's life (endless futile requisitions for petty cash, a decidedly unglamorous secret service HQ), was astonishingly fresh, while the first-person narrative was a sardonic Londoner's refraction of Chandler's Marlowe-speak two decades on. Another radical touch was the refusal to neatly tie up the narrative with a cathartic death for the villain – the shadowy

---

The Ipcress File
dir. Sidney J. Furie, 1965

Although Furie's reliance on eccentric camera angles may look a touch mannered today, it's worth remembering that this was remarked on at the time of the film's initial release. In fact, camera angles and all, this is a career-best for Furie – a perfect reworking of Deighton's quirky anti-Bond novel, with the inspired casting of **Michael Caine** as the low-rent (yet epicurean) spy. The dingy sets are by **Ken Adam** – hard to believe, given the elaborate work he was simultaneously doing on the Bond films for producer Harry Saltzman (whose project this was) – and 007 score composer **John Barry** was also on board. But almost the single most cherishable element (in a film crammed with subtle pleasures) is the late character actor **Nigel Green** as Caine's supercilious, pernickety boss – another career best.

opponent of Deighton's unnamed protagonist is – for political reasons – unpunished. A series of novels in the same vein followed, none quite as impressive as this debut – but all highly accomplished.

Blood of Victory 2002
Alan Furst

Furst's impeccably written *Kingdom of Shadows* (2000) invoked comparisons to **Graham Greene**, **John le Carré** and **Robert Harris**. The invoking of these stellar names was perfectly appropriate: Furst's brilliant recreation of the 1930s and Europe at the time of World War II had the kind of richness and authenticity that only the best writers can boast, and the sense of danger and foreboding that informs this tale of intrigue and betrayal brings back for the reader the all too rare rush of excitement that only the finest novels in this field can convey. That novel dealt with the growing tide of Fascism in Europe, and represented a new vigour for the espionage tale, combining total authority with characterization of the first order. *Blood of Victory* has the same trenchant scene-setting and felicitous grasp of character as its predecessor. The setting is once again wartime Europe, here the turbulent city of Odessa; Furst's protagonist is Serebin, a journalist with aspirations to fine writing. He is making his way to Istanbul to bring about the release from jail of an ex-lover. Serebin encounters a powerful spy network located in the Russian émigré community in Paris, and learns that the network extends to Berlin, Belgrade and even the city of Odessa itself. Furst is an American author who considers himself European, and his lineage as a writer stretches right back to **Joseph Conrad**. He is not afraid to challenge the reader, and his radical reinvention of the espionage novel is the happy result of the authority and fastidiousness of his writing. As in *Kingdom of Shadows*, Furst is careful to ensure that not all loose ends are tied up: that, and the multi-layered characterization of Serebin gives the novel the kind of weight more typical of fine literature than of the thriller genre.

The Ministry of Fear 1943

Graham Greene

Penguin

The scarred and darkened London of the Blitz has never been so memorably created in fiction as in this consummate piece of thriller writing by Greene, who chose to bracket the book as one of his so-called 'entertainments'. As so often, the distinction between his entertainments and more serious work doesn't preclude an examination of moral issues quite as profound and harrowing as anything in, say, *A Burnt Out Case* (1960). The atmosphere of the novel is almost surrealistic in its accumulation of sinister detail. The protagonist is Arthur Rowe, suffering agonies of guilt after having brought about the death of his ailing wife. Ignoring the realities of the war, he guesses the weight of a cake in a charity fête, and thenceforward finds himself pitched into a world in which he is the hunted, on the run from murderous, shadowy figures, with

---

The Ministry of Fear
dir. Fritz Lang, 1944

Given that Graham Greene himself was once a film critic, it's perhaps not an accident that he was so lucky in his choice of directors. His association with the gifted British director Carol Reed produced some of his best work (notably *The Fallen Idol*, 1948, and *The Third Man*, 1949) but here his novel was sympathetically filmed by the great German Expressionist director **Fritz Lang**, doing wonderful work in the crime genre after his move to America (his later gangster thriller *The Big Heat*, 1953, was to anticipate *The Godfather*). The film is lucky, too, in having the ever-dependable **Ray Milland** as the hapless hero/victim.

his only chance of survival lying in cracking the truth behind his predicament. While the mechanics of the storytelling are kicked along by standard thriller imperatives, they have rarely been brought off with the brio that Greene demonstrates here, and the picture of a Blitz-torn London will stay in the mind of any reader of the novel.

Bad Company 2003
Jack Higgins (pseudonym of Harry Patterson)

Bad Company? One can forgive Jack Higgins for trundling out a title that's seen so much service before (as it's no doubt harder and harder to come up with thriller titles that haven't been used previously). In any case, this outing for the tough and resourceful Intelligence man Sean Dillon is quite as fast-moving and uncomplicated as any of its predecessors (even though it's a long way after the glory days of 1975's *The Eagle has Landed*), with Dillon as reliable a protagonist as any in the field. This time, dark secrets from World War II are resurfacing to cast a shadow over the present. Hitler's diary (yes, apparently, there was such a thing – perhaps that discredited *Sunday Times* story was accurate after all) was placed in the custody of a youthful aide, the German nobleman Max von Berger. After the Führer died ignominiously in the Bunker, the canny von Berger parlays his inheritance to achieve much temporal power, not least in terms of consolidating an association with the sinister Rashid clan, implacable opponents of British Intelligence – and specifically Sean Dillon and his colleague Major Ferguson. The diary contains an incendiary secret – details of a clandestine meeting between representatives of Roosevelt and Hitler – and the present-day ramifications may bring down the current US president. Higgins fans will recognize this as standard-issue Sean Dillon territory, and the author doesn't disappoint. All the customary tangled plotting, bursts of kinetic action, and a studied avoidance of nuance, make for reliable Higgins fare.

John le Carré (b. 1931)

More than any other British writer (including even his great influence, **Graham Greene**), John le Carré has made the novel of espionage and adventure a respectable literary form – one that can be a repository for trenchant insights into human nature, politics and the moral bankruptcy of the developed world. It might be argued that another influence le Carré is happy to acknowledge, the novelist **Joseph Conrad**, performed this same feat, but Conrad was long entrenched in the 'classic' category before le Carré began his genre-stretching activities.

As with Graham Greene, le Carré could draw on his own period in the security services when he added a literary career to his civil service one – but his early novels such as the splendid *Call for the Dead* (1961) and *A Murder of Quality* (1962) were essentially detective novels, although the unassuming secret service man **George Smiley** made his first appearance here, before moving centre-stage in the later, far more expansive novels. *The Spy Who Came In From The Cold* (1963) is the writer's first unalloyed masterpiece, and one of the great espionage novels, but more ambitious work was to follow in such multi-faceted books as *The Little Drummer Girl* (1983). The imposing George Smiley sequence beginning with *Tinker, Tailor, Soldier, Spy* in 1974 enriched and deepened le Carré's achievement. While some lamented the loss of the tautness of the earlier books, the massive panoply of the Smiley saga allowed le Carré to transcend the thriller category and produce works of literature quite as profound as more 'serious' literary novels, using the duplicity of his troubled protagonists for sharp insights into the human condition.

The Little Drummer Girl's use of the Arab/Israeli conflict rather than the Cold War demonstrated that le Carré could negotiate the end of the conflict with Russia

The Spy Who Came In From The Cold 1963

John le Carré (pseudonym of David John Moore Cornwell)

The greatest favour an admirer of crime or thrillers could do for themselves is to read John le Carré, and start with *The Spy Who Came In From The Cold*. Even if you've read it – more than once – you'll be

to move on to other threats. In later novels such as *Absolute Friends* (2003), le Carré has given vent to his hatred of recent British and American foreign policy – including the invasion of Iraq. But despite the appearance in his novels of the kind of polemics he would once have shunned, le Carré nevertheless remains one of Britain's greatest writers, on any level.

The George Smiley novels

The seemingly mild-mannered intelligence officer George Smiley will probably be forever associated with **Alec Guinness**'s masterly personification of him in successive, and enormously successful, TV adaptations, beginning with *Tinker...* (1979), although James Mason was memorable in *The Deadly Affair* (dir. Sidney Lumet, 1966), a version of *Call for the Dead*. Smiley pops up as a minor character in *The Spy Who Came In From The Cold* and *The Looking-Glass War* (1965), before re-emerging as the central character in the 'Quest for Carla' cycle.

▶ *Call for the Dead* (1961)
▶ *A Murder of Quality* (1962)

The 'Quest for Carla' cycle:

▶ *Tinker, Tailor, Soldier, Spy* (1974)
▶ *The Honourable Schoolboy* (1977)
▶ *Smiley's People* (1979)

reminded anew how impeccably written is this finest of all modern espionage novels. The story of the ill-fated British spy Alec Leamas achieves a genuine tragic dimension, and there is not another novel in the genre that has plotting as consummate as this, with every piece of sleight-of-hand played on both the characters and the reader supremely satisfying. Finally, though, it's the not-a-wasted-word economy of the book that astonishes. Later novels by the author, however accomplished, are nearly always of epic proportions. This is a reminder that le Carré could work in a much more concise fashion.

🎬 **The Spy Who Came In From The Cold**
dir. Martin Ritt, 1966

It's interesting to speculate how much of his massive popularity le Carré owes to this perfectly honed adaptation of his classic novel. Of course, he would have enjoyed immense success, but that final plateau of celebrity may be down to Martin Ritt's movie. All the key elements of the source novel are incorporated in the top-notch Paul Dehn screenplay, while those elisions that were necessary are seamlessly done. The icing on the cake is, of course, **Richard Burton**, as Leamas. Too often the actor made unfortunate choices in his film roles. Thankfully, he seized this opportunity with both hands.

Richard Burton in one of his finest roles as hard-bitten spy Alec Leamas

The Company 2002
Robert Littell

If you find slim novels insufficiently demanding, and have a taste for *War and Peace*-sized thrillers, Robert Littell's remarkable *The Company* is for you. As it was for many readers: word of mouth has been so enthusiastic that sales are astronomical. Littell has gleaned comparisons as jaw-dropping as De Lillo, Mailer, Homer and Dickens; the general consensus is that *The Company* is the definitive CIA novel. The narrative details the search for a mole in the CIA against a massive panoply of key events in world history. New Haven, 1950: the CIA recruits from the country's most promising students at Yale – but is the KGB recruiting also? Budapest, 1956: what was the CIA's role in the Hungarian revolt against communist rule? Cuba, 1961:

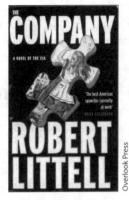

what was behind the debacle of the Bay of Pigs and its catastrophic aftermath? Afghanistan, 1983: the CIA is torn between bankrolling Afghan rebels and giving weapons to Islamic fundamentalists. What did the CIA know about Bin Laden and his ambitions? Moscow, 1991: during the fall of the Soviet Empire, the CIA supports the forces of Boris Yeltsin, while the KGB aims to overthrow Gorbachev. Washington 1995: spooks have been handing secrets to the Russians, but no longer for ideological reasons – filthy lucre is the motivator now. With a vast cast of characters, *The Company* skilfully integrates fictional espionage with an ambitious, panoramic canvas of the latter half of the twentieth century, offering an unbeatable picture of the endless ramifications the secret world has on all our lives.

Littell was always going to find this novel a hard act to follow. If *Legends* (2005) is more compact than its predecessor, it's still a weighty tome. In it, Littell once again demonstrates his mastery of literary espionage, but this time shifts his attention from the Cold War panoply of the earlier book to the dangerous life of a lone CIA operative who finds himself in a wilderness of mirrors. The singular achievement of this notable follow-up novel is the fashion in which the author has allowed it to function on two levels: firstly as a powerfully atmospheric, labyrinthine espionage narrative, and simultaneously as a penetrating study of divided personality. But the latter aspect is never handled in any po-faced fashion, and always remains at the service of storytelling impetus.

The Bourne Identity 1980

Robert Ludlum

Starting with *The Scarlatti Inheritance* in 1971, Robert Ludlum was top of the thriller tree for so many years (with 22 bestsellers) that it was quite a blow to his readers when he died in 2001. Since then, a number of new books have been published under his name, written at least in part by an anonymous ghostwriter, and fans of his blockbuster thrillers have eagerly embraced these crumbs. But the real Ludlum is to be found in *The Bourne Identity*, with all the author's familiar tropes still working nicely. Jason Bourne is a man without a past, pulled from the sea full of bullets. He also has a surgically implanted microfilm, and a reconfigured face. The trick is to find out who he is – and soon Bourne is fleeing from his erstwhile colleagues in the security services. Using his instinctive tradecraft (and a woman with whom he once had a relationship), he decides to test the premise that attack is the best form of defence. And taking the

The Bourne Identity
dir. Doug Liman, 2002

Memories of an indifferent earlier Richard Chamberlain movie were erased by this lean and efficient adaptation of Ludlum's novel, starring **Matt Damon** as the beleaguered Bourne. The film was the progenitor of a successful new franchise, which has already influenced an older series, James Bond, as seen in Daniel Craig's debut, *Casino Royale*. Some have argued that Liman's movie (and its successors, *The Bourne Supremacy*, 2004, and *The Bourne Ultimatum*, 2007) actually improved on Ludlum's sometimes by-the-numbers novels.

fight to the enemy is also a way of finding the missing pieces of his own identity. *The Bourne Identity* delivers all the requisite action set-pieces, and never neglects the essentials of economical scene-setting. If the characterization is rough-hewn, that's par for the course with Ludlum, and aficionados don't turn to him for subtleties of psychological insight. This is pulse-racing stuff, delivered at the gallop.

Old Boys 2004
Charles McCarry

Elegant, pared-down prose. A measured, richly characterized picture of the secret world. A continent-spanning narrative. A middle-aged hero and a largely mature cast of characters. Betrayal and sudden death. Are these the constituent elements of a classic Cold War novel of espionage by John le Carré? In fact, these fingerprints also belong to the *éminence grise* of the American espionage novel, Charles McCarry – a writer whose considerable reputation has been built up since the 1970s in a widely spaced series of diamond-hard, ruthlessly logical novels, positively burnished with high-end CIA tradecraft. McCarry appeared to write *finis* to the career of his protagonist Paul Christopher in 1983's *The Last Supper*, and he was recalcitrant when asked about the CIA stalwart's return (as he was when quizzed on his years at the Agency; unlike certain British ex-spooks, McCarry remains close-mouthed about his earlier clandestine activities). But Paul Christopher was back in *Old Boys* – even if he appears to be dead shortly after the first chapter. His CIA colleague and student Horace Hubbard (with whom Christopher, now in his seventies, has just had a valedictory meal) inveigles other ageing Agency men into finding out if Christopher is really dead – as Hubbard suspects he is not. Was it worth the protracted wait between books? The answer is an unqualified 'yes'. McCarry is not an apologist for his country's less defensible actions, and the moral equivocation of his book, combined with fascinatingly handled spy tradecraft, confirms his place in the pantheon.

Dark Winter 2003
Andy McNab

Corgi Adult

Let's face it – we all once thought that Andy McNab was set to become a one-book wonder, parleying his experiences in the SAS into a single (highly readable) book, *Bravo Two Zero* (1993). But with such popular books as *Immediate Action* (1995) and *Crisis Four* (1999) he has established a strong body of work, marginally more sophisticated than his first outing, but with all the brute force and kinetic action fans want from him. *Firewall* (2000) is a stream-lined thriller in which Nick Stone (ex-SAS, now working for British Intelligence on 'deniable operations') is handed the freelance job of snatching a Mafia warlord and taking him to St Petersburg – lucrative, but highly dangerous work. More kinetic, though, is *Dark Winter*: the narrative has some fresh moves, the bolshie protagonist is sharply drawn and the action is loaded with all the energy that we expect from McNab. Nick is dispatched to Southeast Asia (reluctantly putting up with a female partner on the trip) to tackle a scientist in the pay of Bin Laden. But before the end of the book, Nick is turning up a host of terrorist plots in both Britain and America. One would hope that McNab regulars might be pleasurably surprised by the extra characterization afforded to Nick in this book – especially since it is achieved without impinging on the customary bone-crunching business.

Empire State 2003
Henry Porter

Henry Porter's *Empire State* consolidates the impression made by his earlier *A Spy's Life* (2001): here is an espionage writer with all the panache and assurance of his great predecessors, turning out work as ingenious and exuberant as anything written in earlier eras. Heathrow is the setting for a major assassination: the Special Counsel on Security to the United States is killed, and it is discovered that his family has been similarly murdered in another part of Britain. Robert Harland finds himself obliged to tackle the most complex mystery of his career, but a clue lies in another seemingly random happening: an osteopath in New York (of whom Harland is a patient) is sent postcards of the Empire State Building, dispatched from Iran and Turkey. The man who sent them, Karim Khan, is murdered in Macedonia. Harland has to draw these strands together before another major atrocity occurs. The world is a more dangerous place since 9/11, and thriller writers such as Porter are obliged to take this on board. While the narrative here is quite as discursive and mystifying as one might wish, it's the always felicitous characterization that raises Porter above the level of his less ambitious peers. Henry Porter might well be among those writing the key espionage thrillers of the 21st century.

Land of Fire 2002
Chris Ryan

Chris Ryan writes the kind of books that virtually dictate the pace at which they are read. Many a reader will have settled down for a chapter or two with such books as *Stand By, Stand By* (1996) and *Tenth Man Down* (1999) and found themselves unable to put the book aside for hours. There is a fine balance between assiduously observed professional detail (often military) and the plausibility of the highly dangerous tasks Ryan sets for his tough and resourceful protagonists. We're told just as much as we need to know, and it never gets in the way of the action. *Land of Fire* follows senior NCO Mark Black, a hero of the Falklands war, coming to terms with a conflict that involves his past. During the war, he captured a young woman who was an Argentinian spy. And as a new military junta makes bellicose noises about re-invading the Falklands, Black is forced to confront the girl of his past once again – and possibly even trust his life to her. While all the usual suspense is on offer here, Ryan has built an element of characterization into the novel, demonstrating that at this point in his career he had tired of simply dashing off straightforward thrillers. *Land of Fire* may not always be as plausible as his earlier work, but it's compelling stuff.

Traitor's Kiss 2003
Gerald Seymour

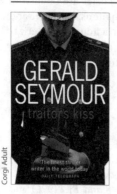

Corgi Adult

Many publishers make grandiose claims for their pet authors, but Gerald Seymour's publishers can put their hands on their collective heart and unequivocally claim: we have the best thriller writer currently working in the UK. Seymour remains, quite simply, the most intelligent and accomplished thriller practitioner in Britain today, and even his misfires (of which there aren't many) are more interesting than most of the competition. When so many novelists in the field are happy with hand-me-down characterization and shopworn plots, Seymour always manages to create fresh and original protagonists, and weaves for them plots that are unlike anything he (or his rivals) have come up with before. In *Traitor's Kiss*, a top-of-the-tree Russian naval officer, Viktor Archenko, is a source of much arcane information for the special services. Alarm bells begin to ring in MI6 when the usual lines of communication with Archenko are abruptly severed. London man Gabriel Locke, like his colleagues, knows that this precious contact was living life at the edge, but he remains an enigma. How to proceed? Locke decides that the best course of action is to get Archenko out – and while the Cold War may be over, this is a course that is fraught with immense danger. Locke is a classic spy hero, forged in the mould created by **Eric Ambler** and **John le Carré**, and he's one of Seymour's most forceful and unusual protagonists, with his combination of cool realism and denatured sensibilities.

The Company of Strangers 2001
Robert Wilson

Wilson's tales of danger and betrayal in foreign settings echo those of **Graham Greene**, but with an added, individual strain that is entirely Wilson's own. When he won the CWA Gold Dagger Award for *A Small Death in Lisbon* (1999, see p.276) he quickly acquired the literary gravitas that goes with this kind of celebrity. He built on this success in his following novel, *The Company of Strangers*. This tale of divided loyalties and a bitter war fought behind polite façades is his most ambitious and sprawling novel yet, set in the stupefying heat of Lisbon in 1944. We are shown a city that echoes Bogart's Casablanca, where spies and informers make every conversation a minefield. The Germans have developed rocket technology, and are on the brink of atomic breakthrough. The Allies are keen to stop the German secret weapon, and their operative is Andrea Aspinall, a young mathematician struggling to come to terms with the sophisticated world she finds herself in, living in the house of a rich Irishman who may

Through a glass darkly

Historical crime

To some degree, reading any crime novel is a form of escape into another world – one in which all the moral codes we may hold are torn to pieces. But it can also be a temporal escape. If you feel the need to read about dark deeds committed somewhere long ago and far away, historical crime offers the perfect passport. Want to dig into conspiracies in Ancient Rome? **Lindsey Davis** and **Steven Saylor** will hold your hand. What about murder inside the Third Reich? **Robert Harris** and **Philip Kerr** both know. Medieval bloodshed? **Ellis Peters** will put you in the muddy avenues. In fact there are now so many guides to mayhem in ancient times that we're coming to know the mean streets around the Coliseum in Rome as well as Marlowe's LA. The challenge facing writers of historical crime is rather similar to that facing science fiction authors: how to fill in just the right amount of incidental detail about this unfamiliar society, so as to firmly establish the story's context without slowing down the forward trajectory of the narrative. A further problem very specific to historical crime is how to persuade the reader that the private investigator (a relatively recent phenomenon) had predecessors spread throughout history. Here's a slew of writers who pull off that sleight-of-hand (and many others) with panache…

The Damascened Blade 2003
Barbara Cleverly

There's nothing like a full-on historical crime novel, is there? Particularly one set in the dying days of the Raj. But *The Damascened Blade* isn't quite that – even though there are some genuinely pulse-racing moments here as James Lindsay, commander of a British squadron in the beleaguered fort of Gor Khatri on the Afghan border, deals with the bloody death of a native prince and its catastrophic aftermath. British policeman Joe Sandilands becomes involved in this incident when he is seconded from London and spends time with Lindsay, an old army colleague. Barbara Cleverly, though, has a keen psychological insight, possibly gleaned from such master observers of this territory as Paul Scott and J.G. Farrell. Both the British and native characters are realized with an acuity that is always perfectly matched to the exigencies of a suspense-generating plot (the set pieces are splendidly exciting) and the moral dilemmas are by no means as clear-cut as they might have been (needless to say, the book is all the more interesting for its careful parcelling out of issues of conscience and commitment). Sandilands is drawn with complexity and skill as he encounters the disparate group of visitors to the fort and attempts (within the week the duo are given) to identify and execute the murderer. Of course, all of this would go for nothing if the historical details were not similarly spot-on, and the author has demonstrably done her homework here. Nothing is ever forced, but all the requisite indicators of time and place are picked out with genuine authority.

A Body in the Bathhouse 2001
Lindsey Davis

The two key practitioners of Roman crime novels, Britain's Lindsey Davis and America's **Steven Saylor**, are not the bitter rivals one might expect. Of course, it would be perfectly understandable if they cordially detested each other. And we rather like it when people ploughing the same field have it in for each other – it's made great copy ever since Brahms and Wagner, Joan Crawford and Bette Davis, Marvel and DC Comics. The truth, in the case of Davis and Saylor, is more prosaic. Both happily acknowledge

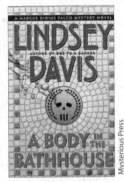

Mysterious Press

the skills of their rival across the pond. As a chronicler of bloodshed on the Domus Aurea, Lindsey Davis is without equal, and *A Body in the Bathhouse* is a splendid outing for her resourceful and sardonic Roman sleuth Marcus Didius Falco. While making improvements to his bathhouse, Falco (fuming at the shoddy workmanship of his

The top five Falco books

▶ *The Silver Pigs* (1989)
▶ *The Iron Hand of Mars* (1992)
▶ *Time To Depart* (1995)
▶ *The Accusers* (2003)
▶ *Saturnalia* (2006)

builders) becomes aware of disgusting smells – and finds that human corpses are the source. But then he is sent by Emperor Vespasian to the murky Roman colony of Britain to examine why everything is going wrong with the building of a new palace for the British King Togidubnus. Soon Falco is up to his elbows in murder and deception – par for the course, in fact. This is wonderful stuff, with impeccable historical detail allied to plotting that is always full of élan.

Garden of Beasts 2004
Jeffery Deaver

Like so many lawyers, Jeffery Deaver decided to abandon one already lucrative profession for an even more remunerative one – that of the bestselling thriller writer. And Deaver swiftly built up a consider-able following for his Lincoln Rhyme crime novels, highly adroit thrillers featuring a quadriplegic investigator assisted by a young police woman, Amelia Sachs (who takes on most of the danger). But while some authors are happy to plough the same furrow for most of their careers, Deaver clearly felt the need to re-energize his batteries by introducing two distinctive new heroes in *The Blue Nowhere* (2001): Frank Bishop, a flawed but ruthlessly effective cop, and his reluctant associate, Wyatt Gillette, a highly talented young computer hacker released from prison to help Frank track down a kind of online Hannibal Lecter. And if that weren't enough, he struck off in yet another direction with *Garden of Beasts*, a period thriller that is among his most accomplished work. Set in New York in the 1930s, the central character is hitman Paul Schumann, who finds himself grabbed by the police when a hit goes belly-up. Schumann is offered a choice: travel to Berlin to murder Hitler associate Reinhard Ernst, or be tossed into jail, with the key thrown away. There would, of course, be no novel if Schumann didn't take the first option – and his lethal hunt through a brilliantly realized Berlin, in chaos as preparations for the Olympics are under way, delivers the requisite tension – particularly as an implacable and resourceful German cop is on his tail (not to mention the assembled might of the Third Reich). This particular Garden of Beasts is not a comfortable place to be (exactly what thriller aficionados want, in fact), with Schumann a strong anti-hero. On the strength of this, Deaver need never go back to his Lincoln Rhyme books. But what's the betting he will?

Fatherland 1992
Robert Harris

Of late, the excellent Robert Harris has moved into other areas of history, but this picture of a crime investigation in a Europe in which Germany won World War II remains his masterpiece. The concept of a victorious Germany is not a new one, of course, and such writers as **Philip K. Dick** have explored it. But by adroitly marrying an investigative narrative to this alternative history, Harris created something very special indeed. The drowned body of an old man is discovered, and a routine investigation is initiated by Harris's dogged Berlin copper. But when he discovers that the Gestapo is involved, things become very messy indeed. He finds himself with a case whose tendrils reach right into the heart of the Reich. As Harris demonstrated

Fatherland
dir. Christopher Menaul, 1994

Most people who bothered to watch it considered this by-the-numbers adaptation of Harris's novel somewhat underwhelming. **Rutger Hauer** (a talented actor more often miscast than not) and the usually reliable **Miranda Richardson** are the protagonists involved in cracking a truly sinister plot, but Christopher Menaul's tepid direction largely keeps tension at bay, and the convolutions of Harris's plot are disappointingly smoothed out into something a touch penny-plain. Some sharp small-part playing provides compensation.

in subsequent books, political intrigue is one of his specialities (Harris is a political insider apart from his writing), and it's that element that powers the motor of the plot here. The trick, of course, is to make the central investigation interesting when the reader is keen to know everything that is different about this world that never happened, and it's the juggling act that the author performs in this regard that is so admirable: information about the victorious Reich is freighted into the plot just at those moments when it is appropriate, no more. For a while, Harris struggled to find the form that he had displayed in this novel, but resolutely recaptured it again in such later books as *Pompeii* (2003).

In the Kingdom of Mists 2002
Jane Jakeman

We all know that dispiriting feeling on realizing that the plot of a thriller is one we know all too well, however much the author may shuffle the cards. So it's genuinely exhilarating to encounter something as fresh and inventive as Jane Jakeman's *In the Kingdom of Mists*. Not only is this a sharply textured piece of work, there is never any sense of straining for effects: Jakeman's unique narrative unfolds with quiet confidence. It is set in London at the beginning of the last century, with the painter Monet central to the macabre mysteries. As the great Impressionist paints his celebrated visions of the Thames, that same river is a repository for hideously mutilated bodies. There are fears of a return of Jack the Ripper. Tyro diplomat Oliver Craston just happens to be present when the bodies are pulled from the Thames, and finds himself drawn (against his better judgement and his wishes) into the investigation. The Foreign Office has jitters over French sympathies with the Boers, and Craston is instructed to follow the doings of the Monet family, who are staying at the Savoy Hotel. But there is a terrifying secret in the rooms above their suite, and grim events in the Stygian slums of Lambeth across the Thames draw Craston into a nightmare from which he'll be lucky to emerge alive. *In the Kingdom of Mists* works on several levels: as a bravura thriller, full of vigorous set pieces; as a fastidiously detailed picture of early-20th-century London; and even as a pellucid examination of art itself.

Walking the Shadows 2003
Donald James

With such books as *Monstrum* (1996) and *Vadim* (2000), Donald James has proved himself to be a master of the large-scale, block-buster thriller in which violent action is set against a vibrantly realized canvas. *Walking the Shadows* carries on that exhilarating tradition. In the village of St Juste in southern France, all is silence and darkness. The village was drowned in World War II, but when a drought drains the reservoir that conceals the town, many secrets come to light. James's protagonist Tom Chapel arrives in St Juste in order to discover why a man from the village left a massive fortune to his daughter in his will. She was subsequently kidnapped and is now barely alive in a coma. Needless to say, Chapel encounters a wall of silence from the local police (when did you last read a thriller in which local police were helpful?), and he is obliged to travel back in history to uncover some unacceptable facts. Under the sway of the hated Vichy government, resistance fighters were helping Jews to leave the country – and Tom Chapel was one of these escapees. But is the betrayer of this organization (responsible for the death of several Jewish women) still alive and prepared to kill to protect his secret? The pleasures of this book are many. One particular skill James displays here is the careful attention with which he achieves the subtle marriage of the past and present so necessary to the narrative. The theme, more serious than his previous books, is handled with responsibility.

The Last Templar 1994
Michael Jecks

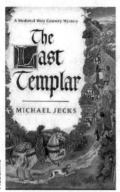

Michael Jecks is known for his historical accuracy – nothing goes into his books which he knows to be wrong. Even the murders and other crimes investigated in his books are taken from the Coroners' Rolls and other contemporary records. The books are intended to be modern-day thrillers that happen to be set in a past century. Cadfael they ain't! Although characterization is very important to Jecks, there are two other planks to his stories. Plot, naturally, but also the countryside. It was a canny move to base the main action in Dartmoor, because the author clearly considers that there is nowhere so redolent of the past in Britain as this wild moorland. In his stories it's fair to say that the countryside is often as important as the people. Set in the years of the great European famine of 1315–16, *The Last Templar* looks at what happened to some of the men who had served in the great religious army, the Knights Templar, after their destruction by an avaricious French king and grasping Pope. The famine caused massive dislocation, and all over Europe bands of men clubbed together to rob, rape and murder. In 1316 in Devon, Simon Puttock, the new Bailiff of Lydford Castle, discovers a body in a burned house. At first it seems like merely an unfortunate accident, but then another man is found burned to death, and this man was burned alive. Could the two deaths be linked? Simon isn't sure, but he is glad to enlist the help of the intriguing new master of Furnshill, Sir Baldwin.

Death in the West Wind 2001
Deryn Lake (pseudonym of Dinah Lampitt)

As so often before, Deryn Lake takes the historical mystery and gives it a much-needed shake. If the characters in her books don't always behave in a strictly plausible fashion (given the 18th-century setting), the assiduously researched detail allows us to accept all the murderous shenanigans, however outrageous. *Death in the West Wind* is vintage stuff, with the author on her most assured form. Lake's customary protagonist, the resourceful apothecary John Rawlings, is enjoying his honeymoon in Devon, but (needless to say) marital bliss is not on the cards for long when the mutilated body of a young girl, Julia van Guylder, is found on a schooner. Then the young girl's brother Richard vanishes, and Rawlings traces a sinister trail to the Society of Angels, a clandestine group that appears to have something to do with the mystery. Thrown into the mix is a highwayman and even a phantom coach, so Rawlings calls for help from the canny Joe Jago and the Flying Runners, his London colleagues. As in her previous books, Lake is adroit at creating a satisfyingly knotty plot for Rawlings to resolve, and the Georgian period has rarely been evoked with such colour, whether in the historical thriller, romantic fiction or even the literary novel.

The False Inspector Dew 1982
Peter Lovesey

Aboard the ocean liner *Mauritania*, sailing for New York in 1921, an unassuming dentist, Walter Baranov, nerves himself to chloroform his domineering wife and push her out of a porthole. The idea is that he and his lover Alma, who has stowed away, will then pose as a police inspector and his wife. It is a refinement of the real-life Dr Crippen case, and with a nice sense of irony Walter borrows the

name of the inspector who arrested Crippen and his mistress at sea.
But before he gets the chance, a body is recovered from the sea and
is found to have been murdered. The ship's captain invites Walter,
the false inspector, to lead the investigation. He is compelled to
make a show of detective work, questioning American millionaires,
professional gamblers and wealthy matrons seeking matches for
their marriageable daughters. What follows is a series of twists and
surprises. *The False Inspector Dew* won the CWA Gold Dagger and
was ranked 27th in a poll of the top hundred crime novels of all time.
But acclaim for Lovesy's sophisticated, dazzlingly plotted Sergeant
Cribb books, such as *The Detective Wore Silk Drawers* (1971), is
most to be found coming from fellow practitioners, such as **H.R.F.
Keating**, **Ruth Rendell** and **Colin Dexter**. Like all the best historical
crime, the marriage between seamlessly incorporated period detail
and dexterous characterization is a harmonious one.

The Frost Fair 2002
Edward Marston (pseudonym of Keith Miles)

Edward Marston has made his mark as a playwright and has run
his own professional theatre company, but this Renaissance man
among crime writers has one real *métier*: his impeccable series
of richly atmospheric crime novels (such as the Domesday series
exploring crime in Norman England). *The Frost Fair* (subtitled *A
Restoration Mystery*) is perhaps his most accomplished and detailed
piece yet: historical crime of the first order. The novel is set in the
terrible winter of 1669. London ignores such hardships as a frozen
Thames by celebrating Christmas with a traditional 'Frost Fair' on
the river. Amidst the carousing throng is a talented young architect
who is escorting the daughter of one of his clients. The architect,
Christopher, has romantic designs on the delightful Susan, and he's
further pleased to encounter his friend Constable Jonathan Bale,

who is also there with his family. Christopher and Jonathan, while saving a boy from a freezing death in the river, discover a frozen cadaver underneath the ice. The corpse is that of an Italian fencing master, and despite Christopher's best efforts, he finds himself further embroiled in the mystery when his brother Henry is accused of the murder. As in all Edward Marston's previous books, there is an assiduously maintained balance between authentic period detail and lively, intelligent characterization. When so much historical crime seems to be dispatched by rote these days, it's refreshing to encounter a writer like Marston, who never gives less than his best.

The Quincunx 1990
Charles Palliser

As a very clever synthesis of **Dickens** and **Wilkie Collins**, Charles Palliser's labyrinthine *magnum opus* is carried off with supreme élan, despite the fact that he dismissed it as a postmodern literary experiment. All the tropes of historical mystery developed by earlier masters are reactivated with great skill, but it's the infusing of a modern sensibility with these dark deeds of the past that makes this arm-straining volume so distinctive. John Huffam and his mother have been leading clandestine lives for as long as he can remember. John's potential inheritance is formidable, but there are many people laying claim to this wealth. The proof of John's right to his estate lies in a missing will – and the search for this proof in the dark corners of a cathedral town is the engine for a vast, baffling narrative which is often as redolent of **Mervyn Peake** as it is of Dickens (though neither author raked in so many carefully orchestrated suspense sequences). While characterization is writ large, the naïve hero

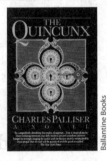

Ballantine Books

is particularly well honed – though it's the fustian period atmosphere that claims the attention.

Hard Revolution 2004
George Pelecanos

Little, Brown

It's the spring of 1968, and Martin Luther King is attempting to preach his message of non-violent change to young blacks who are seething with impatience. Washington DC is a hotbed of resentment – and Pelecanos' tenacious hero Derek Strange is at the start of his police career, not yet the character we've come to know through the author's other books. Then Dr King is assassinated, and all hell breaks loose. Pelecanos' counterpointing of small-scale crime against national disaster within a brilliantly evoked historical episode is powerfully handled, and he once again proves that no black writer – not even the firebrand **James Baldwin** – could show such a single-minded concern for issues affecting black (and other ethnic) Americans as this white writer.

The Golden One 2002
Elizabeth Peters (pseudonym of Barbara Mertz)

At the start of this fourteenth adventure for Amelia Peabody (which continues the wartime theme begun in 2001's *Lord of the Silent*), it is New Year's Eve, 1917. Risking winter storms and German torpedoes, the Emersons are heading for Egypt once again: Amelia, Emerson, their son Ramses and his wife Nefret. Emerson is counting on a long season of excavation without distractions but this proves to be a forlorn hope. Yet again they unearth a dead body in a looted tomb – not a mummified one though: this one is only too fresh, and it leads the clan on a search for the man who has threatened them with death if they pursue the excavations. If that wasn't distraction enough, Nefret reveals a secret she has kept hidden: there is reason to believe that Sethos, master criminal and spy, may be helping the enemy. It's up to the Emersons to find out, and either prove his innocence – or prevent him from betraying Britain's plans to take Jerusalem and win the war in the Middle East. This Amelia Peabody mystery is one of the most adroit. Elizabeth Peters is a highly prolific writer with over 50 novels to her credit, and Amelia, her Edwardian lady-sleuth, is a strong creation. At times, Peters' books have been workaday, but *The Golden One* is a real winner – the pages virtually turn themselves.

A Morbid Taste for Bones 1978
Ellis Peters (pseudonym of Edith Pargeter)

Edith Pargeter wrote such successful historical mysteries as Ellis Peters before her death in 1995 that her name has been adopted for the most prestigious of historical crime fiction prizes. Peters was a writer for five decades and produced nearly 100 books, but it was her Brother Cadfael titles in the last ten years of her life that cemented her achievement in the popular mind. Her herb-growing, intuitive monk, solving medieval crimes in authoritatively rendered historical settings forged (along with Umberto Eco's *The Name of the Rose*) a genre that grows in popularity to this day: the mystery set in the past featuring a detective before there really were such people. Peters' Cadfael books were always slim and beautifully turned, and the first, *A Morbid Taste for Bones*, remains the perfect entry point. At a Benedictine abbey, a young monk has a vision in which he thinks that he sees St Winifred in her pre-celestial incarnation as a young girl in a Welsh village. She communicates the fact that she is unhappy with the state of her grave and wishes to be moved to the

> ### 🎬 A Morbid Taste for Bones
> dir. Richard Stroud, TVM series, Granada, 1996
>
> While certain liberties were taken with Ellis Peters' impeccable plotting, few complained, as the standard of this adaptation was so high. But while a solid cast was assembled, there is no denying that the success of this film (along with all the others in the popular TV series) rested squarely on the shoulders of one of Britain's finest classical actors, **Derek Jacobi**. Brilliantly conveying the hyper-resourceful mind behind the benign monkish exterior, Jacobi also cannily suggested the violent crusader past that makes Cadfael such an intriguing character.

abbey. For the monks, this is an enterprise fraught with difficulties, but they finally agree to travel to Wales to redeem the holy relics. This first outing for Cadfael, the ex-crusader living a cloistered life in Shrewsbury, is brilliantly realized. An influential nobleman who has strongly opposed the monks' plans is killed, and suspicion falls (naturally enough) on the monks. Cadfael is obliged to find the real murderer. Apart from the impeccable historical detail, Brother Cadfael arises as a fully fledged master detective, deserving the place in the pantheon that he was quickly to acquire.

Lying in State 1985
Julian Rathbone

Not as well known as he should be, but highly rated by those who do know his work, Rathbone has been writing thrillers for nearly 40 years. He has attempted on three occasions to write a series but each time after the third book he has declared himself bored with the same character and setting and gone off to do something completely different. This makes it difficult to find a pigeon-hole to fit him into. The common factor, if there is one, comes from his attachment to the work of **Eric Ambler**. As with Ambler, there is usually a bigger arena in the background: the Cold War, agri-business, genetic modification, nuclear energy, and so on. *Lying in State* was inspired by a series of actual events. While exiled in Madrid, Juan Perón taped his memoirs and, on his return to Argentina, he gave them to his actress friend Nini Montiam. Following his death, she found that no one was prepared to pay the sort of money she thought they were worth, and upped the ante by threatening to sell them to an English agent (who happened to be Rathbone's agent). The complete tapes are reputed to have been dynamite – especially regarding the Nazi exiles in Argentina such as Bormann and Eichmann. Rathbone takes this background and imagines the existence of a second set of tapes, even more sensational than the first, and builds a tense narrative around the character of a now-impoverished Argentinian bookseller who is employed to authenticate them. The action takes place in Madrid between the death of Franco and Juan Carlos's declaration to the Cortes that the Franco era is over. The final revelation of *Lying in State* is a real *coup de foudre*.

A Trust Betrayed 2000
Candace Robb

Candace Robb has proved in such books as her debut *The Apothecary Rose* (1993) and *The King's Bishop* (1996) that her Owen Archer investigations are an intriguing development on the theme inaugurated in the novels of **Ellis Peters**. For the first two books in Robb's second series, *A Trust Betrayed* and *The Fire in the Flint* (2003), the crimes centre on the family of her central character, Margaret Kerr. Through this device, Robb is able to deal with the often destructive division in families, as well as exploring the position of women in different centuries. She's particularly sharp on the very different nature of society when no one really possessed 'the big picture' in the modern sense, and society's fragmentation is conveyed here in all its confusion and disorder. *A Trust Betrayed* is set in 13th-century

Scotland, with Margaret Kerr worried that her husband has been swept up in the revolt against the English. When her husband's agent is murdered, Margaret has to act alone on a variety of very dangerous missions. This is writing of real craftsmanship, full of authoritative detail.

Night Crossing 2004
Robert Ryan

Robert Ryan (no relation to the late actor) may have enjoyed great success with his tough, stripped-down modern thrillers written under the name of Tom Neale, such as *Steel Rain* (2005), but his real *métier* emerged in the World War II novels he writes under his own name. The historical detail in these books has a gritty authenticity, despite the fact that the author is too young to remember the period. A recurrent theme, flying, is equally persuasively handled – in this case, the author has physically done his homework and flown in more than a few bone-rattlers. The third Ryan World War II novel, *Night Crossing*, traces the lives of four characters as the war leaves its marks on them: the classical musician Uli (who is Jewish), escaping from Berlin to London, the intelligence man Cameron, an ex-detective, the German U-boat sailor Erich (engaged to Uli) and the sinister SS man Schüller. This multiple perspective is something in which Ryan has few equals, and the dangerous panoply of this dark period in history is vividly evoked with his customary skill.

Dissolution 2003
C.J. Sansom

A much-acclaimed first novel, *Dissolution* gleaned advance praise from the likes of **P.D. James**, and proved to be a historical crime novel that redefined the genre. It is 1537, Tudor England. Henry

VIII has proclaimed himself Supreme Head of the Church. The country is waking up to savage new laws, rigged trials and the greatest network of informers it has ever seen. Under the orders of Thomas Cromwell, a team of commissioners is sent throughout the country to investigate the monasteries. There can only be one outcome: they are to be dissolved. But on the Sussex coast, at the monastery of Scarnsea, events have spiralled out of control. Cromwell's commissioner, Robin Singleton, has been found dead, his head severed from his body. His horrific murder is accompanied by equally sinister acts of sacrilege – a black cockerel sacrificed on the church altar, and the disappearance of Scarnsea's Great Relic. Matthew Shardlake, lawyer and long-time supporter of reform, has been sent by Cromwell into this atmosphere of treachery and death, accompanied by his loyal assistant Mark. His duty is to uncover the truth behind the dark happenings at Scarnsea. Shardlake's investigation soon forces him to question everything that he hears, and everything that he intrinsically believes… Historical details are seamlessly wedded to a powerful narrative gift.

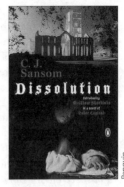

Penguin

Last Seen in Massilia 2000
Steven Saylor

Saylor's highly successful series of books chronicling the murky exploits of Roman sleuth Gordianus the Finder are rich with all the requisite authentic historical detail. Wryness is a key Gordianus characteristic; his sardonic humour flavours his observations on any subject, but he's deadly serious when it comes to his work. Steven Saylor was born in Texas and studied history and classics at the

University of Texas in Austin; his home is now the college town of
Berkeley, California, where he may often be found doing research in
the stacks of the University of California libraries, unravelling the
2000-year-old crimes of ancient Rome. The final years of the Roman
Republic offer a treasure trove of all the stuff that makes for a rollick-
ing read. There's political intrigue, courtroom drama, sexual scandal,
extremes of splendour and squalor, and no shortage of real-life murder mysteries. The greatest challenge for Saylor is to make two things
happen simultaneously at a book's climax – to reveal a solution to
the mystery plot which makes perfect sense, and at the same time
to bring the thematic elements of the story to a satisfying resolution.
In *Last Seen in Massilia*, civil war rages, and Gordianus hears (via an
unnamed source) that his son, Meto, is dead. Meto was acting for
Caesar, and the very personal task of tracking down his killer leads
Gordianus into extremely dark waters indeed. This is both one of the
most polished and most immediate of Saylor's excellent series.

The American Boy 2003
Andrew Taylor

In the period after its publication, barely a week seemed to pass
without Andrew Taylor tucking another award under his belt for *The
American Boy*. The author had re-read **Edgar Allan Poe's** *Tales of
Mystery and Imagination*, and had been struck again by the European
cast of Poe's imagination and by the sense of vulnerability, of wounds
that had never quite healed. Poe had lived in England from 1815 to
1820. *The American Boy* invents a secret history of Poe's childhood,
concentrating on an episode in 1820 – the last year of his stay in
England. Taylor's novel reflects as accurately as possible the manners
and mores of the period. He researched how people spoke, thought
and acted in late Regency England, from the mansions of Mayfair to
the slums of St Giles and Seven Dials, from the leafy village of Stoke

Newington to a country estate in Gloucestershire. He studied that curiously inconclusive war between the world's one superpower and a small, pushy little country half a world away: the War of 1812, the last time the British and the Americans fought on opposing sides. The book coaxes a murder mystery and a love story from scraps of history and the oblique hints in Poe's writings. Most of the book is the narrative of an impoverished schoolmaster, Thomas Shield, who has a chequered past that includes a brief but disastrous military career and a history of mental instability. At the heart of the fictional Shield's story is Wavenhoe's Bank and the families concerned with its fortunes and misfortunes – especially the women. The collapse of the bank is based on a real-life embezzlement case, which led to the Fauntleroy forgery trial of 1824 and eventually to the gallows. Poe haunts the book, though for much of the time he appears to play a relatively minor role. It's an astonishing, epic achievement. Also look out for Taylor's *The Roth Trilogy* (1997–2000), which triumphantly shows that crime novels can deal with serious themes and use innovative literary techniques.

A Vote for Murder 2003
David Wishart

The streets of Caesar's Rome are becoming increasingly crowded with the cunning breed of ancient-world sleuth, and it's a wonder that the anachronistic detectives of **Stephen Saylor**, **Lindsey Davis** and David Wishart are not stumbling over each other. But who cares? All three authors are producing work of the highest quality, shot through with sardonic wit, offbeat characterization and highly plausible historical detail. More than his colleagues and rivals, Wishart seems aware that the whole Roman sleuth enterprise is a confidence trick: we know (he infers) that there were no detectives in this era, but such is his narrative skill that we completely 'buy' the concept and enjoy the outrageously entertaining results. In *A Vote for Murder*, Wishart's canny investigator Marcus Corvinus is having a leisurely holiday with his stepdaughter and generally enjoying a bibulous time (while keeping half an eye on the Machiavellian antics involved in the pending consulate elections). But when one of the two candidates meets a violent death, Corvinus (with no reluctance) summarily ends his vacation and plunges into the murder hunt. Of course, it's too easy to assume that the rival political candidate would be behind the killing, and some labyrinthine plots are ahead before Corvinus cuts the Gordian knot in his usual fashion and brings things to a highly surprising conclusion. The varied denizens of this dangerous world are drawn with great dash, and the one-liners in which Wishart specializes are quite as sharp as anything the author has entertained us with before.

A Small Death in Lisbon 1999
Robert Wilson

Wilson's considerable reputation continues to grow from book to book, with *A Small Death in Lisbon* one of his subtlest achievements. It is 1941. Europe cowers under the dark clouds of war, and neutral Lisbon is one of the world's tensest cities. Klaus Felsen, a reluctant member of the SS, finds himself drawn into a savage battle in the Portuguese mountains for a vital element, wolfram, needed for Hitler's armaments industry. In modern-day Lisbon Inspector Zé Coelho is an outsider in the cliquish world of the Policia Judiciaria. Investigating the death of a young girl, he suddenly finds himself deep in the events of 50 years ago, with ramifications for the Portuguese Revolution which is hardly a generation old. Robert Wilson has carved out a niche for himself as a remarkable writer of distinctive, colourful thrillers written in a striking literary style. Here again he echoes his forebears **Graham Greene** and **Eric Ambler** in a complex and powerfully characterized story that builds inexorably to a breathtaking climax.

Foreign bloodshed

Crime in translation

A hotly debated topic among British crime writers and enthusiasts was brought to a controversial climax by the recent award of the prestigious Crime Writers' Association Gold Dagger. The recipient? **Arnaldur Indridason**, for his novel *Silence of the Grave*, originally written in his native Icelandic. 'Shouldn't all entries for this prize be written in English?' was an oft-heard, irritated cry.

All the fuss was unsurprising. Few crime readers on either side of the Atlantic can have failed to notice the avalanche of foreign crime novels flooding into bookshops – most of them greeted with massively enthusiastic reviews. But these hotter-than-hot new writers (**Henning Mankell**, **Fred Vargas**, **Karin Fossum** *et al*) were not just taking readers into fascinatingly unfamiliar new climes – they were also gleaning applause for the freshness and invention of their approach to the genre and their undeniable literary values. Foreign crime writers could simply no longer be sidelined. However, these new voices are only the latest literary combatants in a crime fiction war that began quite some time ago with some remarkably talented writers…

The Winter Queen 2002
Boris Akunin
(pseudonym of Grigory Shalvovich Chkhartishvili)

While Akunin's series of historical thrillers had been something of a publishing phenomenon in the author's native Russia, they were virtually unknown in the West. The title chosen to be the first published in English, *The Winter Queen*, was not the first in the series, but served as an excellent calling card for a very accomplished writer. In a short time, Akunin found himself on many reading lists. The books deal with the young and high-minded Moscow policeman Fandorin, a character who actually changes as the various books progress, with his early idealism somewhat under siege from the realities of his job. *The Winter Queen* is set in Tsarist Russia in the late 19th century. After a suicide in a Moscow park, Fandorin begins to unravel a tortuous plot involving seductive women, labyrinthine conspiracies and a sinister figure with designs on global power. The young policeman's quest to untangle a dark mystery takes him to London (as well portrayed as the Moscow of the opening scenes), then back to his own country, where he realizes to his dismay that everything he thought he had deduced has taken him in quite the wrong direction. Comparisons have been made to both **Dostoyevsky** and **Ian Fleming**, but Akunin is his own man, and these light-hearted, vividly pictorial period thrillers have great charm, even if they steer clear of more serious issues and are slighter than we were led to believe.

The Night Buffalo 2005
Guillermo Arriago

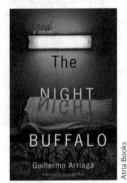

Already celebrated as the Mexican writer behind *Amores Perros* (2000), *21 Grams* (2003) and *The Three Burials of Melquiades Estrada* (2005), Arriago as usual disdains genre for something much more individual in a brilliant analysis of personal and moral guilt; this novel bears comparison with **Patricia Highsmith** at her best, or **Hitchcock** at his most subtle. A first-person narrative, it draws the reader into the apparently normal everyday life of its narrator, Manuel. But as he tells his tale of a *ménage à trois* which ends in fatality, the increasingly dark levels of culpability are revealed like layers of onion skin. What horrifies is the narrator's inability to see his responsibility for the events which unravel.

Atria Books

Celle qui n'était pas/Les Diaboliques/The Fiends 1954
Boileau-Narcejac

The writing team of **Pierre Boileau** and **Thomas Narcejac** enjoyed a spectacularly successful dual career writing highly efficient thrillers in their native France. The surprise for most readers when reading this taut and ingenious thriller is the gender-switch in the narrative from the famous Henri-Georges Clouzot film (see below). Ravinel is a killer. His wife Mireille has been drowned in her bath, and (along with his mistress Lucienne) he has dumped her corpse into a river to give the impression of suicide. But if Mireille is dead, how is she

---

> ▦ **Les Diaboliques/The Fiends**
> dir. Henri-Georges Clouzot, 1954
>
> As well as being one of the most accomplished crime films in the history
> of the cinema – one that retains its power to shock even in our jaded age
> – Clouzot's classic was immensely influential. Its scene of terror in a bath-
> room, for instance, is a clear influence on *Psycho*: Hitchcock was an admirer
> of the film and wryly noted that his own techniques were being parleyed
> into something quite as effective as the original. Apart from the impeccable
> cinematography, it is, of course, the wonderful performances that make
> the film work so well: the matchless **Simon Signoret** and the unpleasant
> **Paul Meurisse** as the adulterous lovers, and (most of all) **Vera Clouzot**'s
> incarnation of the cowed wife. Never was nepotism put to better use than
> Clouzot's casting of his spouse in this role. An indifferent American remake
> with Sharon Stone quickly sank without trace.

---

writing to him from beyond the grave? Unfortunately, the plot for
Les Diaboliques has been plundered so often that the original has lost
something of its novelty. It's worth remembering (if you ever knew
this) that Hitchcock's classic 1958 movie masterpiece *Vertigo* was
based on Boileau-Narcejac's *D'entre les morts* (*From Among the Dead*,
1957). It's worth seeking out other work by the team, notably such
slim and effective thrillers as *The Victims* and *The Evil Eye*.

The Terracotta Dog 2004
Andrea Camilleri

As more and more crime in translation began to break through
into the mainstream, certain names quickly established themselves
as implicit guarantees of quality. One of these names is Andrea
Camilleri, and *The Terracotta Dog* is as good a sampler of the
author's work as any. This is a police procedural delivered with all
the consummate skill that has always been a speciality of European
writers in this field, and features the author's Inspector Montalbano,
one of the most distinctive Italian coppers on the scene. Montalbano

has received an invitation to meet a killer, and decides to accept the invitation, even though it may be dangerous. In fact, the meeting is a setup, and leads to Montalbano finding out about a clandestine relationship between a whole host of crimes. These involve dirty doings within the Sicilian Mafia and religious institutions (both Christian and Muslim) that stretch back into the past and even involve the American landings in Sicily in World War II. In *The Shape of Water* (1994), the first book in the series, Camilleri had established Montalbano as a highly distinctive protagonist, and he continues to develop him here, not just in his professional dealings (where his laser-sharp mind makes a series of outrageous connections) but also in his relationship with the woman in his life. But while the characterization here is as adroit as one could wish, it's the plotting that remains the masterpiece of *The Terracotta Dog*. So popular is the former film director in Italy that his home town changed its name to that featured in many of his books – Vigàta.

The Pledge 1959
Friedrich Dürrenmatt

One of the most important European writers of the modern age, Friedrich Dürrenmatt is best known for such plays as *The Physicists* (1962), but among his novels this psychologically complex tale of an obsessive detective is a classic of the genre. A little girl is found dead in a Swiss forest, and her murder is similar to several committed years earlier. Inspector Mattei is put in charge of the investigation, but is forced into retirement before tracking down the murderer, and becomes adviser to the Jordanian police force. The moment when he must tell the parent of the dead girl the terrible news is highly significant for him: he is forced to make a solemn promise to track down the killer. And this – over a very long time period – he feels obliged to do. He takes over a service station in an area of the Canton

The Pledge
dir. Sean Penn, 2000

When Sean Penn shed the tiresome adolescent antics that characterized his early career, he metamorphosed into one of the finest actors and directors of the modern American cinema. This stunning adaptation of Dürrenmatt's novel plays fair by its source material, and retains the sense of the passage of time which is so crucial to the narrative. Of course, having **Jack Nicholson**, one of the most accomplished actors in modern film, as the obsessed detective was the icing on the cake.

near where he assumes the killer must live. And waits. And waits. As this synopsis conveys, we are by no means in standard police procedural mode here: the psychological state of the relentless pursuer is centre-stage in the narrative, and his obsessiveness shades over into something approaching mental illness. As well as steadily building his arresting narrative, Dürrenmatt allows his interest in the mental states of his characters to be paramount.

The Name of the Rose 1985
Umberto Eco

In the 21st century, it's possibly hard to remember just what impact Eco's remarkable novel had in its day. Certainly, it was literary fiction of an uncommon order. And the success of this Italian novel (by a celebrated academic and historian of popular culture) was something of a Trojan horse for the sales of foreign fiction in translation in both the UK and the US. This was, of course, due in no small part to the remarkably sympathetic translation by William Weaver – one of the few occasions on which the translator's achievement was loudly celebrated. And despite its dense and allusive prose, Eco's novel was also a classic historical detective story (the name of its monkish sleuth, William of Baskerville, was something of a clue to the book's antecedents). The setting is Italy in the Middle Ages, and

---

🎬 **The Name of the Rose**
dir. Jean-Jacques Annaud, 1986

Sean Connery makes a rather more muscular Franciscan friar than most people will have envisaged from Eco's novel, but any thoughts that William of Baskerville might be a medieval 007 are quickly banished by his charismatic performance. The production design of the film is stunning, and the hiring of the great F. Murray Abraham (Salieri in the Milos Forman 1984 film of *Amadeus*) as a sinister inquisitor was a masterstroke. All of the novel's intricate religious discourse is, of course, jettisoned.

---

as the Franciscan foreigner William cracks an impenetrable mystery in which six monks are found murdered in a variety of ways (involving sinister religious sects and ecclesiastical corruption), we are given a picture of the religious wars, a detailed history of the monastic orders and a complex and multilayered vision of the Middle Ages. William himself is, frankly, something of a cheat: a modern sensibility hides behind the medieval trappings, and his modernity is the perfect conduit for the reader. Even here, though, Eco plays around with this conceit: for all his modernity, William has a desperately medieval view of women (they are there merely to tempt men from the ways of God). The phenomenal success of this often inaccessible book led to a positive avalanche of far less distinguished historical mysteries.

He Who Fears the Wolf 2003
Karin Fossum

There is no room for debate: the most important female writer of foreign crime fiction at work today is the Norwegian Karin Fossum. In many ways, her unprecedented success has opened the floodgates for other foreign writers in translation who have been re-invigorating the field. *Don't Look Back* (1996) was a dark piece of interior writing quite different from the standard fare that many readers had become accustomed to, and *He Who Fears the Wolf* continued Fossum's subtle re-invention of the genre. Her first reviewers in Norway spotted parallels with the British crime writer **Minette Walters**, but **Ruth Rendell** (a favourite writer of Fossum's) is nearer the mark – Rendell, that is, in her decidedly non-cosy mode as a cold-eyed examiner of the darker reaches of the soul. In *He Who Fears the Wolf*, a savagely mutilated body is discovered in a secluded village, and the apparent killer is subsequently committed to an asylum. Shortly afterwards, a bank holdup results in a hostage situation – and it's the strange relationship between the criminal and the female hostage that is the crux of the book, brilliantly developed by Fossum, always moving in directions that take the reader by surprise. The idiosyncratic picture of Nordic society – both like and unlike Britain – is one of the key elements in the success of the book (and most of Fossum's work).

Voices 2006
Arnaldur Indridason

Harvill Secker

Many felt that Arnaldur Indridason would be the first writer to break the stranglehold that **Henning Mankell** maintained on foreign-language crime fiction. And so far, the signs are that this remarkably talented writer is doing just that. British and American readers may have problems pronouncing his name, but they are fully aware of the highly distinctive characteristics of his Reykjavik-set thrillers. Following the remarkable successes of *Jar City* (2003) and *Silence of the Grave*

(2005), this is another taut and beguiling thriller. Indridason's detective Erlendur comes across echoes of his difficult past when the doorman at his hotel is savagely stabbed to death. The manager attempts to keep the murder quiet (it is the festive season) but Erlendur is, of course, obliged to find out what happened. As he works his way through the very bizarre fellow guests who share the hotel with him, he encounters a nest of corruption that gives even this jaundiced detective pause. The particular pleasure of Indridason's books is their combination of the familiar and unfamiliar – while the detective is cut from the familiar cloth, the locales and atmosphere are fresh and surprising for the non-Scandinavian reader.

Rider on the Rain 1992
Sébastien Japrisot

Among his compatriots, Sébastien Japrisot has gained the epithet 'the Graham Greene of France'. The remarkable success achieved by his highly engaging crime novels in his native country has not really been repeated outside that country. But the fact that two of his best books, *Rider on the Rain* and *Trap for Cinderella*, have enjoyed elegant translations makes these striking books even more cherishable. The comparisons made with the earlier novels of **Georges Simenon** are not high-flown: as a storyteller, Japrisot has the same steely grasp. *Trap for Cinderella* has a remarkable premise:

The Harvill Press

the protagonist is detective, murderer, victim and witness all at once. Who is the scarred, amnesiac survivor of a beach house gutted by fire – perpetrator or target? But *Rider on the Rain* is one of the key Japrisot books. A deserted Riviera bathing resort is the scene for a brutal rape. When an enigmatic American meets the victim, Mellie, he seems to know the full story of that night – and the desperate young woman finds herself in a whirlpool of fear. The reader has to figure out if he is an ally or enemy. The book (with nary a wasted word) is vintage Japrisot.

Almost Blue 2003
Carlo Lucarelli

Italy is fast becoming one of the most attractive destinations for literary bloody murder, particularly among writers not native to that country. Of the Italians, Carlo Lucarelli has already established a considerable reputation as one of the most accomplished (and disturbing) writers in the field. His first book was *Carta Bianca* in 1990, which featured his male protagonist, Commissario Da Luca. But *Almost Blue* has at its centre the female inspector Grazia Negro, and the genre of the book is firmly in **Thomas Harris** territory, ie the tracking down of a ruthless serial killer. The setting is Bologna, and a blind young man, Simone, hears the voice of a murderer on his ham radio setup. As Grazia attempts to corner a very dangerous maniac, Simone becomes an essential tool in her armoury. The real coup of the novel (and the one that has brought it much attention) is the three-way split in the narrative: the ever-accelerating momentum of the plot is carried forward by three voices: young Simone, the policewoman Grazia, and the brutal killer himself. Needless to say, it is, of course, the murderer's sections which most rivet the reader's attention. Despite the praise the book gleaned outside Italy, there were dissenting voices. But most would agree that Lucarelli is a name to watch.

Firewall 2002
Henning Mankell

Loud was the wailing and gnashing of teeth when Henning Mankell announced that he was retiring his laconic detective Kurt Wallander. Crime aficionados had long taken the Scandinavian copper to their hearts, and the news that Wallander's daughter was to take centre stage (working long Ystad nights cracking the mysteries that were her father's speciality) didn't exactly whet the appetite. And when the initial outing of Wallander *fille* didn't match the panache of the earlier books, Mankell fans wore expressions

Vintage

as bleak as the Scandinavian winters. But we still have those early Mankell books! The excellent Wallander novels have been the standard bearers for foreign crime in translation (and he's been very lucky in his translators). But although many British and American readers soon became aware that some of the finest modern crime

The top five Mankell/Wallander books

Overweight, diabetic, and carrying the woes of the world on his shoulders, Kurt Wallander proved particularly appealing for the baby-boomer generation, who could identify with his distractions and concerns.

▸ *The White Lioness* (1998)
▸ *Sidetracked* (1999)
▸ *The Fifth Woman* (2000)
▸ *One Step Behind* (2002)
▸ *Firewall* (2002)

fiction was being produced by this Swedish writer (in such books as *Sidetracked*, 1998), Mankell's work still encountered some resistance. Understandable, perhaps, for like one of the most acclaimed of all filmmakers, **Ingmar Bergman**, Mankell is from a country noted for Nordic gloom, and the lazy-minded are not always prepared to go beyond stereotypes. That's their loss: like his cinematic compatriot (Mankell is, in fact, married to Bergman's daughter), the writer is a man of rare skills. In *Firewall*, Wallander is trying to track down the perpetrators of a series of bizarre deaths in very disparate circumstances – and finds that he's being led to the Internet, with technocriminals bent as much on destabilizing society as on mere monetary gain. Once again, he has to motivate his recalcitrant team (while worrying about his uncertain health) – and the results (for the Mankell fan) are as compulsively readable as one could wish.

All She Was Worth 1992
Miyuki Miyabe

Miyuki Miyabe is probably the most interesting modern Japanese thriller writer, and the most widely translated. In *All She Was Worth*, Shunsuke Homma is a widowed Tokyo police inspector, with a 10-year-old son. While on leave after being wounded on duty, he is asked by his nephew to look into the disappearance of his fiancée. Ashamed of being so out-of-touch with his family, Homma agrees and soon finds himself in an increasingly nightmarish world of murder and stolen identity. This is a classic Japanese theme, but *All She Was Worth* has nothing to do with the traditional fox-spirits. Miyabe explores the world of spiralling debt, the loan sharks that prey upon it and the price exacted from Japanese society for its obsessive consumerism. Along the way, she explores the official Japanese mechanisms of social control, as well as changing attitudes to women, money and debt. The nature of reality is also explored here and in several of Miyabe's other books. It is, of course, another favourite Japanese theme – the best-known example in the West being the mysterious *Rashomon*, both the story by **Ryonosuke Akutagawa** and the 1950 film by **Akira Kurosawa**. Another of her works available in English is *Shadow Family* (2001), in which she explores the nature of the family and reality in modern Japan, where the cyber-world may well have more appeal than the real one.

The Queen of the South 2002
Arturo Pérez-Reverte

This is a key entry in an impressive line of quite mesmerizing novels by Arturo Pérez-Reverte. He has demonstrated himself to be a master of finely honed storytelling techniques, impatient with the thin gruel we are so often served up today. His historical Captain Alatriste series (1996–2006) is more Dumas than Highsmith, but a clutch of novels – including *The Flanders Panel* (1990), *The Dumas Club* (1993) and *The Seville Communion* (1995) – explore much the same territory as **Dan Brown**'s *The Da Vinci Code* and *Angels and Demons* (and roundly trump them in terms of intelligence, credibility and sheer quality of writing). *The Queen of the South* has all the panache of its predecessors, with a new ambition: apart from the trials of his beleaguered heroine, we are given the intriguing insights of her mysterious biographer. Güero Dávila and his lover, the initially docile Teresa Mendoza, are caught up in the drug-smuggling activities of the ruthless Mexican cartels. But when Dávila tries to play both ends against the middle, he ends up dead – and Teresa finds herself on the run, fearing for her life. In Spain's sultry and dangerous city of Melilla, she encounters another man engaged in the drugs trade, the dispassionate Galician Santiago Fisterta. He draws her into his activities, and Teresa is soon involved in the hashish trade. It isn't just the impeccable scene-setting of this dangerous Latin world that makes *The Queen of the South* such an impressive read, but the perfectly judged dialogue (of which there is a great deal) – Pérez-Reverte is a master of idiom, and everything here rings true. The compelling central narrative of Teresa is set against the perceptions of her anonymous narrator, and the result is a fascinating *mélange*, if a little over-ornate at times.

The Man Who Watched Trains Go By 1946
Georges Simenon

Georges Simenon's readership was worldwide (although the author had no interest in the translations of his work, considering them virtually different books by different authors). Those who admire Simenon often venture the opinion that his finest work lies not in his **Maigret** books, but in the more literary psychological thrillers in which the perpetrators or victims of crime are at the centre of the narrative. Of these, *The Man Who Watched Trains Go By* is generally considered to be one of the best, shot through with a bleak and evocative atmosphere. The novel's protagonist is the Dutchman Kees Popinga, a man secure in his family life until the shipping firm for which he works goes under. This catastrophe effects a terrifying change in Kees: all trappings of normality fall away, and he sinks into a morass of paranoia in which acts of casual violence and even murder become possible for him. Simenon brings home to the reader just how close to chaos ordinary lives can be, and this lean and tense novel makes for very uncomfortable reading. If this takes your fancy, try Simenon's unique variation on Highsmith's *Strangers on a Train*, the extraordinary *The Blue Room* (1964), a chilling demonstration of the unknowable qualities of those we choose to make love to.

Georges Simenon (1903–89)

Georges Simenon wrote that he'd slept with over 10,000 women – and while one may be sceptical of this rather boastful (or careless) claim, it's fortunate for the world of crime fiction that he found time to write one of the greatest bodies of work in the genre anywhere in the world. Belgian-born Simenon was a one-man fiction machine, and his prodigious output included some dark and existential psychological crime novels as well as delicious puzzles featuring his celebrated pipe-smoking sleuth Maigret. More than most, he made a case for the literary crime novel, and such literary giants as **André Gide** held him in very high esteem. In his early career, he mass-produced a great variety of work, before his trademark *romans policiers* achieved their immense finesse. *The Case of Peter the Left* in 1953 was the first official Maigret title, and 75 other books over the next two decades would feature this detective. But, like **Ruth Rendell** in Britain, he saved his finest work for non-series titles, such as the marvellous *The Stain on the Snow* (1953). After putting down his crime-writing pen in 1973, Simonen began his voluminous memoirs – where that jaw-dropping claim of sexual hyper-activity appeared.

The Man Who up in Smoke 1969
Maj Sjowall and Per Wahloo

It is a cause for real celebration that the complete works of this most celebrated duo of crime writers are now available in English. Their neglect until recently is remarkable, given that the critical start of the Swedish duo could not be higher, with most fellow crime writing practitioners rating them as the very best exponents of the police procedural. So if you haven't yet familiarized yourself with the Martin Beck series, now is

HarperPerennial

the time to start. He is, of course, the ultimate copper, gifted with the powers of ratiocination that distinguished his predecessors, but the novels are also powerful human dramas. In *The Man Who Went up in Smoke* Beck is on an island holiday with his family but soon finds himself involved in the case of an unpleasant journalist who has vanished. Read this and you will find yourself wanting to collect the other books in the series as quickly as possible.

Wash This Blood Clean from My Hand 2007

Fred Vargas

There are those who find Vargas' highly unorthodox detective stories just too outrageously plotted, but aficionados know that this is her special ability: she invariably creates narratives that resemble absolutely nothing else in the genre (and her novels are all the better for it). This example of peculiarly European crime writing starts with an unusual premise: between 1943 and 2003, nine people have been stabbed to death with a curious weapon – a trident. While all the murderers had been (apparently) brought to justice, there is one bizarre detail: each lost consciousness on the night of the crime and have absolutely no knowledge of their act. Commissaire Adamsberg has decided to look into this long-running mystery, and has settled on the imposing judge Fulgence as his prime suspect. Soon, of course, history is repeating itself… This is Vargas' weightiest and most ambitious tome, but shot through with that nervy and sardonic Gallic humour that is her *métier*.

When Red is Black 2004

Qui Xiaolong

The author's debut, *Death of a Red Heroine* (2000), caused quite a splash when it first appeared, and *A Loyal Character Dancer* (2002) was a highly individual read, handling its culture-clash theme with real aplomb. For once, the 'cops from different backgrounds' concept was treated with real freshness. Here again, we meet the resourceful Inspector Chen Chao, who has agreed to do a translation job for a Triad-connected businessman. When a murder is reported, Sergeant Yu is obliged to take care of business – but both men are soon knee-deep in a baffling mystery. This third Inspector Chen mystery set in contemporary China is quite the equal of its predecessors.

unashamed of his admiration for **Ian Fleming**'s Bond, it isn't true that he helped finish the incomplete *The Man with the Golden Gun* (1965); but he did write both *The James Bond Dossier* (1965) and *The Book of Bond* (also 1965, under the pseudonym of M's chief-of-staff, Bill Tanner). He was also responsible for the first 'successor' Bond novel, *Colonel Sun* (under the pseudonym of Robert Markham, 1968). His son **Martin Amis** is on record enthusing over **Elmore Leonard**'s literary standing. His own attempt in the field, *Night Train* (1997), is not one of his best, but it is interesting nonetheless. Meanwhile his contemporaries, such as **Ian McEwan**, the versatile **Iain Banks** and the exemplary London-obsessed successor to Derek Raymond, **Ian Sinclair**, have all delved into the unpleasant, criminal symptoms of modern-day Britain. Indeed, it is rare to read a modern novel in which crime does not play a prominent part. In the US we saw **Norman Mailer** trying it out with *Tough Guys Don't Dance* (1984), while modern Western supremo **Cormac McCarthy** produced an extraordinary existentialist modern crime novel in *No Country for Old Men* (2005). When the *enfant terrible* of modern American letters, **Bret Easton Ellis**, published *American Psycho* in 1991 (see p.173) – which he claimed as a satire on the Manhattan 'me' generation – there was confusion and uproar in the literary columns. Result: easily his best-selling book, but it was nevertheless consumed behind closed doors or brown paper wrappers.

What lies in the future for a genre in which every conceivable plot twist, elegant conceit or highlight of *grand guignol* must have been recycled a thousand times and wrung dry? The principal problem is reinventing anew the conventions of the genre – or at least rejigging them so that we don't mind meeting yet another novel about a feisty young female pathologist or a recovering alcoholic copper with marital problems. This is the stuff of acquisitions meetings in publishing houses the world over, not to mention crime writing seminars. Many crime writers are ploughing new furrows, examining locale, confronting social issues and delving into history as a means of extending the range and longevity of the genre. If crime fiction can find that delicate synthesis between classical form and totally modern sensibility, the possibilities for growth may stretch indefinitely onwards.

It is undoubtedly true (as many observers of crime fiction have noted) that the sheer amount of product out there makes it difficult for new individual voices to be heard. But how many new individual voices are there? And what of the old guard? Thomas Harris seems to be becoming increasingly baroque, and other recent best-selling crime authors frequently teeter on the edge of formula and self-parody. While we relish the fact that a maestro such as Elmore Leonard entered his eighth decade seemingly unabated, no one lives for ever. And the demons which have pursued **James Ellroy** ever since his mother was found eviscerated on an El Monte roadside in 1958 may finally have been laid to rest. In *My Dark Places* (1996) the author recounts his attempt to reopen the unsolved investigation with the help of a retired detective involved with the case. The result is an extraordinary and searing account of self-discovery which many felt would end his creative career. Not so, but he has been quoted as saying he is through with 'genre fiction'. And maybe that is the future. Crime is, however unfortunately, an endemic aspect of the human condition. Thus, as long as literature continues to be produced, crime will inevitably form a central aspect of it.

Picture credits

22 © Bettmann/CORBIS; 39 Moviestore, Warner Bros Pictures, MGM/UA Home Entertainment; 87 Moviestore, Monarchy Enterprises B.V., Regency Enterprises, Warner Bros Pictures; 93 © Rune Hellestad/CORBIS; 106 © Rune Hellestad/CORBIS; 117 © Jessica Kovaks/Sygma/CORBIS; 122 © James Leynse/CORBIS; 128 © Will & Deni McIntyre/CORBIS; 144 © Sophie Bassouls/CORBIS SYGMA; 166 allenandunwin.com; 168 Moviestore, Paramount Pictures, Universal Home Entertainment; 175 Moviestore, Orion Pictures Corporation, Strong Heart/Demme Production, The Criterion Collection; 196 © Rune Hellestad/CORBIS; 248 Moviestore, Salem Films Limited, Paramount Pictures, American Broadcasting Company.

Index

Index

Index

Index

Index

Index

Index

Index